This is the first book by an ex-sailor, fisherman and farmer, in his early eighties, who on leaving school at the age of fifteen joined the Royal Navy. An interesting and often hilarious few years, followed by the Merchant Navy and emigration to Australia where he travelled extensively. Working in a copper mine, various labouring jobs and back to sea again on a Tasmanian lobster boat. In later years he worked in Aboriginal communities in the Gulf of Carpentaria and the Red Centre. Currently settled in a quiet coastal town on 90 Mile Beach in Gippsland, Victoria, where he is surrounded by the sea.

To my wife Rosalin, whose love and belief in me inspired this memoir.

# Hugh Rose

# Don't Go Into Town, Tonto!

AUSTIN MACAULEY PUBLISHERS™

LONDON · CAMBRIDGE · NEW YORK · SHARJAH

A CIP catalogue record for this title is available from the British Library.

ISBN 9781398460379 (Paperback)
ISBN 9781398460386 (ePub e-book)

www.austinmacauley.com

First Published 2022
Austin Macauley Publishers Ltd®
1 Canada Square
Canary Wharf
London
E14 5AA

# Part I

# Chapter 1

## Sibford Gower

I was born during the winter of 1937 at Stornoway in the Outer Hebrides. Well, that was the plan anyway. But due to unforeseen circumstances, my mother did not make it. Deep snow apparently was one of the reasons of my being born at Bank House in the village of Sibford Gower, Oxfordshire. The town of Banbury and the indecisive Civil War battleground of Edgehill were close by. Banbury was also famous for its cakes, its Cross and an ancient rhyme that went like this:

> *Ride a cock horse*
> *to Banbury Cross*
> *To see a fine lady*
> *on a white horse*
> *Rings on her fingers*
> *and bells on her toes*
> *She shall have music*
> *wherever she goes.*

It was never mentioned whether the fine lady wore anything else. Where this lady rode from could well have been Sibford Gower or the adjacent village of Sibford Ferris. Sibford from Sheepford, pronounced 'Zibberd' by the locals. I was forbidden to use the dialectal form. If she hailed from either village, she would have had plenty of competition in eccentricity. There were two inns in Sibford Gower. The 'Bishop Blaze', not far from Bank House. At the other end of the village, a short distance from the bungalow that my father, Stuart Rose, had designed and built, was the 'Whykam Arms' where my father enjoyed the ale and shove halfpenny with the villagers before enlisting in the Gordon Highlanders.

My father left in 1942 for North Africa, never to be seen again by me or my mother who loved him. Killed in the desert advancing on Rommel, I was led to believe. Not so, I found out seventy years later. Advance on Rommel, he did, coming through unscathed physically. Army records state that he died in Cairo in 1951 fighting insurgents. Faded newspaper clippings revealed that at war's end he had married a German woman in Nairobi where he had spent some time as a young man. His wife and two children left Kenya to live in London, where according to a newspaper article, they picked up the pieces and eventually found happiness, I hope. There was no mention of my mother and the three sons he left. I have never judged him. He fell in and out of love, that's all.

I spent the first five years of my life at the bungalow. They were happy years with my mother and brother Gordon, two years my junior. There were two trips away during this period, one to the Garrison town of Huntly in Scotland where my father had family and the other to Tottenham in North London where my mother came from. WWII was well under way by this time. What duration these trips were, is difficult to say. I know I hadn't begun school then. In Huntly, we stayed with my Aunt Mary and there was an Aunt Polly in the background who may have been the mother of cousins Neil and Minka. There was a boy called Martin that I used to play with who swiftly taught me the local dialect which kept the family in stitches. Another boy Dombey whom I played with once only, shat behind his mother's sofa for which I got the blame. My mother stoically defended me and that was the end of that friendship. A 12-year-old girl called Sheila McKay would bring a can of milk at four in the afternoon in time for tea. One day, she arrived at five and another phrase was picked up, 'the coo was'naemilket'.

Aunt Mary's house was adjacent to the Gordon Highlanders' barracks so we were well used to the skirl of pipes and the tattooing of drums. Army lorries, armoured cars and despatch riders sped constantly in and out of the depot on their way to manoeuvres. An old man with one leg spent a while every morning watching the goings on. I stood with him. One day, he wasn't there. "Son blown up on the 'Hood'," they said all day. The old man was there the next day.

"What is blown up, what is Hood?" I pestered.

"Dinna fash yourself, laddie," he said gruffly. I seldom saw him anymore as they deemed it dangerous for me to be there. Instead, we went for picnics to the rivers Deveron and the Bogie and watched the salmon fishermen casting. One warm day, we saw the regimental parade before leaving for the war. Crowds of folk managed to maintain silence for prayers until the leopard-skinned drum major gave his instrument an almighty thump which caused my brother Gordon, who was dozing in the sunlight, to be thrown out of his push chair. He was bleeding a little but didn't cry. A woman said he was a brave lad. Looking back, I'd say he was concussed.

Up to this point in Scotland, I do not remember seeing my father, but he must have been around. I presume it was my father who arranged for mother, Gordon and I to meet the driver and fireman on the footplate of the 'Flying Scotsman' at Waverley Station in Edinburgh. A privilege indeed. The train then sped south with hundreds of semi-inebriated squaddies who were very nice to us and gave us lots of chocolate; we fell asleep despite the bedlam. The exact dates when anything took place in those early years, I am incapable of recalling. I was soon five years old and began school, which turned out to be a waste of ten years of my life, apart from weekends and holidays.

For a few days before my first day at Sibford school, I had been concerned about a thing called a headmaster, as my mother had failed to point out that a headmaster was a human being. I had imagined a headmaster was like a telegraph pole or a Belisha beacon. I was quite disappointed that the children in my class didn't know their A, B, C and couldn't read. I, who knew my Beatrix Potter and while not fully understanding 'Treasure Island', was conversant with the main characters such as Long John Silver and Jim Hawkins but also minor players like Mr Arrow and George Merry. Here was I chanting mumbo jumbo about Henny Penny and Chicken Licken. At that precise moment, I ignored all lessons and proceeded to educate myself. I used to walk to school on my own. It was not far, about a quarter of a mile.

One morning, the lane was jammed with American tanks on the wrong side of the road, when a speeding armoured car covered me and my new school blazer and shiny shoes in mud. My school cap, which sat on my large round head like a yarmulka with a peak, also suffered badly. A soldier wiped my face and attempted to clean me up, which made things worse. When I got to school, a big girl called Isobel took me home. I don't remember if my mother made a fuss, but I do know that Isobel called for me every morning from then on. I was very embarrassed. I had never mentioned anything about the tanks so they probably thought I had fallen in the village pond, a constant source of interest to me.

My mother's eldest brother, Uncle Wal, visited on several occasions before joining the Royal West Kents as a stretcher bearer. He would carry me on his shoulders and draw pictures and cartoons with his fountain pen. He was a very good artist and also a journalist and of course, a pacifist. Uncle Wal didn't survive the war and is buried in Athens. His wife Margaret Gunn, my Aunt Peggy, had selected letters he wrote to her which she had published after the war by Faber & Faber, titled 'Letters from a Soldier'. He was a fine man and I have never forgotten him. On leaving for the war, he gave me his set of Encyclopaedias.

Our nearest neighbours were Mr and Mrs Chambers. Their son Harold was in the Royal Navy. Harold shovelled deep snow from the front gate to the house so I could get to school. When on leave, Harold would frequent the Wykham Arms and on return secrete a bottle of stout in the potting shed for Mr Chambers, as Mrs Chambers frowned on Bacchanalia even in its mildest form. However, she turned a blind eye for Harold's sake because how could one chastise a man for drinking when he had recently been torpedoed in the North Atlantic? One Christmas, a Mrs Lingard came to the village. She was Harold's natural mother and came from Central Europe and was fluent in several languages. She kept us spellbound in the dark evenings around the fire with tales of being chased by wolves while galloping through the snow in a troika with her father, mother and big brothers shooting at the wolves while she drove with the steam of the frightened horses mingling with the snow. Mrs Lingard also knew many folk songs and dances. Her husband was hanged by the Nazis. Why? I don't know. I don't suppose they needed a reason.

One windy morning, the French windows on the veranda slammed on brother Gordon's finger. Dr Barnard drove him to Banbury Hospital to have it put in plaster. My mother had a sack of coffee beans sent by my father from Kenya some years before and unprocurable at the time. The good doctor immediately caught a whiff of Kenyan coffee beans freshly ground and percolating when he and Gordon arrived home and treated the cup my mother poured him as if he were holding the Holy Grail. After that, we never had to go shopping in Geoff Jenner's bus and were subject to house calls several times per week to check on our health.

The paper delivery man went by the name of Tarmadook because when I met him at the front gate with the tuppence for the News Chronicle, that's what he said. It was his way of saying 'Thank you, my duck'.

My favourite person at Sibford after Uncle Hector who lived at Bank House, was Theodore Lamb. Theodore came from a well-to-do family of farmers and landowners. Why he chose to live in a shack of corrugated iron, dressed in rags and hessian bags, we never discovered. There were several rumours of course; the most popular that he had been left at the altar like Pip's nemesis from Great Expectations. He rode a rusty old bicycle sans tyres and his approach could be detected half a mile away. When we went for walks up Pound Lane on the way to Whychford Woods to pick hazelnuts, his shack could be heard rattling in the wind behind the high hedge that gave his humble abode some privacy. One day, he was eating eagerly his ration of dried fruit in the shop. He dropped a sultana and a dog pounced on it. Eventually, he was requested to wait outside the shop as some customers complained about his lack of hygiene. The dog was allowed to remain inside the shop. On several occasions when he was in the village, I saw him engaged in earnest conversation with various people; Uncle Hector being one of those who found his company enjoyable. My mother said that Uncle Hector had walked with kings and it was only natural for him to talk and walk with Theodore. I only found out what she meant when I saw 'IF' printed on the bulkhead of the training ship 'Ganges' ten years later. Theodore died in 1950 after contracting pneumonia. He broke a leg while fetching water from a spring and spent the night exposed to the elements. The hospital heeded his last request that they leave his shoulder-length dreadlocks unshorn.

The garden at the bungalow was a delightful wilderness except for the flowerbeds which my mother looked after, and a potato and root crop section that was tended by a Mr Kite who came for a few hours now and then. The remainder was left to nature and where a large nettle bed was allowed to flourish. It took roughly a bushel of nettles to feed the three of us, and small as I was, I soon got used to them. When the word spread, by Mr Kite I suspect, villagers were shocked and sympathetic that a lone woman with two children in their midst had been reduced to eating nettles and began leaving cabbages and other vegetables on the doorstep overnight, along with rabbits and pigeons. Most small children dislike greens, I was not one of them; my brother Gordon was and when mother wasn't looking, I ate his. I don't think he ever appreciated this gesture. I even loved parsnips. I really was odd. Still am.

There was a garage which I never saw the interior of and a row of dog kennels where my mother had kept her Borzois before I was born. Their pet names were Boris, Kish and Nan, and their pedigree names Ruski Carl Kirolov, Kish of

Kazan and Podra Dainty Anna. Borzois are a large breed so their kennels were like barns. My brother and I defended those kennels against Red Indians and Zulus. My mother had loved her dogs but decided to give them away when I was born. She never let on that she regretted the decision in spite of my weighing in at eleven pounds, four ounces at birth. It was a difficult birth she said. I seemed to be all head. This didn't put her off giving birth to three more sons whose heads were of average dimensions, thankfully. She laid the blame on walnuts for my weight which she ate by the stone.

There were a family of rough boys who I both feared and admired. They ambushed small children who had been sent to the post office-cum-shop. I say admired because on one winter's afternoon they broke the ice on the pond and were punting on great slabs in bare feet, blood from knees to ankles. Heroic! Feared, because when they were not doing daring deeds, they were capable of being quite feral. One of the brothers, Alf, unbeknownst to me was on one hot day concealed in a tree and peed on me from a great height as I passed below. My mother, unsure as to what term to use, challenged Alf's mother with, "Your son micturated on my son."

Alf's mother looked dumbfounded, but Alf defended himself stoutly, "I never, I only piddled on him." My mother then burst out laughing and everyone went home. Fifteen years later when home from the sea, I paid a visit to Sibford. I caught a bus in Banbury and sitting in the only seat available, sat next to Alf who immediately apologised for pissing on me. Alighting from the bus, we then spent a pleasant evening in the Whykham Arms, among those present was Mr Kite. An enjoyable evening ensued, full of happy reminiscences. I slept in a hay shed near Tadmarton on the way home to Duns-Tew.

Strange things began to occur a few months after I began school. We left the bungalow and moved in with Uncle Hector and Aunt Ethel at Bank House for a brief period. But the night before we did, I heard a crunch of boots on the gravel path and the sound of talking and quiet laughter and then silence. I suppose that night the seed of my brother Murray was planted in my mother's womb. Next day, I saw my father for the last time. I cuddled his leg as he was warming himself by the fire; I tried to wrest the Skean Dhu from his stocking top. He didn't pick either Gordon or I up. He didn't say anything. Not a goodbye or a hug. And then he was gone.

At Bank House, Uncle Hector and Aunt Ethel were fostering evacuees. They were children from the large cities who were temporarily fostered out to escape the blitz. Uncle Hector was an educated man. He came from Stornaway, on the Isle of Lewis, in the Outer Hebrides. A kind man whose generosity somehow ran in conjunction with a fiery temper. Red hair and moustache flecked with silver; piercing blue eyes that would mesmerise a stoat. On a wild wet day, hair awry, he resembled an escapee from an asylum for the criminally insane. Aunt Ethel reminded me of a cuddly mother bear. Among the evacuees were two Cockney brothers named Heggarty and there began a new phase in my education. Benny and Jerry Heggarty were cobblestone-schooled exciting rascals. I was delighted with them and wondered what the outcome would be if a chance meeting occurred with the red-headed crowd at the other end of the village. It never happened in my time at Bank House but took place many times in my head. Benny and Jerry had never seen a live cow before arriving at Sibford or anything that village kids took for granted. Adaptability was their strength, and they soon had the best birds' egg collection in Sibford. They'd been used to earning money by collecting practically red-hot shrapnel and spent cannon shell cases split seconds after the ALL CLEAR and quite often before the ALL CLEAR because there was plenty of competition apparently. They were as clearly disappointed by the lack of booty as they were amazed that the cottages in the village still had their roofs attached. One day, Gordon and I were dawdling two hundred yards astern of the boys over a newly cut wheat field when we came upon eight feet of live German cannon shell and cemented a firm friendship, and until we left Bank House, they served us faithfully. Shoplifting from the Co-Op, scrumping the best apples and knocking walnuts out of other folks' trees. My mother in her innocence accepted those gifts although raising an eyebrow at some dried fruit once, and of course, she had been off walnuts for some years.

Back to the bungalow for a short period during which time my brother Murray was born at Chipping Norton, a town not a great distance away. When we did leave the bungalow for the last time, it was an overnight evacuation to Wigan in Lancashire. It was hot I recall because my mother had brought our ration of butter and cheese which was in an advanced state of liquescence. We woke up in what appeared to be a community hall and the strangest sound that I had ever heard. Understandably, a lot of people were afraid and children began crying. The clatter got louder and louder until it shut out all other sound. Curiosity overcame fear, and quivering in my sandals, I ran to the door and saw hundreds of women and girls in clogs hurrying to begin work at the cotton mills. Later on, that day an older boy on his way to school gave me a Mickey Mouse book. I thanked him and gave it to Gordon. I was becoming a literary snob even then. In the afternoon, we were billeted with the kindest old couple I had ever met, apart from Grampy and Nanny. Their three sons were merchant seamen, and we said prayers for them every night before going to bed. We stayed about two weeks I believe, and I barely understood a word they said, so thick was their accent, yet I hear their voices still.

### Tottenham

Then it was south once more and senseless as it seems, we stayed at Grampy and Nanny Robson's again in Tottenham. The nightly raids were on in earnest. My brother and I would hang out of the bedroom window waiting for our grandparents to wend their way back from the 'White Hart'. The skyline in the Port of London a Turner masterpiece.

Gordon had not begun school at this time, but the local school which was two hundred yards away decided to fit him in as our grandparents were at work during the day. I have no idea where my mother was at the time. Then she was here once more and we felt much safer, and it was fun sleeping in the dugout, in our pyjamas. Once, we were on the underground waiting for a train to Turnpike Lane when there was a raid. Panicking folk crammed around us. We slept there that night. My brother and I, along with assorted unwashed kids, giggling and farting as the sirens wailed, the ACK ACK blasting away and the distant crump of bombs. We usually arrived at school very early as there was nowhere else to go. Same with most of the pupils. One morning, we found a big hole in the playground with children sitting on the perimeter with their legs dangling down the crater. A teacher arrived and immediately fled and a little later an Army lorry came and shooed us away. The children booed them and called them spoilsports.

On weekends, our mother would take us on bus rides. Once, she said we were going to the zoo. It was not a real zoo, more like an animal enclosure. I did not care for zoos, cages full of dejected animals pacing up and down and a condor in a cage not five miles up in the thermals was the saddest sight I had seen. That is until I read about the extraction of bile from bears and the despicable things people did to tigers. I don't think there were many animals in residence because how could the lions be adequately fed? I hoped that most of them had been taken back to the jungle. One interesting scene was a goat, munching gratefully on a cardboard box.

Why we spent that period of the war in London, when thousands of kids were being evacuated by the trainload will forever remain a mystery. On weekends, I would help Grampy tend his allotment and feed the stinking bonfire that seemed mandatory among the gardeners. I would also feed his goldfish which were in a large glass tank. One night, a stray bomb exploded not far enough away and the house shook. Grampy told us that it wasn't a raid as the siren had not sounded. Just a lonely bomber lightening his payload in order to make his escape and get home in time for breakfast. At first light, we all inched into the back garden. The goldfish were lying dead, gaping in the shards but carrots, turnips and lettuce remained upright and on parade. A row of houses about a mile off had toppled like dominoes. Grampy walked across the allotments with some other men. He came back an hour later looking as if he had just revisited the Somme. There were kids from school that had been sleeping in those houses.

First V1 and later V2 rockets were aimed at London during this time. None fell near us, but two Doodlebugs flew overhead. Whilst their engines could still be heard, we knew we were safe, but when the engine cut out, it was time to move very fast because they simply fell out of the sky. We were lucky there also, as none did land near us. We could differentiate between various aircraft. Spitfire, Hurricane, Wellington, Fokke-Wulf 190, Messerschmitt and many others, and of course, we all knew the sound of the murmuring Luftwaffe passing overhead at great height to hammer Coventry and beyond. The daylight raids were the most exciting, for when a fighter had shot down a bomber or been successful in a dog fight, the pilot would do a victory roll over the houses, rattling the slates and sending housewives cheering into the streets.

I suspect that Grampy was at loggerheads with his father for most of his life, because whereas his brothers all became butchers, Grampy was a carpenter and worked in a timberyard, which explained why I only met my great-grandfather twice. The first time was at their 60th wedding anniversary when I was seven, and some years later when Grampy and I paid him a visit. We didn't stay long as the sun was setting and Great-grandfather was in the habit of going to bed early to save electricity. Also, he wished to turn on the wireless for the evening news. The morning news was at nine o'clock and they were the two occasions the wireless was switched on. On leaving, he gave us two shillings each, saying, "I suppose you'll waste it on drink." He was in his nineties when I last saw him. When he died some years later, my great-grandmother followed him three days after. At the age of eight, he had walked from Scotland with his six-year-old sister, sleeping by the wayside. On arrival in London, he soon found that the streets were not paved in gold. He got a job as a butcher's boy.

In the Great War, Grampy spent four years up to his neck in mud and blood on the Somme. Like many thousands who returned, he never spoke of it, apart from an amusing anecdote he would recount when pressed. It was as if hearing it for the first time the way he embellished it.

It's been well documented that there were occasional front-line truces, at Christmas, Good Friday and for the evacuation of the wounded and the burial of the dead. Grampy's story began when a crazed horse strayed between the lines and collapsed kicking in a barn of a ruined farmhouse. A volunteer was called for to put the animal out of its misery and to garner from it what could be easily obtained. After shaking hands and exchanging cigarettes with a volunteer from the opposite trench, they fell upon the horse with knives and bayonets. With time running out, loaded with slabs of horse flesh, they said their goodbyes but not before simultaneously spying a large Spanish onion hanging on a nail on the remaining barn wall. This was halved and soon the signal to re-engage was given and men stood to with the smell of frying horse and onions mingling with the cordite. Grampy came back to his family. I like to think the other fellow did likewise.

My grandmother who we called Nanny came from a family of twenty-two girls. A bit rich, even in Victorian times. There were four sets of twins of which she was one twin. I never met any of my great-aunts personally though; I suppose most of them must have been in attendance at my great-grandparents' Diamond Wedding Anniversary, where my attention was entirely focused on the five-tiered cake and the numerous salivary comestibles which surrounded it. That the vast majority of the madding throng were blood relations held no interest for me. I may as well have been at a rugby match. Apart from the cake, the only things I remember were Great-grandfather on stage singing a song in an understandably weak and quavering voice and my small brother Murray swinging on the stage curtains, causing great mirth, which drowned out the old boy's serenade. My mother was acutely embarrassed of course. I was surprised that she didn't deny all knowledge of him.

## South Newington

After this short but interesting period with Grampy and Nanny during the blitz, my mother packed our bags and we were soon on a train but not for long.

We alighted at a station and sat in the refreshment room around a table. I see it now, Gordon to my right, little Murray opposite with my mother nowhere to be seen. I don't recall how long we waited, but soon the air raid siren wailed and a little later, bombs were dropping not far off and plaster fell from the ceiling on to the table. We sat there as mother instructed until a kind policewoman took us to her station, put us in a cell, gave us cocoa and covered us in blankets. We awoke next morning in the children's ward of a hospital, and after a couple of days of anxiety and uncertainty, our mother came for us and we left for the country once more.

I didn't have to wait long to see what was going to happen to us. Torn apart again, Gordon and I were taken to the village of South Newington and billeted with an elderly couple who had spent many years in India. Tiger skin rugs complete with heads, gun cabinets packed with shotguns, elephant guns, rifles, Mausers and a beauty called a Flintlock, which was engraved and studded with semi-precious stones and primed for action. Colonel and Mrs Robertson lived in a large, thatched cottage on the edge of the village with roses and honeysuckle around the door.

Our new foster parents were quite intimidating. He, very gruff; she, very severe. Showing us around the house, pointing out where not to go or touch, she led us up the creaking stairs to our bedroom. "You are really being spoilt," she said. "The mattress is of goose down and the bed hasn't been used since Mummy died twelve years ago, and we weren't intending to use it until that brute of a billeting officer thrust you two upon us," she said witheringly. Chilling moments like these were interspersed with unexpected tenderness as she lighted us up to bed that evening and warmed the bed and mattress with a long handled brass frying pan, with a lid filled with hot ashes. That was that, she didn't help us into bed, the mattress being about three feet from the floor. In fact, neither of us was touched by either of them for the duration of our stay. Untouchable, I suppose. Low caste.

I used to climb up a bed leg and haul Gordon up, who kept talking about the lady's dead mother until Morpheus took over. I think we were probably with this eccentric couple for about three months. The weather was blustery and wet when we arrived so it was most likely spring. Our stay was largely uneventful; the war a long way off until a hot summer afternoon found my brother and I lying in long grass making daisy chains watching hundreds of aircraft, Flying Fortresses, Wellingtons, Lancasters and many others on their way to Europe. I know I didn't sleep very well that night thinking of the many German kids that would not be attending school the next day. My mother would visit every so often, and we would take her for a walk around the village. We never asked where Murray was and she did not mention him. Somehow, inside me I knew he was safe.

### Upper Tadmarton

One day, mother came for us in a car and took us to another village, Upper Tadmarton. We were together once more, never to be parted, I hoped. I was familiar with the names Vicarage, Parsonage and Manse as terms given to the residences of Men of the Cloth. These were mostly nice places where church fetes were held, as well as Christmas parties where we could stuff ourselves with cakes, buns and trifle. The rectory held no such promise. The rector was no longer living there, but he had left behind the smell of old Bibles, musty cassocks, boiled cabbage and mouse shit. We were the first to take up lodging. My mother compared the ambience with a badgers' sett. Another family, a woman and her two daughters, arrived about midnight. The following day was spent cleaning and dividing the huge house into four sections as two more families were expected. Another family came the next day, a woman and two more girls. That made four girls in all. For us two boys, aged six and four, they were uninteresting indeed and we studiously avoided them.

Two days later, we hit the jackpot when a French-Canadian couple arrived and the stench of antiquity was blown away. Within hours, the aroma of wine and perfume mingling with the stink of garlic and Gauloise cigarettes completely exorcised the austerity and gloom of the past. The man was a pilot recovering from wounds. He and his wife had been in England at the outbreak of war. He immediately joined up. My mother had kept quite a strong hold on what was left of the Kenyan coffee beans, as she had learned the value of them and we became great friends with his odd couple. They both knew much of the verse of Robert Service and the writing of Jack London and sang songs of adventure in the frozen tundra. They enjoyed reversing the roles of the brave unimpeachable Mountie, who always gets his man, the man usually a French-Canadian fur trapper called Black Jacques or Rene the Rat. Where the Mountie was rotten and corrupt and the much-persecuted Jacques-Rene being 'awfully nice chaps'. We must have stayed at the rectory for six months at least. I remember a warm summer catching minnows and sticklebacks in the brooks and a snowy Christmas when the Canadian pilot made an igloo for us. We played in it every day until we all caught measles. By the time we recovered, our igloo was a pool of slush and the exciting couple had left.

I haven't mentioned my younger brother Murray in the previous pages because from the time of the railway station incident he came under the foster care of a Mr and Mrs Sherwood whose own children were grown, fully fledged and had left home. He was only a baby really, and they loved him very much. So, when we made our next move to the village of Bloxham, Murray came with us and left the Sherwoods heartbroken. Murray never forgot them and visited them often. He also kept in touch when he joined the Navy and throughout the remainder of their lives.

## Bloxham

Our next abode in the village of Bloxham was a huge decaying mansion with orchards, garden, barns and stables, unattended for decades. There were two other families living on various levels. Our bedrooms were four floors up the back stairs, the servants' quarters in years past. No beds, but dozens of musty mattresses, cushions and pillows, none of which lasted much longer when the glorious pillow fights began. Pillows lodged in trees after they had sailed out of the big sash windows. The gardens were a jungle and a delight, fruit trees of every kind imaginable, a walled vegetable garden with espaliered peaches, apricots and plums clinging to the walls. A nut grove of walnuts and hazel, scary and spooky nooks and gazebos. Parts of the barns and stables were continually caving in, usually after we'd just left off playing in them. Preserved fruit and old wine bottles filled the dark and menacing cellars; they were covered in cobwebs and the dust of ages. Gordon dropped a bottle of fruit; it made a terrific bang as it exploded and the smell persuaded us to leave, although a dipsomaniac would have appreciated it, I'm sure.

# Chapter 2

My mother came from a large working-class family. She did well at school in both athletics and the general curriculum, as did all her siblings. In those days with her background, it was very difficult for her to go any further with her education, so she finished school at fifteen years of age and worked to help support her numerous younger siblings. She educated herself by spending as much time as possible in libraries, art galleries and museums and was an insatiable reader all her life. How she met my father remains a mystery as he was an architect and surveyor and had spent some years in Kenya. Photographs of their wedding and subsequent references to him years after, indicates the love she had for him. She kept every item of his life in Africa: python skins, 'heffalump' tusks, daggers and carvings. His tropical wear, a topee, came with us on our travels, plus kilts both hunting and ceremonial, along with a sporran which I proudly wore in which I stored my marbles and conkers. The coffee bean sack was considerably lighter by now. My mother never once wept openly, but now and then when she thought she wasn't being observed, I saw tears in her eyes, which must have been when the divorce proceedings were going ahead in my father's absence.

It was about that time she began going out most nights, in all weathers. She had a bicycle which she rode to Swalcliffe and 'The Stag', a pub frequented by Air Force personnel from all over the world. I was under instruction to look after my brothers until she got home. I did, and we had fun. She did confide in me her reason for going out every night in a shy sort of way – translated she was on the hunt for a father figure for us boys. One day, she blushingly showed me a photograph of an Australian pilot called Jack who came from a part of Australia called the Riverina in New South Wales. I have never held her endeavours against her, if anything, I wished her success. I knew that she was a good woman and a devoted mother. Many years later, I had an astonishing meeting with Jack.

One bright sunny weekend, my mother ran to the top of the stairs and welcomed Commander Robert James Wynne R.N. into our lives. We called him Uncle Bob and life was never the same again from that moment. As a young boy, I had no idea how influential he was to become in shaping my future both professionally and personally. Uncle Bob was in command of a fire fighting and salvage sea-going tug operating out of the Port of London and the Thames Estuary. He had been decorated by King George for boarding and extinguishing a fire on an oil tanker and rescuing most of the crew. Ships that safely ran the gauntlet of U-boat packs were still subject to intense bombing and strafing in the English Channel and the Thames Estuary. Ships that were sunk in the comparatively shallow waters of the estuary, with difficulty and danger could still be salvaged of a fair proportion of their cargo. I am not ashamed to admit that we benefited occasionally from this booty, and for certain, we were not the only ones who did.

One day, my mother, who never wore hats, borrowed one from a friend. She and Uncle Bob went to Banbury and she returned with Uncle Bob, who thenceforth became Pop, my hero. Pop came home as often as his dangerous job permitted and he would take us fishing in South Wales, where his mother was living in a cottage in the Brecon Beacons. He taught us to shoot rabbits and pigeons for the pot; never for fun. I have never forgotten that lesson.

About this time, I began to notice a difference between Bloxham and the other villages and places I had lived in. There was little sign of war except when we went for walks past Barford aerodrome, not far from Bloxham. Occasionally witnessing a Spitfire or Hurricane taxiing across the road which the runway traversed, so close were we that we could see the pilot looking left and right in case there was a haywain or the district nurse on a 'sit-up-and-beg' bicycle bearing down on him at speed. So close was he that my mother and he managed to mouth a few words to each other. He was an Australian, she said, where kangaroos and Eileen Joyce came from. Barford was used to give air protection to beautiful Oxford. However, the Luftwaffe steered clear of the city as Hitler intended having himself installed as Chancellor when victory was his. But in case he decided against the idea at any stage, the Royal Air Force were not taking any chances.

The news that the war was over came with the pealing of church bells and farmers driving their tractors and hay wagons through the village, picking up excited children and whoever else chose to clamber aboard and thence to a farmyard where a huge bonfire was blazing and to a surfeit of cakes and cider.

Not long after, Pop came home for good and took a position as Director of the winding down operations at the aerodrome. The rear wall of the gardens at 'Stone Hill House' in Bloxham overlooked the playing fields of the local college. There I saw rugby played for the first time. Apart from running and jumping, I was quite useless at sport. At football, I never knew which direction the ball would go once I'd kicked it. In rugby, I could pick up the ball up without being penalised and run with it. What could be easier?

I learned to ride my mother's bicycle but could 'sit-up-and-beg' only when whizzing down Barford Hill and other heart stopping slopes, otherwise I stood on the pedals, tiring work but beneficial for my calf muscles, which made me the speedy runner I was to become. I chose to play on the wing when I began to play rugby in the Navy rather than run the risk of having my head rearranged in the scrum. There was a gambling phenomenon at the time called the 'Pools', whereby for a small outlay a fortune could be won by predicting the outcome of football matches. Smaller sums could be won also. Pop decided to indulge and collected one thousand and eighteen pounds and sixpence. He gave me the sixpence, bought a pre-war Standard Vanguard, registration number CER677. My mother bought a baby grand piano and things that she thought had a fair chance of retaining their value for a number of years and not fall to bits in a fortnight, as she forecast the car would. Her eccentricity really reared its head when she had fitted wall-to-wall carpet in our part of the crumbling mansion. The carpet did complement the baby grand, I had to admit, but it also convinced me that we would be spending the rest of our lives in the house provided it didn't collapse. More by luck and not his mechanical aptitude, Pop nursed the battered vehicle through the country lanes to South Wales and down to Devon, packed with fishing and camping accoutrement, his family and as many village kids that we could squeeze in and who so far in their lives had never laid eyes on the sea.

On January 12, 1948, we all had a belated Christmas present when my mother brought home from Banbury Hospital, Robert John Wynne. A remarkable baby brother who walked at nine months. As a baby and toddler, Bobby was spoilt by us all, but he never grew up to be a spoilt child. By the age of three, he was well aware of the boundaries and rules which were not to be transgressed. Never once did Pop refer to us older boys as his stepsons. He treated us equally. Punishment for stepping across the line meant deprivation of privileges such as trout fishing, shooting and no pocket money. Had we the choice, we would have opted for corporal punishment every time. But Pop knew what hurt most.

Bringing up Bobby did not prevent my mother to begin taking piano lessons with Mr Chidzey in Banbury during the daytime. Soon after, I too began the weekly journey to Mr Chidzey, which started at seven o'clock in the evening, pleasant enough during summer, in winter another thing altogether. It was dark and freezing by the time of my return. Despite the piano practice and the lessons interfering with my social life, I was pleased with my progress and passed my exams with ease. I also knew that it pleased my mother to whom I owe my love of classical music. We both were aware that I would never be a Vladimir Horowitz. Pop had shown me the sea that would be my life for a number of years.

As far back as I can remember, my mother loved classical music. It took several records to play a symphony; they were stacked on top of each other, and when one was finished, somehow another dropped down and the music continued. We went to charity piano concerts in Banbury; among the soloists were Moira Lympany, Myra Hess, Irene Scharrer and Moisevitch! Benno Moisevitch was a member of the dart team of a pub in a nearby village; he went everywhere in carpet slippers due to a chiropodic ailment. Listening to him play once, I was squirming and fidgeting with the back of the chair in front to see if he was wearing his slippers, when the quite justifiably annoyed lady asked my mother to remove her demented child. Fortunately, she did not. My curiosity satisfied, I behaved myself and we sat back and enjoyed the recital.

As we boys grew older, we wandered and cycled for miles around Bloxham. A favourite spot was a many roomed, fortified mansion with leaded windows and gargoyles, and to my mind only qualified as a castle by virtue of the wall and moat surrounding it. A bridge over the moat took one through an archway and guardhouse where the portcullis and the mechanics for the drawbridge were once housed. The castle's owners and ancestors must have been sympathetic to the Parliamentarian cause as Oliver Cromwell was a guest the night before the Battle of Edge Hill. The castle was open to the public for a few months of the year. Fetes, Gymkhanas and other events took place also. One of our wanderings found us near the castle one day. It was closed to the public at the time, but we decided to approach anyway. We knocked and kicked the door until it was open by a very old lady who informed us kindly that the castle was closed to the public until the summer. We had the sum of one shilling and seven pence-halfpenny in coppers between us and offered it as a sort of bribe. She refused to take the money, but just as it began to rain, the old lady relented and invited us into the hallway to shelter. I had been to the grounds before but never entered the Hall of the Mountain King. There was no one else in residence apart from a maid, and I think that the old lady was beginning to enjoy the company of this troop of scruffy village boys. Suits of armour stood about the hall. Pikestaffs, Halberds and lances clung to the walls, and there were chests of rusty blunt swords which we were permitted to wield. Gordon was adamant that the rust on the sword was dried blood. I allowed him his morbid fantasy. On a strange iron frame, there was hanging a short sheepskin coat, covered in dust and very close to disintegration. I asked to try it on. The lady said that no one had in her memory, but it was about time someone did. We carefully and with difficulty removed the coat, which she draped around my shoulders, saying that Oliver had forgotten it when he left to meet the King's Men. One would have thought that she had been on intimate terms by the manner in which she caressed Oliver's name.

An impertinent boy called Brian asked if we could go upstairs. The lady obliged and led us very slowly up several flights to where the nuns once lived. She then lifted up a small trapdoor and taking a pebble from a bowl nearby, dropped one down the hole. There was a splash seconds after echoing from the well, which was where 'the nuns disposed of their babies' she said blithely. "That's not true," interjected cheeky Brian. "Nuns can't have bubbies cos they ain't married." I was old enough to know that the lack of a marriage certificate didn't preclude giving birth. Gordon concurred with Brian of course. When the short and fiery debate had run its course, we found that the old lady had fallen asleep in an armchair. We left her there, then ran down the stairs. After wresting a sword from Brian's tenacious grip and dropping it, we rushed out the door without closing it and ran like antelope till we could barely breathe.

Bloxham's village school was no different from the others. With much patience and fortitude, I sat out my stretch one row in front of the dunces. There was ample space in the dunces' row where the clowns, agitators and misfits whiled away the hours. Either the teachers had detected a spark of hope in me, or they were concerned that my relegation to the back bench might lead to anarchy, could be the reason I was kept apart.

# Duns-Tew

In the late summer of 1949, Pop excited us with the news that he had secured for us a new council house in the village of Duns-Tew, five miles from Bloxham. Pop said we would take a look at it soon, as we would not be moving in until the following February. Soon, not being soon enough for me, I immediately left on a reconnaissance mission on my bicycle, returning after dark with a glowing report, a rough topographical map of Duns-Tew and an estimation of the distance from the house to 'The White Horse' and other less important information. Pop was very annoyed with me for leaving without telling anyone. However, he was soon back in his usual good humour, and on discovering that it was not a day's march to the pub and a pint, we were the best of friends once more.

On one bitter, windy February day, the same men who grunted and groaned with the baby grand up the stairs of Stone Hill House, grunted and groaned down with it. With the rest of our goods and chattels, including the rolled-up carpet we left without looking back for Duns-Tew and our brand-new council house. With the aid of a tail wind and leaving ten minutes before the convoy, I was waiting for them at the front gate of the house. There were three pairs of semi-detached houses, we were in the middle. The site was on a piece of high ground overlooking a valley to the North and Siberia. There were ample grounds both front and rear which resembled frozen tundra. The builders had done their best to clean up, but sand and gravel, spilt paint and plaster stained the earth. My mother immediately put the sight out of her mind with the positive words. "Well, at least it's ours and spring's not far off." The removalists began off loading and running backwards and forwards in order to get their circulation going. Pop was taking the front door off its hinges to accommodate the piano. Mother was lighting the fires and we boys were making sure that wee Bobby didn't get under the men's hob-nailed boots.

Finally, everything was crammed in, mostly in the correct rooms. The beds were upstairs but so was an armchair. The piano was in place with the rolled-up carpet on top of it. But we were warm and happy at last. Pop sent me to the pub for two quarts of cider, which the removalists soon polished off. They then left saying that they hoped we wouldn't think of moving again for at least two years, by which time they would have retired. To add to the pleasure of the day, I had missed a day's school. It was a Thursday, and as no one mentioned anything about school for the next day, I decided not to also. Three whole days to reconnoitre the village and pick out the best fruit trees, although leafless, wouldn't escape my hawk eyes. Monday and school were a long way away and the world could end before then.

Next evening being Friday, with the family dinner money in my pocket I awaited the fish and chip van. I could hear the tolling increased as the van swept its way through the village, rounding the bend in the lane, lit up like a cruise liner in the Arctic, an-hour and a half past dinner time. I warmed my hand on the side of the van and drooled like a bloodhound.

Monday arrived only too quickly. Gordon and Murray were enrolled at the village school and I caught the school bus to Steeple Aston, about three miles of winding country road, pulling up at Dr Radcliffe's 'Dotheboys Hall'. All weekend, my bottomless well of optimism had supplied me with plenty of hope. That something would be different, but it was no different. Was my optimism crushed? No, I was a born optimist; the word pessimist was not in my vocabulary. There was no room for pessimism in my head. Three years to go I thought and shrugged. Like the other schools I had been to, more than half of the teaching staff were well over retirement age, called up from the tranquillity of their twilight years to fill the ranks of the slain. I admired them and I knew they would do their best for me. There was one young woman teacher who had not long left college. She was very pretty and when playing netball with the girls, anything else held little interest for us boys. She was the friendliest teacher I had had so far. During the dinner hour in the summer months, she would sit on the grass on the playing fields surrounded by girls and boys; the girls to talk, the boys to look up her beautiful legs whenever she changed position, to ascertain the colour of her knickers. When the bell rang, we would stagger back to class, the air charged with pubescent heat.

The art teacher, Miss Molly Dickson, at a confident guess would have been in nappies at the outbreak of the Crimean War. She was the oldest looking person I had ever seen. Imagine how stunned I was when ten years later when punting down the Cherwell at Lower Heyford with friends, full of rowdy Sunday lunchtime beer, there was 'Molly', standing at the water's edge under a willow tree at the bottom of her cottage garden. She was wearing a long black dress, high necked, with a Cabochon brooch at the throat identical to her school attire. Surely, it was a different dress! "The Navy doesn't seem to have changed you one bit, Hugh Rose," she said, and I detected what could have been a little smile. I gave her my best salute and nearly fell overboard.

One day at school, Molly asked the class to bring two shillings each and she would take us to Oxford for an historical excursion. I was the only bringer of two shillings, the rest of the class preferring to squander their money on the annual visit to St Giles' Fair, so the visit was cancelled. But like me, Molly was undefeatable. "You and I will go during the holidays," she informed me, and we did.

We drove off one morning in her car, which I think was called an Austin Seven. She was a hesitant driver and peered intently with bespectacled eyes close to the windscreen, as if examining an ancient manuscript. I was not worried because I knew that she probably had one of the first driving licences issued in England and possibly the world. First stop was the Bodleian Library followed by the Ashmolean Museum and Merton where she had been a student. Then a tour of many buildings including the 'Eagle & Child' Pub a.k.a. 'The Bird and Baby'. The inn had been used as the Royalist pay office during the Civil War. C.S. Lewis stood in the doorway. Molly said hello to him and he said hello to me and patted my head. Molly apprised me of this honour later. A wonderful day, rounded out with tea and cakes at The Randolph. Thank you, Molly, I wish I had appreciated you more.

One of the repercussions for a minor misdemeanour in class was the order to sit with the girls. I was 12 years old, no longer embarrassed by their presence as I was at 7. Sitting next to sweet-smelling girls was no punishment for me. However, I did not play the role of the repentant very well and they soon caught on.

Dr Radcliffe's was the first school I had attended that had woodwork as part of its curriculum. Mr William Fulton was the Woodwork Master, and if he hadn't been as bald as a billiard ball, I am sure he would have torn his hair out in his valiant efforts to teach me carpentry. Boys were making walnut veneered cigarette boxes, whilst I was struggling with a spade scraper, which was the sole piece of my 'joinery' that he deemed worthy of my taking home. I intended displaying it on our piano for all to see. I was not allowed to varnish it however, as Pop was going to use it for scraping spades. I shrugged yet again.

Unlike the rest of the staff, Billy, as he was known to us, was a rustic; we loved him; he was one of us. If he showed any favouritism at all, it was to the farmers' sons, whose fathers allowed Billy to go ferreting and pigeon shooting on their land. Generally, he treated us equally, from the potential cabinet makers, to the hopelessly inept, like me. The school hall and one other building were seventeenth century. The school had been gradually extended with prefabricated classrooms, one of these being the woodwork room which was some distance away on sloping ground to the vegetable garden and surrounded by huge elm trees. Billy had smuggled his dismantled twelve bore shotgun into the school and would shoot pigeons in the elms, out of the windows, then quickly stow the gun under piles of wood shavings. The headmaster, a Mr Pleasance a.k.a. 'Pheasant', would appear soon after to find out who the ineffable barbarian was causing the infernal racket during his mathematics class. We boys of course said nothing and just stood around looking like Hogarthian idiots. The headmaster must have been suffering from a malfunction of the olfactory organs as he seemed oblivious of the acrid reek of gun smoke. Both Murray and Bobby were to enjoy the company of this gentleman of copse and heath; Bobby going on to become a master carpenter and stonemason. When I left school to join the Royal Navy, Billy told me he was greatly relieved to know that modern day warships were no longer made of timber.

The school library consisted of about forty books stuffed carelessly into a cupboard. Seeking permission to take a book home, Miss Blyton, the English teacher, was quite taken aback and certainly lost for words. I was the first boy who had enquired about the library in years. Permission granted, one by one I removed *Coral Island, Lorna Doone, The Children of the New Forest* and several others and took them home to add to my growing bibliotheca, a rescuer of literature, not a thief. I got on quite well with Miss Blyton. On a day when the class monitor – a dog's body who filled up the ink wells and collected the exercise books for marking – was absent, Miss Blyton gave me the much longed for task of sharpening a box of new pencils, issued that morning. I scarcely could contain myself. It was akin to trusting an alcoholic footman with the key to the Tantalus. The fascinating little weapon was screwed to a small bench in the corridor, with a wicker work basket underneath to catch shavings. Normally, the basket needed emptying no more than once a term. This was about to change. There was nothing malicious about my enthusiasm. No malice aforethought. I was wholly in a grip of an obsession. Miss Blyton poked her head out of the classroom after twenty minutes had elapsed, in time to salvage half of the pencils. The rest were sharpened and short, an inch long in fact. I regretted my action; I had expected to be sent to the headmaster's office. Her eyes were moistening. "Why do you do these things, Hugh Rose? You show so much promise," she pleaded. I ducked a half-hearted slap which felt more like a caress. Possibly, a resentment of having to attend school, for which I harboured a deep and abiding loathing.

The headmaster, 'Pheasant', took arithmetic, my nemesis, hence his intense antipathy towards me. The Cold War was on at the time and oddly enough provided me with much comic relief during some of the lessons. Across the valley was the village of Upper Heyford and adjacent to it was the US Airbase of the same name on the plateau. Night and day, giant B52 bombers would take off every few hours, occasionally during the maths torture. We heard the menacing growl of their taxiing, followed by the thunderous roar of take-off as it swept over the valley and clearing the school by about two hundred feet. It was so low that we instinctively ducked while laughing our heads off at 'Pheasant' shaking his fist at the bomber, his face a rictus of hate. Hilarious episodes like this lightened up the day considerably.

The Cherwell ran at the bottom of the valley just mentioned. Occasionally, especially at the end of winter and the beginning of spring, there would be floods, and watching the swirling water carrying dead sheep and cattle and once an entire haystack, I got to thinking about the various schools I had reluctantly attended. I realised that these schools all had one thing in common. They were situated on elevated locations. Nothing interesting ever happened to any of them, certainly no flood. No direct hit from a meteorite, no outbreak of Lassa fever, no incendiary attack by the Irish Republican Army. Nothing. Even the Luftwaffe were way off target. Never a teacher's strike. Just a decade of purgatory. I thank Odin I left with original thought intact.

'Curly' Morgan was the music master. As his soubriquet suggests had wild curly fair hair. He was a couple of decades younger than his older colleagues and in spite of a portly figure became very animated and energetic when he conducted the school choir. At the Christmas concerts, he referred to himself as Choral Master on the programme, which I thought was an unjustified self-promotion considering we sounded like a gaggle of geese. At one concert, twenty boy sopranos were singing *Nymphs and Shepherds* when one boy, without warning, decided to become a man. Nineteen Jenny Linds and one Fyodor Chaliapian, a fiasco. Poor Curly, I truly empathised with him.

Older boys in their penultimate or last terms before leaving, worked for an hour in the vegetable garden a couple of times per week. On one of these days, it was announced that King George VI had died. Exactly a year later, I was on the Royal Naval training ship 'Ganges', marching up and down with rifle and fixed bayonet at the Coronation Parade. But of course, I didn't know that then.

# Chapter 3
## Joining the Royal Navy

My much-anticipated birthday came on December 11, 1952 and a few days after the school broke up for the Christmas holidays. I boarded the bus for the last time. The bus rumbled off, excited children shouted and waved. I did not join in, unfettered at last. It was a little disconcerting. I had three months to while away before my induction into the Navy. During this time, I had plenty to do. Preliminary medical checks, intelligence tests, character references from local dignitaries. Literacy paper, easy. Numeracy, nothing Euclidian. Then to Portsmouth for an interview with a Navy psychiatrist. Pop had forewarned me about the importance of this interview. "Don't say you want to sink a Bismarck or win the Victoria Cross when he asks you why you want to join the Navy." I had no intention of doing so, so when the inevitable question was posed, I said that I wanted to see the world, get duty free tobacco for Grampy and wear the sailor's uniform to enable me to meet lots of girls. The psychiatrist apparently thought those reasons were normal from a 15-year-old boy.

The big day came at last. I don't remember saying goodbye to Pop who had gone to work, or to Gordon and Murray who had left for school. I must have done. Bobby was rugged up and playing in the mud with a puppy. I could not say goodbye to him or I would have cried. It was a Monday. I know this because my mother waved from the laundry door and the soap suds from the boiler were surging past me down the lane to where I caught the bus to Banbury and the rest of the world, with Portsmouth being the first port of call.

### Ganges

Upon arrival at Portsmouth, I reported to the Seamen's Mission where I met a dozen other boys. Dinner was at six o'clock, after which we went to the pictures. Early next morning, we were on a train to London, then by underground to Liverpool Street station where a larger contingent was gathered. From there, we went to Ipswich and thence by bus to Her Majesty's Stone Frigate, 'Ganges'. We spent the first six weeks in the Annexe, a boot camp, learning how to face life without our mothers.

First up was the 'Shotley' haircut, each haircut taking forty seconds to complete. London Teddy Boys locks with the Tony Curtis quiff over the forehead together with the 'Duck's Arse' and sideburns fell sacrilegiously in sheaves, leaving the shorn embarrassed and dismayed. Boys like me with the unimaginative short back and sides only needed a twenty-second trim and the orphanage boys were already shaven like Buddhist monks.

The communal showers were next, followed by what was called a short arm inspection, where our genitals were thoroughly examined for signs of venereal disease or any other indication of perverse behaviour. The weather was freezing and the water only lukewarm, but that didn't stop one boy who had had enough of the Navy. Attaining an erection, he attempted to mount the boy in front of him. "Get orf of 'im, you dirty little sod!" shouted a Petty Officer. The boy got his wish, slept in the cells that night and was discharged the next day.

The much-anticipated uniform and kit issue followed the disturbing incident in the showers. Much hilarity occurred while we were trying to figure out how to not resemble a bag of shit tied up in the middle. No easy task, but we eventually got the hang of it. My hat, naturally enough, was the largest size issued and difficult to locate in the stores. To my relief, a hat was found, precluding the need for a bespoke one. Boys of every size, shape and accent all talking together and sounding like a flock of budgerigars. Worzel Gummidge boys from Zummerzet and Devon, Welsh, Irish and Scots. I felt comfortable with the Scots although the Glasgow patois was a wee bit testing. The Geordies were the most incomprehensible, with one of them in the bunk next to mine. We got on well, and after a couple of weeks, I was able to understand half of what he said and guessing the other half, saved me from appearing a congenital idiot. There was no one from my area in my class, but I did meet a boy from Bicester later on, who agreed with me that most of my schoolmates were busy muck spreading and following the plough, the sole occupation I was fit for had the Navy rejected me. Had that been the case, I knew that I would have ploughed straight furrows. All in all, they were quite a likeable bunch, apart from an annoying cretin from Chichester who held court at the far end of the mess fortunately. There he was praising the school he had recently left. I, who was so pleased to be shot of school, listening to another, overcome with worship for his alma mater, an amalgam of pity and admiration swept over me. Physics, geometry, algebra, calculus and trigonometry. I, who spent my school years baffled by fractions and never knowing where the bloody decimal point should be placed. Instantly, my spirits rose when he announced to his mesmerised courtiers that he intended transferring to the US Navy when the first opportunity presented itself, because to his mind they wore snazzier hats.

The hospital complex catered for boys who suffered from various complaints, cuts and bruises, and where one could be 'turned in' for more serious ailments, such as broken limbs or a severe cold. The facilities were where one received one's jabs. On returning from each leave, we were subject to a health inspection, usually focussed on our genitalia. These examinations were normally carried out by a male doctor or nurse, but often embarrassingly by a female nurse. I can vouch that on one occasion several of us boys, aroused beyond measure, had our passions quashed by a sharp rap on the raging member with a pencil. We were fifteen years of age. The significance of these procedures baffles me still.

After six weeks of marching up and down with wooden rifles, lots of sport, information films and inoculations, the instructors were satisfied that even the densest and moronic of us knew his left from his right; we packed our kit bags and transferred to 'Anson' division on the good ship 'Ganges'. Our mess was at the bottom of a long covered way which sloped down to the sea. Other divisions were also named after notable Admirals of the past, Drake, Blake, Grenville, Benbow and Collingwood. Anson division being at sea level, in cold weather was usually submerged in a North Sea fog in the early morning. The Port of Harwich was directly opposite and foghorns sounded constantly to assist the ferries from the Hook of Holland to dock. In the previous weeks, there had been biblical floods in East Anglia and Ganges boys helped fill sand bags and were engaged in rescue work. This occurred while we were at the Annexe learning how to wash our clothes and spit and polish boots. We missed out on this adventure.

Instruction and training began immediately. Knots, bends and hitches, splicing rope and wire, and memorising the flags of all nations, as well signalling, semaphore and the morse code. At the rifle range, we fired 303 rifles. We had just mastered the phonetic alphabet, i.e., Able, Baker, Charlie, etc. when their Lordships of the Admiralty, under international pressure I suspect, stunned us with a revised version i.e., Alpha, Bravo, Charlie, still in use as I write this over sixty-five years later. Soon we came to grips with the sea. There were cutters and whalers which we were taught to pull and sail in all weathers except fog. Sometimes we sailed down to Felixstowe about ten miles away. My first real taste of the sea.

On our first Sunday 'aboard' Ganges, we met the Naval Chaplain with the Dickensian name of Clutterbuck, Church of England. There was also a Roman Catholic priest. How Boy Montefiore attended to his devotions, I could not say as there probably wasn't a rabbi for miles. The Rev Clutterbuck on his new flock of shorn lambs enquired kindly as to whether any of us had not been confirmed, assuming that we had all been baptised. Thank you, pagan mother. I was in my seventies when my brother Gordon sent me my Confirmation Prayer Book. Unbaptised. I treasure it.

The first bit of trouble I encountered was on the foreshore. There was a large area of rough grass before the sea, where we practised rigging sheer legs for Jack Stay transfer at sea and where the field gun crews trained. Three gun-emplacements remained from WWII and were out of bounds but not for the reason I imagined. I had heard from senior boys of the picturesque graffiti decorating the interior, such as, 'What Goering could do with his Doodlebugs?' and 'what Himmler could do with his testicles?'. Apparently, poor Goebbels had no balls at all. One Sunday afternoon, I saw several senior boys head towards the forbidden concrete structures and disappear within. Assuming that they were swatting up on WWII history, I followed them in and discovered how wrong I was. Girls from the village of Shotley, a short distance away, were in the habit of trysting with any boy willing to risk corporal punishment. It was the worst piece of timing in my life up to that point. Whistles blew and shouting was heard and I was grabbed by a huge regulating Petty Officer and scooped up with the guilty ones while knicker-less girls shrieking and laughing, made their escape dropping items of apparel as they fled. One boy managed to souvenir a pair of knickers in the melee, which he proudly showed us sixteen months later when on our way to join ships. Summary justice followed; we were to be dealt with six cuts each as punishment. I was face down over a vaulting horse in tandem with an ardent Sinn Fein lad when the tannoy announced that Joseph Stalin had died. "Who the fooks he?" my heroic fellow offender blurted out. The pain vanished instantly and I sobbed with joy. Despite this event, life was strict but not severe. The food was dull but plentiful. There were lots of sports and I learned to swim. Every week, we had a picture show at the gymnasium. The show started with a month-old newsreel which was our sole source of information of the outside world. It was followed by a cartoon, then either a short featuring the Bowery boys, the Three Stooges and often *The Lone Ranger*. *The Lone Ranger* was very popular with us and we enjoyed its predictability. Without variation, the Lone Ranger and his mono-syllabic Red Indian partner Tonto would reconnoitre a town at dusk. The Lone Ranger would then instruct Tonto to go into town, in order to glean information of any nefarious goings on, saying, "Tonto, you go into town and see what you can find out." We all knew that these supposedly undercover operations were destined to fail.

At the name Tonto, two hundred rowdy boys rose as one, shouting, "Don't go into town, Tonto!" But Tonto never failed to go into town and for various reasons always ended up in jail. Maybe his headband had something to do with it. The ever-vigilant Lone Ranger, noting that Tonto was overdue would mount his well-rehearsed rescue crusade which also never varied. He would then saddle Silver his horse. In the quiet hours of early dawn, arriving at the rear of the calaboose, he would attach his lariat to the window bars, take a turn or two around the pommel, and with a 'Hi, yo Silver' remove the wall of the jail in a shower of dust and bricks. Tonto, coughing and spluttering, would come stumbling through the rubble, leap upon 'Scout' his faithful Palomino who was conveniently tethered and saddled nearby. The doughty pair would make their getaway in a hail of bullets. On many of my forays ashore in the Royal Navy where I seemed to magnetically attract trouble, I was to recall our boisterous advice to Tonto.

During my time on the Ganges, we were granted four periods of leave of three weeks each. Very generous, I thought. Excitement mounted as our first leave neared. Reveille was sounded at 0600 Hours. This bugle call was known as 'Charlie'. We were usually up and dressed by then as the Duty Petty Officer had pulled us out of our bunks at 0530 Hours, shouting and banging anything that made a noise with a large stick and often accompanied by a lewd ditty:

*"Rise and shine the morning's fine*
*You've had your sleep and I've had mine*
*Come along you hardy tars*
*Hands off cocks*
*Pull on your socks"*

Two boys were then delegated to go to the galley every morning, returning with a two-gallon bucket, known as a fanny, of scalding cocoa with the viscosity of custard. With a mug of Kai, as it was called, inside us and a couple of ship's biscuits which needed dunking constantly for us to have any hope of getting our teeth into, we set to scrubbing, polishing, sweeping and dusting until 0800 Hours, when we repaired to the central mess galley for breakfast. Great dollops of porridge oats, followed by a cooked dish and two one-inch-thick slices of bread stuck together with edible axle grease. The tea was disgusting and was laced with a mysterious compound designed to stop boys from thinking about girls. Living amongst them for sixteen months and listening to their vulgar and intriguing discourse, the additive appeared to have little effect.

Another ritual before breakfast was 'Mast Party' where classes took it in turn to climb the mast, climbing outwards over the Devil's Elbow. Great fun, except in winter when the shrouds and ratlines were thick with rime ice. On descending, we flew back to our Kai mugs to thaw out our blue and numb hands.

On leave morning, we were out of our bunks by 0300 Hours. Cleaning still had to be done and we needed the extra time, being shorthanded as the boys from the Hebrides, Ireland and the Channel Islands had left the day before. Then it was off to breakfast where the excitement and expectancy did nothing to diminish our appetites one bit. Breakfast over, a packed lunch was handed out consisting of two, two-inch sandwiches, a large chunk of fruit cake and an apple and orange. These lunches had little chance of surviving until lunch; in fact, very few made it to Ipswich, where we packed into a train bound for Liverpool Street station, London and dispersed to the far reaches of the British mainland. Let loose, in a sailor suit, I tipped my hat on to the back of my head and rolled down the platform to the underground railway as if I had recently returned from Trafalgar, a hero, a salt encrusted Jolly Jack Tar.

Since my arrival at Ganges, I feel that I have been guilty of referring to my mess mates as 'them and they', as if I was an innocent observer. This was not the case. I was complicit in all their crudities and lewd behaviour; we were as one. 'Them and They' included me.

The train from Paddington was a non-stopper to Banbury, and as we neared familiar landmarks, I thought of Molly, Pheasant, Billy, Curly and the pretty teacher with the beautiful legs. We passed Somerton where the Cherwell and the Canal ran along-side the railway and there was the dangerous 'Lasher' sparkling and splashing in its fury where fat chub & perch could be caught. I wished the train had stopped, when I could have walked or run the mile and a half to Duns-Tew. But it sped on for a few miles to Banbury, where luckily, it was cattle market day, and I secured a lift home in a local farmer's lorry. The farmer was full of market day beer and all I could think of was Robert Louis Stevenson's poem, 'home is the sailor, home from the sea and the hunter home from the hill'. The lorry screeched to an unaccustomed halt outside No. 5 Duns-Tew finding Bobby where I had left him playing in the mud with a much larger puppy.

It was mid-afternoon when I walked into the house with an excited Bobby at my heels when the strangest thing occurred. My mother hugged me for the first time. I can feel the intensity of that hug even now and knew that she could sense the reciprocation. I felt that she was trying to tell me something, but she failed to find the words. She had tears in her eyes, then we both knew that we had to turn this impromptu display of mother and son affection into a joke for Bobby's sake and we began laughing with different tears. I made a fuss of Bobby and gave him a squashed Mars bar. Then it was small talk; we both did not know where to begin until my mother fetched a quart bottle of Woodpecker cider from the larder, and by the time we had lowered the bottle halfway, we were both chattering like woodpeckers.

She asked me what I had been reading. I knew she would. I said that Ganges was without a library, and unless one was studying the seamanship manual, such pursuits were actively discouraged, not that we had much time to read. A few dog-eared Westerns did the rounds and a much-read Mickey Spillane novel, which was fast approaching disintegration. Funnily, my well-read mother 'claimed' to have no knowledge of Mickey Spillane, so I and the cider enlightened her with a lurid description of a Los Angeles Gumshoe who, having just been whacked on the mastoid bone with a baseball bat, survived a car smash, fallen four storeys down a lift shaft, been thoroughly exhausted by a beautiful blonde nymphomaniac, found that the panacea to full recovery was four fingers of Rye. She was really crying now. I had never seen her so happy. Our first real talk together. Bobby was laughing too, but I am sure that he didn't know why.

The children at Duns-Tew Primary were released from their chains at 3.30, but my mother never expected Murray to travel the few hundred yards home in less than an hour as he had a tendency to quarter the ground like a beagle. It was with feigned surprise that she greeted him at 3.45 with, "God, is it 4.30 already?" Murray had grown five inches, so it seemed, and together with Bobby thoroughly examined my sailor suit and its trappings in the manner of primates searching for vermin. My civilian clothes had arrived home a couple of months before, but I knew that I would have to wait for Gordon and Pop to get home before I changed. As it happened, I bowed to Pop's request to remain in uniform for the rest of the day in order for him to parade me about the village like a performing bear. At the 'White Horse', numerous sons and daughters of the soil eagerly bought me half pints of shandy. I stood out like a penguin in the Congo. Henrys, Freds and Percys shook my hand and Brendas, Bessies and Phyllises roughed me up in a rather pleasant way.

During the next three weeks, apart from fishing at Sow Brook with Bobby, reading Thor Heyerdahl's account of the Kon Tiki voyage and putting on a few pounds with my mother's pastries, I don't remember much about my first leave. Only that they sped by. In subsequent leaves, I was old enough to enjoy the camaraderie of the village inn and got to know elderly villagers whom I had helped to keep fit by their having to chase me out of their orchards.

Fred Tench, a quietly spoken man, whose lawn I mowed on Friday afternoons in summer, was a veteran of Flanders and had been much affected by the experience. In season, his garden was ablaze with poppies. His house adjoined the ancient forge, where his forefathers had smithed for generations. Tongs and hammers lay as if just left on the forge, and I was always tempted to feel for warmth in the long dead coals. Buckets of rusty nails, horseshoes, and great horse collars hung on the walls, beams dripped with farrier's accoutrement and all festooned in countless years of dust, spider webs and memories. The lawnmower, handmade of course, was kept in the forge. Every Friday was a new wide-eyed experience, always something fresh to wonder at. In winter as the school bus passed, I was the only one who looked at the massive doors and knew what was behind them, and I would still be dreaming of Pip and Joe Gargery having larks when the Tumbril arrived at the school.

The lord of the manor, a Major General, and Pop were friends. They met in unusual circumstances, although recalling what Pop was all about, maybe they were not so unusual. Pop lived his life with a fervent belief that he had the right to wander and forage as he wished. There was nothing political in this belief. On one of his early investigative poaching forays around Duns-Tew, he was apprehended and marched at gun point to the Major who was busy skinning rabbits for his hounds. The Major must have heard about Pop, he dismissed the gamekeeper and invited Pop inside for a whiskey. Pop never had to poach again, which removed most of the pleasure, he would often lament.

During the summer leave of 1953, the Major enlisted the help of Pop, and I to assist him in doing something about the belfry in the Norman Church, next door to the manor. Elderly parishioners had complained of the feebleness of the bells on Sundays. A few had reasonably concluded that deafness was coming upon them, while the pious among them thought that their offertory contribution should be put to good use. No money was needed, however. There was no record of the belfry having been cleaned since William the Conqueror. The Major, Pop and I climbed the belfry stone stairs and proceeded to remove seven feet of bat shit and jackdaw nests. It took hours to lower the detritus in buckets to the ground where folk were eager to cart it off for their vegetable gardens. When we had finished, the lady of the Manor served strawberries and cream to three blackened faces whilst bells tolled in celebration. The cacophony was brain disturbing; I wondered why the church did not collapse. Soon after, the fire brigade and ambulance arrived from Deddington, two miles away. The bells probably had not pealed as lustily as this since the Armada was sighted.

The Reverend Small conducted the services at Duns-Tew and also at an adjacent village where he resided. He had an explosive temper and his nerves were very much frayed at the edges. His war experiences were very much in evidence. He also officiated at other nearby churches. His village was one of those oddities that England was full of; it was bereft of an inn, which undoubtedly explained why Duns-Tew's Sunday morning service was last. No shaking hands with parishioners at the ancient doors. Bang on midday, the reverend bolted for the 'White Horse', sometimes forgetting to divest himself of his surplice and cassock. The locals gave special countenance to his eccentric behaviour, as is common among English folk. Pop knew him well, referring to him as the 'Sin Bosun', an epithet the good man rejoiced in.

Another villager, whose name I never knew and whose face I never saw, played sleepy nocturnes in the evenings and boisterous mazurkas by day. He was a Polish émigré who had fled Europe and had served with the allies. Farmer Frank Brough was a rich, hardworking old curmudgeon. On my last summer holiday before leaving school, I turned up early one morning at his beautifully carved sandstone house, which was about half a mile from the village down a deeply rutted lane. I began slashing dew-soaked thistles in the orchard with a sickle. From the corner of my eye, I could see the cranky old man peering at me from his breakfast window and expecting any moment what everyone had forecast would happen. But I bent to the task at hand, and the thing that everyone said would happen did not happen. There were plenty of windfall apples, and every so often, I would hop over an adjoining fence and tend Mrs Brough's strawberry patch, removing weeds with as many strawberries as I could secrete among them. I found other jobs to do that probably did not need doing but were a welcome change from thistle slashing. It was hay making time and when the sun had been on the newly mown hay for a couple of hours, I would hitch up the hay turner to the gentle farting horse and turn hay until hunger drove me back to the thistles once more. Every Friday afternoon, he gave the labourers a pay envelope. I got nothing. On the Friday of the last week of the holidays, I too received an envelope, as I felt sure I would. "If I'd paid you every week, you'd have nothing," he said quite correctly. "Now you have something. I've charged you six pence per punnet of strawberries Mrs Brough estimates you ate, which is why you'll find ten shillings less than what you would have been paid. Your enthusiasm has been noted and you can begin working here after Christmas. Come on January the second."

"Thank you, Mr Brough," I said, "but I am joining the Royal Navy."

"God help England," he said as he turned and marched away.

I will cease looking back for the time being and return to Ganges where life was repetitive but never dull. We were super fit. No Billy Bunters on board our ship. We ate voraciously, anything and everything that was dished up to us and spent our weekly seven shillings and sixpence pocket money on chocolate from the N.A.A.F.I. Boys were sent food parcels, including me, as if we were P.O.Ws. These were always shared out so the orphan boys were included.

Christmas 1953 arrived and three weeks leave again. Home to Duns-Tew where I thought of Frank Brough's illustrious career offer. I would have excelled as a ploughman, plenty of time to cogitate the meaning of life, but Pop had altered the course of my destiny and I never gave the meaning of life a moment's consideration.

Frost was covering the ploughed fields and mist clung to the village and its leafless elms, where rooks' nests froze. We walked home across Frank's fields at dusk with a haversack of wood pigeons that we had waylaid as they had flown home to roost in their fir tree copse. Dirty, hungry and tired. First a bath, then mother's cooking and then bed to the sound of sparrows fidgeting under the eaves and the rattle of a goods train in the valley. Next morning, I wondered where I would be next Christmas. Would I be stuffing myself with goose and pudding washed down with cider and mulled ale? I doubted it. I loved it all but felt a pang of guilt that I was consumed with the thought of the final six months on Ganges and wanting it to begin.

A week into the New Year, we were back on Ganges. Our class was 'Mast Party' on the first morning. A North Sea fog had rolled in like gun smoke and the figure head of the old ship of the line that stood nearby, eyed us with a malevolent gaze. Up and over the Devil's Elbow we clambered. The ice on the rigging necessitating haste so as to get to grips with our cocoa mugs for warmth. No one fell. There was a safety net but so great was the height that I am sure a plummeting body would have been diced.

Our final term ended with Easter leave, which was sometime during April. We had learned new tricks from more advanced boys, some who had older brothers or a father serving, or had served. In order to create the illusion when on leave that you were a salt encrusted sea dog, it was necessary to scrub one's dark blue collar until it was as insipid as Cambridge blue. Many boys were over-zealous and their collars, had they bleached naturally, meant that those boys would have sailed with Jellicoe at Jutland. My collars had a look of serious sea time about them, but I did not have to buy new ones as others did. One article of our kit was a Housewife, a sewing kit. On packing for leave, our Petty Officer instructor suggested we would not need our Housewife as our mother could sew on buttons, etc., but he relented when he found that most boys wanted to show their mothers that they could darn socks. Once on the train, out came the Housewives and an array of badges which was supposed to be earned. Marksman, Coxswain, Frogman, Bugler and even a deep-sea diving badge. There was barely any sleeve showing that did not display a badge of merit. Campaign ribbons emblazoned chests, some on the wrong side. One boy had a ribbon belonging to his great-grandfather, issued during the Boer War. I respected Pop too much to indulge. He had a great sense of humour, but he also respected and loved the Royal Navy. That leave at Duns-Tew was fun and fattening and the sun shone every day for Bobby and me to fish in Sow Brook. Everyone knew that upon my return I would be drafted; something I had looked forward to for sixteen months. What ship – where bound? No one knew anything more than that. I would be either in the Home Fleet, the Mediterranean or the Far East.

# Chapter 4
# HMS Urchin

Back on the Ganges, I found that I was to join a ship of the Home Fleet. Far from being disappointed about not going to the Far East for two and a half years or the Mediterranean for eighteen months, I was pleased to join the Home Fleet. The far-off foreign stations would come later. The Home Fleet meant regular leave to watch Bobby grow up and begin school. It also meant visits to Scandinavia, France and Germany and with luck, a voyage to the West Indies.

On draft day, I was woken at an early hour and with another boy whom I had never met, a telegraphist; we were taken to King's Cross station in London bound for Edinburgh and from there via Aberdeen to Frazerburgh, a large fishing port in north east Scotland where my first ship, an anti-submarine frigate, lay at anchor. It felt like I was returning after a long absence to the land of my blood. Arriving at Aberdeen, there was time to spare. A kindly gentleman in our carriage, who noticed our weariness and youth, invited us to his home for a couple of hours. We drank copious amounts of proper tea and successfully dismantled a Dundee cake to the utter joy and amazement of his wife. Loaded with sandwiches and more cake, we boarded the Frazerburgh train and fell immediately to sleep. At Frazerburgh, we were picked up at the station and driven to where the ship's boat took us to the appropriately named HMS Urchin. I had never been so excited in my life. We had been travelling for well over twenty-four hours, but as shaving was an activity, we dreamed of we still look fairly smart. Our arrival on board coincided with the ceremony of 'Sunset' when the White Ensign was lowered for the night to the sound of a bosun's pipe. We stood to attention for this and then were shown below to the boys' mess. A leading seaman showed me how to sling my hammock, but I have no recollection of getting into it. I was well and truly out for the count.

The Urchin had called at Frazerburgh on its way back from showing the flag in Holland and Germany, to its base in Northern Ireland. No warship had visited in years as only fishing boats, etc. could be accommodated in the harbour, making our length of stay dependent on the weather. Next day was a Saturday. There was a football match in the afternoon in which the local schoolboy side had little trouble defeating our hung-over team, to be followed by a dance in the evening.

I had never been to a dance before apart from the embarrassing country capers in the infants which entailed touching girls, of all things. It is amazing how a few years can completely rearrange one's thinking. The fact that I could not differentiate between a tango and a tarantella did not concern me in the least. Girls to dance with, girls to hold by the waist, girls to kiss, possibly. I was in the shower; I turned the water to cold. With a clean and pressed suit, a touch of aftershave for effect, I went ashore in the first liberty boat with as many crewmen as safety regulations permitted. At the hall where the dance was to be held were about two hundred women and girls; there was scarcely a man in sight. Most of the male population were hauling nets in the North Sea and Iceland. It was a wonderful welcome. We were clearly outnumbered, but one and all we decided to brave the situation. Well, we jigged, reeled and schottisched for a couple of hours until the heat, the heady heavy perfume, together with the four pints of McEwan's brown ale drove me out into the fresh sea air where I regurgitated the contents of my stomach. A Petty Officer had rounded up the underaged who had to be back on board by 2100 Hours. I had overlooked this and was glad I happened to be hanging over the sea wall when the Petty Officer noticed my plight. I never got to say farewell to the dozen girls I had fallen passionately in love with. I had given many of them my address, together with my pledge of eternal love. All this on four pints of brown ale. I did receive several letters, one from a girl's father defending his daughter's honour, which she still possessed as far as I could remember. He called me a bloody Sassenach. That really hurt.

The following Monday morning, we weighed anchor and headed north. Rounding Duncansby Head and west into the Pentland Firth, passing the Viking Island of Stroma. An area of violent tidal races, but calm, as Her Majesty's frigate sliced through the swell. Not even the 'Hurricane' performing the victory roll over the rooftops would eclipse this feeling of exhilaration. Spray exploded over the bow and hurled itself at the bridge, and as she dived into another wave, the ship shuddered aft as the screws neared the surface. During the voyage, I was sent to different parts of the ship in order to familiarise myself with the locations and general layout. I was given a chit of paper for various people to sign. One of the tasks was to climb the mast to light the Saint Elmo's Fire, though I was informed to leave this task until we were safely alongside. Left-handed hammer, steam driven screw driver; who did they imagine they were dealing with? I knew about St Elmo's Fire when I was six years old. I went along with the ritual in good humour; it was a rite of passage. I desperately needed to be a part of it.

We passed Loch Eriboll, then Cape Wrath and turned south through the Minches with the Isle of Lewis and Stornaway where Uncle Hector came from, on the starboard side, then set course for Lough Foyle in Northern Ireland. Entering Lough Foyle, the land was mountainous to begin with, gradually flattening out to farm land, fields and meadows. Black and white cattle munched on every shade of green grass. White farmhouses stood out against the emerald background. Cormorants sunned and dried their plumage on the banks that were being splashed by our gentle bow wave. Very slow now or we would have submerged the meadows and panicked the cows.

We eased closer to the right-hand bank in order to pass some mothballed Men of War, when another heart-stopping surprise appeared. There she was, the brave wee Amethyst, pock marked all over from Chinese gun fire. I had always wondered what had happened to her after the Yangtze incident that had been big news a few years before. Sitting sedately and patiently, plastered in seagull and shag shit, she resigned to her fate. Maybe they could not break her up. I felt a lump in my throat which I usually only suffered from watching Lassie pictures. I would see her many more times during the next twelve months. We berthed at Londonderry – Derry from here on – at the Naval dockyard. There was no facility for a major refit, no dry dock, but running repairs could be carried out. There were submarines also at the berthing, soon to become friendly adversaries. Ships were required to berth facing downriver for an easy and speedy departure should the occasion arise and did not require the aid of tugs as turning around did. The manoeuvring to turn and face downriver took us very close to the heart of the city, only a ten-minute walk from our berth. Cassidy's pub was just outside the dockyard. We quickly downed a pint and burped our way to the city, where the ragamuffins lay in wait. These ragged boys begged politely but boldly for pennies. We always had plenty, in fact a pocketful of the heavy coins to distribute, sharing the pleasure on their wan faces as the weight lessened in our pockets. We would buy fish and chips; double chips in fact. The urchins had to be fed. Tearing open the steaming newspaper, they squabbled like herring gulls. Then it was to Doyle's pub, a favourite. Jimmy Shand and his band, with Bridie

Gallagher at maximum decibels. We were young, our leave expired at 2100 Hours. Two pints and we were gibbering like macaques. The landlady would place a huge plate of sandwiches on the table to entice the older crewmen to stay. Unnecessary, as they did not intend going anywhere. On a blank week when money was scarce, they would top up the pints with ruby red port. I drank a pint of this potion one day for a dare. My reward for daring was another pint, which I regurgitated ten seconds later, along with the fish and chips. Moira, the voluptuous bar attendant whom I had been trying to impress, cleaned up the psychedelic mess with a scowl on her face. The road back to the ship had many bends and curves that were not there on the way in. Cannoning into walls and tripping over non-existence objects, I was an hour adrift getting back on board. By the time my punishment was up, Moira was smiling at someone else.

I did not reach Able rate on the Urchin, hence the trip to Dublin to visit the places that Yeats, O'Casey, Joyce and Gogarty had roamed and written of did not eventuate until some years later. When I did finally get to that fair city, I had no desire to kiss the Blarney stone. I was revolted by the thought of the thousands of pints of Guinness that must have blackened the Liffey at that hallowed spot.

I did manage to get over the border once; I borrowed some civvies from an Irish stoker and accompanied him to where he lived with his sister at a village called Bally something or other. He weighed around sixteen stone, four more than I did. I changed at Cassidy's Pub where we were quite well known, and without looking in a mirror or glancing sideways at shop windows, we proceeded by bus to the border. No passports. I didn't have one any way. The Garda wished a thousand welcomes to the stoker who they recognised, and looking me up and down several times, straining to keep a straight face, wished me a thousand welcomes too and probably condolences also. The stoker's sister took one look at me and collapsed in a fit of hysterical laughter, which thankfully lessened to giggles and sniggers after fifteen minutes had elapsed. I removed my coat, which was the main cause of her hysteria, and with my trousers hidden under the table, she made tea in the kitchen from where I could still hear the odd guffaw. We had a pleasant couple of hours, and before leaving, she had found clothes that almost fitted, and we returned to the border stopping at several pubs enroute. The border Garda had not changed as I had hoped they would have, they looked at me in a puzzled way, then congratulated me on my sartorial elegance. I did not mind their fun. I had been to my first foreign country.

We spent one week in Derry before slipping our moorings and heading downriver. A reverse view, so I decided to keep my eyes riveted to port but for the few moments when we passed the Amethyst. I wanted to know all about the river, every white farmhouse, cow, horse and sheep, also the cormorant that stood sentinel on its shit stuccoed rock, motionless as we glided past. What did he imagine we were? The Foyle widened to an oily smoothness under the protection of the hills, but out to sea, a white frothy horizon beckoned, and we were soon dipping into the swell and forging ahead to hunt the submarines which had left some hours earlier. No longer under the lee of the land and steering roughly south east with a beam sea, I had my first dose of a ship with a heavy roll. Constantly changing course, rolling one minute, hogging and sagging the next in pursuit of the enemy. Occasionally, I would be sent with a message to the Operations Room which was darkened, stuffy and stunk of cigarette smoke. ASDIC operators with earphones, pinging for a contact. Officers over a chart table plotting the possible course of the submarine. At the time, ships were being built using asbestos as lagging for the many yards of pipe, which ran the length of the ship. Many years later, I witnessed a Senior Officer in Australia officiating at a ceremony, dying at attention, chest heaving. A victim of mesothelioma. The Navy would have been unaware of the dangers associated with asbestos; I am not so sure about the companies that mined and manufactured it. How fortunate I was to spend most of my time on deck.

When a contact with a submarine had been made, we would change course quickly causing sudden upheaval below, especially in the galley. The submarine knew we were up above somewhere and was constantly taking evasive action. When we estimated that we were within limbo range, we would drop grenades overboard to claim a sinking. An Able Seaman was on duty on the flag deck with a box of these odious pieces of ordnance. He was solely responsible for them. They were primed and dangerous. I pestered to be allowed to drop one overboard when the bridge ordered it. The poor fellow relented and got into trouble over the incident of which I was truly sorry.

We usually exercised all week, covering a lot of ground. Wonderful scenery became a part of life. I was never tired of it. The Giants Causeway. Rathlin Island and beautiful massive, majestic Ailsa Craig, a seabird haven, where comical puffins scudded through the troughs. Occasionally, we would have a weekend break in another part on the Mulls of Kyntire and Galloway. During a particularly foul period of November weather, we visited Campbelltown where a six-foot herring lassie who quaffed pints like an Irish navvy offered to show me around. It was pitch black when we ventured into the winter's night and up a brae to where there were several WWII Nissen huts. One of them had no ends in it and was like the scientific wind tunnels for testing rockets. By now, it was obvious that she was after my virginity, which I may say, I was not trying to protect. I had heard about knee tremblers up against a wall but for this to take place at all in a Nissen hut with an icy blast making it impossible to remain erect on two counts. One needed a low centre of gravity. Quasimodo came to mind. Another failure. I remained a male virgo intacta. I would be seventeen the following month, plenty of time yet, I said to myself, as I fled the clutches of the Caledonian amazon for the safety of numbers in the pulsating pub.

Leaving Campbelltown where we were farewelled by the Amazon and a few of her brawny workmates who cheered and waved. Sometime later, we received a signal to proceed to Loch Eriboll which we had sailed past on our voyage from Frazerburgh. There had been a severe snow storm which had buried the local community under deep drifts and needed our assistance. We rendezvoused with an aircraft carrier that had been operating with the Naval air station on the east coast. Two days earlier, a Surgeon Commander and a Sick Berth Attendant had delivered a baby, but the mother was unable to breastfeed. Upon arrival, we began removing snow with our hands and life raft paddles which one thoughtful crewmember had decided could take the place of shovels. The mother who had no milk and her baby were flown to hospital in a helicopter but not before her baby had sufficiently sated itself at another mother's breast. I took several photographs whilst in Lock Eriboll with a Box Brownie, retail value thirty-two shillings and six-pence, a present my mother gave me when I was drafted to the Urchin. I was no Cecil Beaton or Karsh of Ottawa. I knew nothing about lighting, exposure and apertures, etc. I merely found the object, or panorama or a bunch of grinning idiots and clicked. The camera served me faithfully in all weathers for a number of years. Dozens did not come out, of course, but it was amazing how many did. Once after finishing a day's exercise, a submarine had not made the mandatory signal to indicate all was well. We were at anchor when the alarm sub-alert came through, followed by sub-miss a short while later. Signals were flying back and forth to the Admiralty. When taking a turn around the quarter deck in the twilight with a couple of mates, I espied the conning tower of the submarine coming through the entrance of the loch. I ran to the bridge to report but not before pointing and clicking. A perfect photograph came out.

We returned to Derry after this incident for the Christmas leave where we took a train to Belfast, then the ferry to Stranraer and somehow found my way back to Duns-Tew at the ripe old age of seventeen. In my travels on the Urchin, I had bought quite a few souvenirs and trinkets, most of them quite useless, as I think gifts should be. I had saved the astronomical sum of eleven pounds, which I had changed into ten-shilling notes, so as to increase the thickness of the wad and therefore feel richer. Ten shillings was usually sufficient to have a top night ashore, meaning about seven pints of beer, fish and chips and some change still in your pocket. The finer things in life were to come much later.

In those days, there was a delivery of mail on Christmas morning. The postman, in all-weathers, cycled from North Aston on his bicycle with a large wicker work basket fitted in front. It was the custom to wish him the compliments of the season in whichever manner you chose. Normally, he was sober and diligent on his round, but at Christmas, he was easily cajoled into letting his hair down, figuratively speaking, because he hadn't any. No one knew how many fuelling stops he'd had before arriving at 'Wuthering Heights', but watching him navigate his trusty two-wheeled steed through the slush, it was obvious that he had worked up a full head of steam, crimson-faced and snorting like a Pamplona bull. Pulling up at Number 5, my mother wisely gave him a cup of tea and a mince pie and well wished him on his round. He was later seen being driven home in a lorry with his bike in the back.

Christmas dinner never changed or varied. There was always a goose. Very Dickensian, very Tiny Tim, and always surrounded by Frank Brough's wood pigeons, roast potatoes and brussels sprouts picked frozen solid from their stalks. Quart bottles of cider and ale, plus lemonade, ginger beer and brandy for the pudding to burst into flame. I should point out that during the 1950s, when I was in my teens, a naval uniform was a passport to any pub, regardless of my youth.

My mother shopped in Banbury no more than once a month. The village was well serviced with delivery vans calling weekly. The baker, the butcher, the milkman and the green grocer, who was very welcome in winter when the vegetable garden was not producing enough. In summer, preserved fruit, jams and pickles filled the larder which always had a cool breeze passing through it during the summer, dropping to sub-zero in winter. A refrigerator was not needed. We were sans telephone also. The coalman would call, look in the coal shed, assess our requirements, dump his assessment and be on his way. The bill came in the post. Life was different then. Despite the facilities making life easier, my mother always found a few items missing for her weekend cooking. This meant being sent to the shop-cum-post office, a dreaded, daunting task which before I joined the Navy fell to me to undertake. Looking back, the weekly ordeal of the shop was a good enough reason to run away to sea or enlist for life in the Foreign Legion. The shop and post office were operated, which is a very generous description, by Mr and Mrs Wallace. In all his years in Duns-Tew, Pop called at the shop only once, to buy a stamp and post a letter. He entered the shop armed with a five-pound note while I remained in the car. He emerged twenty-five minutes later looking rather shaken, exasperated and bewildered. He got in the car, sat for a minute regaining his composure, then turning to me, he said, "You do this weekly, don't you, son?" He then patted me on the back. Being invested with The Order of the Garter could not have pleased me more. For those old enough to recall the 'Goon Show', a weekly radio comedy during the fifties, Mr and Mrs Wallace were Henry Crunn and Minny Bannister respectively. A pedantic, dithering, mumbling, bumbling pair, who were not just old, they were pre-historic. Another horrifying thought when dawdling to the shop was the chance of other customers ahead of me wasting away precious hours of their lives. If this was the case, I would wait outside or check on the walnut windfall at the White Horse, keeping a hawk eye on the shop and up the street in case someone should get ahead of me, anything but inhale the effluvia of the shop any longer than necessary. Not that I suspected it of being life threatening as the Wallaces had stomached it for decades. An asthmatic would have succumbed in seconds. The obnoxious cloying atmosphere emanated from sacks, bags, boxes, bins and barrels, which contained sugar, salt, washing soda, flour, cheese, butter and bacon. Everything was in bulk. Purchases were weighed as if they were gold dust then tipped onto a stack of stiff blue paper which was then secured by a well spittled thumb and forefinger and laboriously wrapped up. Your shopping list was then perused for about three minutes and the price of the item written down. I was mesmerised by their sloth. The Irish monks inscribing the Books of Kells would have outpaced him. Things hung on walls, brooms, brushes, mops, buckets and from the rafters, rat and mole traps dangled. It seemed that every other item on the list was stored in the loft, which was reached by climbing a ladder, permanently in place for the frequent forays into the dark recesses, a job usually undertaken by Mr Wallace. I would like to say that he sprang up there like an orangutan, but I can't. The ascent together with much puffing and groaning was accompanied by periodic fusillades of musketry from cracking joints until his great buttocks disappeared from view. Often his florid face would reappear to enquire if anyone could remember what he had come up for.

The White Horse Inn, the social hub of the village, dated from the 1600s. We boys would hang around the door on summer evenings after a few hours ferreting, hoping to cadge a half pint of shandy from a cheery, half sozzled farm labourer. As a boy, I knew nothing of the inner sanctum of the inn. The back door was used as a dispensary for hangover restoratives and cigarettes between opening hours and where I would call for the quart bottle of cider for Sunday dinner. On leave from the Navy, I began a custom of having a pint or two at lunch time in all seasons. The pub was very quiet during the working day and we frequently had to serve ourselves. The landlady was usually engaged in her housework while her husband was away at his day job. Apart from the weekends, I never saw more than four regulars at lunchtime. Two stalwarts, Fred Tench, the blacksmith who plied his trade years before in the mud of Flanders and Jack Riley, the head gardener at the manor. Jack was an Irishman whose voice carried through the village like a gunnery officer's. He had served in the Royal Ulster Constabulary during the troubles and was the narrator of blood chilling tales. I suspect he sought asylum in England. Two other occasional drinkers were a travelling salesman who stopped for a pint and a sandwich and a lugubrious octogenarian known as Tomkin who apart from a boyhood visit to Banbury Fair had been nowhere. He sat in the ingle over a pint, which he studied dubiously, sometimes tentatively taking a sip. I had never seen Tomkin finish a pint. One lunchtime when the landlady entered the snug, wiping suds from her arms in order to replenish our glasses, we were all stunned by Tomkin's request for a refill. "I'm drowning me sorrows, me wife's gorn to forrin parts," he whined. Tomkin's wife had left to nurse a sick sister who resided at Hempton, a hamlet no more than two miles distant.

The entrance to the inn was through a flagstone passage, well worn by a million hobnailed boots. Toby jugs, tankards and horse trappings hung from rough-hewn oak beams. In winter, steaming ex-Army great coats dried in the ingle and rubicund-faced men played darts for half pints and fun. The smell was of horses, smoke and humanity and the continuance of a tradition defying the inevitable change, which was fast approaching.

Annually, the gypsies or Didicoi as they were often derogatively referred to, visited. I would dawdle near their smoky encampment hoping like Toad of Toadhall to get a plateful of stew. Sometimes they spoke to me. Other children kept away as the gypsies were reputed to steal youngsters. The idea had a certain appeal, for a couple of days anyway. Their arrival was always in the autumn, when on windless days their smoke clung to the caravanserai and the leafless trees. They would crowd the pub. The men wore trilby hats and coloured neckerchiefs and from their crumpled outdated jackets pulled bundles of fivers that would have choked a goat and played the villagers at darts, never losing a game. The gypsy women took over the roaring fire, separate from the village women. The young gypsy women coyly whispering and giggling; the old women with their long, lank, rainy hair wore ankle-length fur coats with their diamond encrusted raptor talons clutching tumblers of gin. As quietly as they came, so quietly they left. Not a lurch in their step. Their freedom and independence had a palpability which captured my soul.

At the end of this leave, I left Duns-Tew on a Saturday as I had no idea how long the journey would take. It is always more straightforward travelling home. Bobby walked the mile to the bus stop, with Bob his dog leading the way. We stood in silence until the top of the red double-decker bus rose over the brow of the hill. It was time. I wished he hadn't come. We shook hands. Boys didn't hug then. On the bus, I wished I had hugged him, I loved him so much. As the bus chugged off spouting diesel fumes, the mercenary wee bugger called out, "Bring me back a Japanese fishing rod," and rescued my day.

The crossing to Ireland was made in rough conditions with most passengers huddled on deck, braving the elements, rather than suffer the stench below where the decks were awash with land lubbers' lunch and beer. I kept the barman company; he seemed to be glad of it as he wasn't busy. He was from Birkenhead, which I supposed qualified him as a Scouse as he spoke like them. We regaled each other with bullshit and lies, all the way across. I thought I had seen the worst the Irish Sea could offer, but this was the roughest yet. I have to admit I was as pleased as all onboard when Belfast appeared on the horizon. Soon I was back on the Urchin and the same anti-submarine exercises were resumed. The Amethyst was still in once piece and the cormorant seemed not to have budged from his rock once. Between exercises, we paid courtesy visits. The first was up the Clyde to Rothesay on the Isle of Bute. It was February and freezing. In my eagerness to get ashore, I missed my footing boarding the motorboat and into the harbour I went. I was pulled out on the end of a boat hook, and nearly rigid from the ducking. I was put under a hot shower and given a tot of rum, three years before I qualified for my official ration. I remained on board that night; my superiors considered the rum quite sufficient. Things had a habit of happening to me; I was loving it.

We took a bus trip around the island, which was very beautiful and then did our best to drink the 'Black Bull' dry. The landlord was very glad of the business as there were not many tourists sailing the Clyde in February, a statement that was not too difficult to understand. A few weeks later, the Port of Liverpool was honoured by a visit. We had several Liverpudlians on board, one and all were called 'Scouse' and all answered readily to it. Scouse is also the name of a popular stew in the area. The Royal Navy had a similar stew also for which there was no known recipe, formula or antidote, called Pot Mess. This stew was cooked to use up anything and I repeat, anything, left over from the previous week and dished up on Mondays. This concoction could never be duplicated, and it depended on the cook's imagination as to whether it was fit for human consumption or thrown to the seagulls or shite hawks as they were commonly called in the Royal Navy. Pot Mess also had dumplings or doughboys floating on top. Well, they were not exactly floating; they were just there, as nothing could sink in the bubbling morass.

Naturally, I tagged along with Liverpool boys who had promised to show me Lime Street where the notorious Maggie May used to shake down newly paid off seamen. I was usually aware when having my leg pulled. I just went along for the ride; I had no wish to be a spoilsport, but to be on the safe side, I took ten shillings to spend or be robbed of and put the rest in my shoe. There were plenty of Maggie Mays about, most of them supplementing their pensions by the look of them and lots of gorgeous Scouse girls who I did not stand a chance with, due to my smooth cheeks. I had a toilet bag bursting with razors, brushes and after-shave but nothing to shave off. I would lather up before a shower and go through the motions of shaving on the advice of the hairy Able Seamen in order to stimulate the hidden reluctant follicles, which I religiously did, ignoring the bastards who were pissing themselves with joy in the showers. I envied the dark-haired Celts of the same age who could have been cast as Blackbeard. "Time, patience, you'll not die a virgin," I told myself as convincingly as possible.

A month later, we were the guest of a port in Wales, the name of which I fail to recall, where we were plummeted down a mineshaft and shown the workings of a colliery from the adit to the torturous coal face. With sweat leaving pale streaks down his blackened body, a glistening muscular flyweight working on his knees put down his jack hammer, removed his goggles and stared, reminding

54

me of a nocturnal primate. We shouted at each other for a couple of minutes, and I understood that he played scrum half for the pit on Saturday afternoons and drank beer until he could not stand unaided on Saturday night, then sang in the chapel the next day. I would have done the first two but playing on the wing instead of scrum half. I thought of Pop and remembering him saying that coalminers were the cleanest men in the country. When they went off shift, their wives had a tin bath of suds by the fire and sponged and scrubbed them until their babies recognised their fathers and ceased howling.

Leaving the Land of Our Fathers, always a wrench and steaming south to Portsmouth to pay off, the electrifying order came to proceed to the city of Nantes some way up the Loire. A real foreign port at last. Flat farm land on either side a little like the Foyle, but this time, we exceeded the speed limit and sent several million gallons of the Loire over the paddocks, scattering cattle and damaging small boats. The Navy was fined two thousand pounds damage. The smell of Nantes took me straight back to the rectory in Tadmarton and the adventurous French-Canadian couple. In Nantes, we drank vin rouge for the first time and ate baguettes stuffed with salami, cheese and onion and then tried vin blanc with which we washed down more baguettes stuffed with unknown ingredients. After the wine and baguettes, it was time for Pernod followed by Cognac, all the time puffing away on foul-smelling Gauloise cigarettes. Schoolboy French causing great hilarity among the many mademoiselles we had attracted, who had mysteriously begun to spin around the bar with the furniture. I had the good sense to navigate to the three doors that stood between me and much-needed fresh air, chose the middle one wisely, staggered across the boulevard and crashed through bushes and into a park and passed-out on a bench, when I lay comatose until three o'clock in the morning. Six hours adrift. Stoppage of shore leave followed, plus extra work. Until we reached Portsmouth, I was ship bound. But what the heck. What an introduction to the land of Hugo, Voltaire, Proust and Brigitte Bardot.

The mayor and the Naval Attaché saw us off, or maybe they were there to ensure we left. Lots of girls and effeminate men waved tearfully. A different pilot this time who very carefully rang slow ahead and we eased downriver, scarcely a ripple. With the suggestion of a bow wave, we slipped down the Loire, dropped the pilot off, ran out to sea for a few miles. Turning to starboard, the thought of reaching Portsmouth and the chance of giving Nelson's flagship a thorough going over was foremost in my mind. We rounded Ushant Lighthouse, the sea all turbulence and menace, the grave of a thousand ships and set course for Pompey, the Naval term for Portsmouth, passing the Isle of White on one side, over the resting place of Henry VIII's 'Mary Rose'. The scenery was more interesting than my first visit for my medical and interview, which seemed an eon ago. Frigates, minesweepers, destroyers, submarines, tugs, cranes and the entire maritime bustle I had expected were there. My stoppage of leave had run its course; I had a toxin-free body and had my skates on.

With the paying off pennant at the masthead, the decommissioning ceremony took place less than a week later, with the crew dispersing to other ships and some to barracks, of which I was one of the latter. I spent a dull couple of weeks doing menial tasks and learning to keep out of the regulating staff's way. Perchance you exposed yourself to their sight, it was necessary to smarten your step, make a beeline for anywhere in a straight line with a piece of paper gripped purposefully in your hand. Failure to observe this cardinal rule invariably resulted in a stentorian, high-pitched shriek that would have stampeded cattle and ordered to carry out stultifying moronic useless bloody jobs that did not need doing, because they had already been done about a dozen times that morning.

### HMS Victory – Royal Naval Barracks

My residency at Her Majesty's Royal Naval Barracks Victory stretched to three weeks due to another lapse in my usual behaviour. I had been ashore with a couple of 'old salts' to sample the refreshments at a pub known to be once frequented by Lord Nelson's crew. In between gleaning as much historical information from a congenial landlady and disseminating the shite that was being fed to me by my companions, the beer kept flowing, and as usual, things began to be a bit hazy once more. Sober enough to locate the escape hatch, I found myself steering an erratic course back to barracks. I had an hour to go before my leave expired at 2100 Hours and finding myself alongside the 'Victory', which reposed in all its glory in a sort of dry dock. Apart from a Royal Marine strolling around in the vicinity, there were no guards. I stumbled aboard, saluting of course, and I was soon bashing and bumping my head in a gun deck. With blood trickling from a cut over an eye, I retraced my steps and eventually found what I desperately sought: the place where the Great Admiral of the White breathed his last. I then laid down on the hallowed spot and lost consciousness, waking with the sun well above the yardarm. This incident brought more stoppage of leave and a period of sobriety, which did me no harm.

During this latest period of leave deprivation, I had a few serious discussions with myself and resolved never to transgress again as stoppage of leave is bad enough but confined to Victory barracks was tantamount to life in a monastery. All work but without the wine. Surely, I had the character to reform until my eighteenth birthday, I enquired of myself.

Stoppage of leave over, free at last to explore the sights and goings on of Pompey. Drinking sparingly and dismissing seventy-five percent of the licentious thoughts that were perpetually saturating my brain. I spent my time ashore in libraries, bookshops and studying the Naval history of the Port. So careful was I to get back on board by 2100 Hours that I had to forego the final movement of the 'Eroica' at a concert. Besotted as I was with my new exemplary lifestyle, I found it easier and more enjoyable writing to my mother where I could recount the truth and not having to leave out the unpleasantries. I wondered how long I could keep it up.

One morning whilst polishing and burnishing the garbage bins behind the galley, the Tannoy, known as 'Big Brother', requested my presence in the administration block. It was really quite difficult trying to march like a Grenadier Guardsman across a quarter of a mile of parade ground, heart pounding with the fear and dread of one's sphincter muscle losing power.

"What the fuck have I done now? I am innocent. Not guilty. Not me, sir. Seagull shat on the boom, sir. Were they on to me regarding the night spent on Horatio's flagship? Our Father which art in Heaven, Hallowed be Thy…"

"Rose," an unfriendly voice bellowed, "march straight back, pack your gear and get back here on the double in five minutes."

## HMS Mercury

It didn't take long to pack as I had not unpacked much in anticipation of being unexpectedly sprung from the bloody penitentiary that I had spent the best part of a month in. With kit bag and hammock, it was a tussle returning to the administration block, but with the certainty of change about to take place, I found the necessary strength and pace to sling my gear into the van that was waiting to transport me to God knows where.

The van driver was Tess from Ayrshire. She spoke with a soft voice and smelled of soap. I immediately and heavily fell in love with her. I was jolted out of my mesmerisation by the bellowing voice with an order to proceed to another stone frigate HMS Mercury, a few miles north of Pompey in the county of Hampshire, to do a refresher course in communications. Mercury was one of those estates that the government commandeered when the owners are unable to pay for the upkeep because of crippling death duties and are reduced to residing in a caravan park with a bit of silver and maybe a Titian or two. The house was huge and was used as the officers' quarters. It was set in rolling undulating green grounds with beautiful oaks and elms in clumps standing defiantly here and there.

On the drive up, I had been acutely conscious of my whisker-less face. Tess was twenty-two and I had never seen any girl so lovely let alone sit in close proximity to one. Half of what she said held future promise but the other half she sounded like an aunt. The trip did not take long, which pleased me. Normally, I would have liked it to have been five hundred miles, but with Tess alongside and her soapy smell plus my fantasies, I was experiencing extreme discomfort in my tight uniform, as I found it impossible to avert my gaze from her black stockinged legs and calves. The van pulled up at a red brick barrack room, retrieving my gear from the vehicle, I said thank you and see you around; clutching my kit bag up close to hide my embarrassment. She smiled and drove off. I dumped my kit on the allotted bunk, stripped off, got in the shower and as usual, ignored that puzzling advice from the Bible.

The assuagement for the time being of my ever-present lust, I dressed and repaired to administration to make my arrival known. There was a much more relaxed air about the place, and with the pleasant feeling that Tess could not be far away, I confidently and happily went to find out what was on the agenda, glancing left and right at every form of transport that passed. At administration, I was told to report at 0800 Hours the next morning, but for now, I could bugger off, which I took to mean I was free to reconnoitre. First stop was the transport compound. With its location established, I relaxed and hunger pangs began niggling away. I had missed dinner by an hour so I called at the NAAFI, stuffed two quarter pound bars of chocolate (nutty) into my failing body and sluiced them down with a disgusting bile-coloured beverage called a goffer, ubiquitous throughout the Navy. It is available on all ships, shore establishments from Scapa Flow to the brave wee bastion Malta, and Gibraltar to Hong Kong.

There was a wet canteen at Mercury, and after tea, I partook of a couple of pints of scrumpy, which apple cider is affectionately called. I was aware of its sneaky ability to sandbag the innocent without the slightest warning. It had

58

powers that other drinks lacked. For example, a chap I met that evening was known as 'Piss in Boots' because after jousting with the cider keg for an hour he would stagger or crawl back to his quarters and collapse on his bed, as you would expect. Several hours later, he would stir from his stupor in order to open the sea cocks of his bursting bladder and proceeded to fill the footwear of careless mess mates with his lengthy micturition. His own shoes remained high and dry as he had not removed them. Forewarned, I slept with my shoes under my pillow the first night until I discovered that there was a communal locker to stow one's shoes in, for which 'Piss in Boots' was denied a key. One night, I saw him venture forth in his usual inebriated state; a kelpie water sprite guiding him to another mess and different footwear. In daylight and before the hour of the apple, he was quite normal and recalled nothing of his nocturnal urinations. No one reported his behaviour; after all, we were all of us weird in our own way.

The next morning, I arrived half an hour early for the course I was undertaking in order to create an impression of zeal and on the off chance of catching a glimpse, however fleeting, of the girl I was almost out of my mind over. The course, I soon discovered to my joy which I attempted to conceal, was for two hours per morning; the remainder of the working day, we were assigned to various jobs such as cleaning the officers' quarters in the big house, gardening or scrubbing pots and pans in the galley. I did not mind the work one bit because I could concentrate on my fantasies and trusting that Tess lacked the power of telepathy. With my state of mind, it was impossible to concentrate and digest anything that the instructors were babbling about and subsequently failing test after test and guaranteeing a lengthy stay in close proximity of my lovely Tess. It was summer time; the weather was fine and sunny. Crowds gathered after dinner on the spacious lawn and it was here that I saw her for the first time since my arrival. The memory was still causing private embarrassment. She was sitting on the grass with other girls and a couple of men who both shaved. Next to her was a Chief Petty Officer. The horny old goat was in shirt sleeves, his ribbon bedecked jacket displayed to an advantage and wearing shiny shoes which concealed his cloven hooves. Suddenly, something was crushing my chest, a pain I had never experienced before. A new pain which I angrily identified as jealousy. Striding off over the undulating grass, I walked away the sin that had momentarily consumed me and returned to the business at hand where I discovered the aging Lothario had edged closer to the future mother of my children. My daydreaming had taken me thus far. To my delight, Tess jumped to her feet and asked me how I was getting on and touched me on the arm saying that she had to get back to work, brushing the grass from her uniform and legs; a job that I would have taken the pledge for. I watched her walk quickly away, never snapping out of my trance until she rounded a corner that took her out of my sight only. The whiskered one whose eyes had lusted after her now swung upon me like gun turrets. "Name?" he half sneered. I told him, and instinct warned me to give the randy old bastard a wide berth. I knew that Tess had used me as a means of escaping the advances of her pathetic suitor, and it mattered not. I was Sir Galahad; it was my purpose in life to rescue her from varlets and keep her safe.

The nearest village was Hambledon, famous throughout the cricket world as the birthplace of that drawn out sport, with the Bat and Ball the aptly named inn. It was quite a hike to the village so I never attempted it as getting back in the dark with a belly full of cider by 2100 Hours held no appeal whatsoever. The wet canteen which boasted a snooker table, darts and a TV set was a popular venue. Knowing the toxicity of scrumpy only too well, I would stick to a couple of pints, in case Tess made a sudden appearance. She never did. 'Piss in Boots' nightly quaffed an incredible eight pints, a constant reminder to all not to leave their footwear loafing about. They were fun evenings, hearing stories from older men and some three-badge Able Raters with WWII service. Mostly, I drank with fellows my own age, with an elderly 25-year-old sitting just outside our circle but never part of it.

It was quieter than usual one evening; two boys were playing cribbage. The 25-year-old who had had his National Service deferred whilst at Cambridge was hovering nearby. I had just picked up two letters, one from my mother and the other from Bertrand Russell. I had written to him a couple of weeks before asking him to rewrite the first page of his book called *The Analysis of Mind*, in layman's term as I had found it impossible to comprehend. I had borrowed this book from the library while I was at Victory. God knows what it was doing there. In his response, he was kind and sympathetic to my plight and broke down the text so that I understood half of what he meant. I had begun to re-read the letter, when one cribbage player noticing my gaping mouth, enquired, "Bad news, Hugh?"

"No," I said, "Bertrand Russell sent me a letter."

"Bertrand fucking who?" he said disinterestedly, concentrating on the game.

At this point, the Cambridge man sprang alive and begged to see Bertie's letter. I gave him the prized letter, which for some reason he took to the far end of the room. The cribbage boy momentarily took his eye off his hand and said, "Watch him, Hugh, he's a fucking brown hatter."

I had not heard this term before and along with queer, bum bandit and turd burglar were cruelly and insensitively used to describe those unfortunate men who chose the company of their own sex over the enchantment and mystery of women. It occurred to me at that moment why some of the younger fellows were absent and took me back to the several close encounters I had had with these isolated men. Older men were only too pleased to drink the endless supply of booze that would flow their way and laughingly tolerated their company, if not encouraging it. That evening was the last I saw of the Cambridge man; he was rushed to hospital during the night, presumably with my prized letter. Unrequited love, it was rumoured. I knew all about unrequited love, but I wasn't about to open a vein over it.

One Saturday morning around midday, I thought that I would try the walk to the village and sample their apple juice for a change. Striding out in the sunny day, head held high with the usual Quixotic fantasies flooding my brain. How many children would Tess and I have; would she be happy travelling and living like the gypsies in a brightly painted caravan, drawn by an ancient plodding horse through the Western Isles? Suddenly, my reverie was disturbed by an approaching vehicle. Not trying to hitch a lift, I was surprised when a van slowed down and halted just ahead of me. The van was full of young Wrens out of uniform. "Going to the Bat and Ball?" I was asked. With a pounding heart, I squeezed in with the giggling, sweet-smelling bevy of female bodies, searching for the one face that mattered in the entire world. She wasn't there. We exchanged names which flew in one ear and out of the other as they are inclined to do.

"Do you know Tess?" I unashamedly demanded.

"Yes, she's coming on her bike."

If the van had had an ejector, I would have hit the button. What with the cigarette smoke and perfume, I asked politely if they would drop me off about half a mile from the pub as I badly needed some fresh air.

"Thanks a lot for the lift," I said. Through the smoke that was billowing out of the sliding door, I saw the smirks on their faces.

"See ya, don't get lonely, luv." And laughing, they drove off.

Now what to do? I needed a strategy, a ploy, anything to appear not to be lying in wait. I undid a shoelace and slowly began retying it as I had caught sight of her in the distance. How to remain nonchalant when fumbling with bloody shoelaces which won't obey your fingers due to the blue funk that possessed me. Rising as she slowly came to a halt, panic left me when I saw her smiling.

"Did you walk all the way?" she enquired.

"No, I got a lift but abandoned ship because of the smoke," I lied, trying to sound nautical.

"That's why I cycle here," she said. "Also, I can leave when I wish as the girls only leave when they are drunk. You can sign for a bike at Transport."

I made a furtive study of her bicycle for any particular mark or blemish that would simplify future identification. The thought of sitting on the same saddle that Tess's bottom had caressed up hill and down dale had my head throbbing and my nether regions asking questions. It was also extremely hard to avert my eyes from her slightly tanned legs, which from her ankles to where they disappeared into her short white shorts were glistening in the sun. There were her bold pert breasts thankfully hidden. Enough was enough. I wondered where she sunbathed. We walked and talked to the pub where we sat in the sun with half pints of scrumpy and bags of crisps. As a small boy, I had often wondered what heaven was like. I was no longer in doubt. The other girls, apart from welcoming us with a few ribald remarks, left us alone. She spoke of her father, mother and four strapping older brothers. Whether this was a subtle warning I cared not as I would have taken on the All Blacks to win her. I told her of my childhood, emphasis on the Scottish connection of course, leaving out my father's desertion and having him dying in the Western Desert with the Gordon Highlanders. I had intended learning about the origins of cricket just for the heck of it as the game held little interest for me so apart from entering the bar for refills I never saw much of that ancient hostelry. Time stood still as we talked and sipped until I'd guessed an hour of bliss had elapsed, when she said we ought to be going. Did she say we?

"Do you intend walking back with me?" I stuttered, thinking I had misheard.

"Well, my bike is a ladies' bike and doesn't have a cross bar and I am not letting you traipse back on your lonesome, especially after a lovely time with you."

I said, "I wouldn't have traipsed back but marched like a Royal Scots Dragoon." She laughed, but I knew she liked that.

We didn't walk but meandered the way back where I had the privilege of pushing her bike, never once touching the saddle. We talked of music and what books she had read. She said that she liked folk music. I had already told her of my love of classical music, instantly realising it may have been unwise to do so. I acknowledged a love of folk too, particularly Scottish. I mentioned Loch Maree, The Lovely Dark Island and several others to add weight to the veracity of my idle boast. If the sweet girl had been an aficionado of the Easter Island Nose Flute, I would have been with her all the way. She had read a lot of books but none that I had heard of. I told her I mostly read history, which seemed pretty safe, as I was not about to mention Proust or Voltaire, but as an afterthought, I suggested Sir Walter Scott, who I was positive a Scottish lass would be familiar with. She had heard but not read anything of his, so I expounded not, on the merits of Ivanhoe.

The last half mile of the walk was the private road that led to the great house. It was nearly over. We had walked side by side all the way nearly, just once I feigned a stone in my shoe. She took the bike and walked slowly ahead up a slight incline. I thought of the king in centuries past, thrown from his horse, offering his kingdom for a remount. Not having my Kodak Box Brownie, the tantalising vision has been indelibly etched in my brain.

We said cheerio at the door of her quarters. Thank yous, no kisses but agreeing to meet again. Little did I know how soon, or I would have gone insane with euphoria. I then cooled off my ardour under the shower, a necessary procedure in order to focus my mind on other things, such as eating, drinking and sleeping.

There is an annual event called Navy Week when ships of the Home Fleet visit towns and cities of the United Kingdom and are open to the public. Shore bases from Rosyth to Portsmouth and Chatham to Devonport are also open and entertain the public with demonstrations of life in the Navy, leaving out the nasty bits. Mercury intended organising a crew to take part in Portsmouth dockyard. Running my fingers down the list of compulsory volunteers on the noticeboard; a mandatory morning procedure, I felt a pang of pleasure when I came to my name. I was surprised that the dipsomaniac 'Piss in Boots' was selected into the team and shook with anticipation at Tess's inclusion, along with four of her fun loving 'Bat and Ball' colleagues. I was dismayed at seeing the randy old Chief Petty Officer's name along with two of his leading signalmen underlings. A Sub-Lieutenant was in charge of the expedition.

I reminisced on old Fred Tench's rhubarb that he was so proud of. "For a beautiful harvest one must apply manure." Training and rehearsals began the next day when we all packed into a minibus and drove to Portsmouth dockyard. Not once did I sit next to Tess on the daily return trip. The girls sat together as the young Sub-Lieutenant was still an unknown force, so caution was exercised, until it became clear by the end of the first day that his enthusiasm and fanatical patriotism, coupled with his general ignorance and greenness convinced one and all that what he was planning would be dull and boring. However, the girls who had him completely under their thumbs and who obviously terrified the recently promoted midshipman convinced him to allow farce to thrill and amuse the madding throng.

Our base was in a tidal basin where a rusty old minelayer lay coming apart at the seams. This Naval Review was the old girl's last hurrah. One of the first tasks was to rig a Jack Stay. This was an apparatus for transferring personages and other objects to another ship at sea. The day was hot, and as we had been told that our activities would be aquatic, swimming attire would be the order of the day. Forewarned, I borrowed a pair of trunks, which turned out to be two sizes too large, instead of risking the briefs, I was issued with at 'Ganges', where the pubic bulge was always in evidence. That did not concern anyone on the training ship, but with Tess and her buxom mates cavorting around half naked, I knew that my hyperactive appendage would behave indecently and that the trunks would offer some protection against a possible court martial, I foolishly surmised. With the Jack Stay secured to the only stanchion that seemed as though it would not break free of its moorings, we borrowed a tender and ran the Jack Stay wire to the other side of the basin, a distance of about sixty yards. With wire fastened in place, there were plenty of willing hands eager to zoom back and forth, occasionally letting go halfway to cool off. We had run an electric cable ashore and plugged it in somewhere in order to boil a kettle and to get some lights between decks which were well worth exploring. Tea made, but Tess was not around. I just had to ask her whereabouts of one of her mates, a jolly bawdy Glaswegian.

"She's down in the engine room," the merry tart said, giggling.

"Go find hers," she said thrusting a torch in my hand.

No one else appeared privy to this exchange so I slunk off in search of her. What is it I wondered about Scots and engines? James Watt and Stevenson of Rocket fame started it all. Scottish engineers served on at least a dozen ships I later sailed on in the Merchant Navy. I met them in bars all over the world where they were endeavouring to coax some life out of clapped-out Costa Rican and

Liberian tankers that should have been scrapped decades before. Hearing faint sounds coming from below, I climbed down into the engine room and found Tess with a torch examining intently what was to me a heap of scrap metal.

"Hello, look at this," she said and proceeded to bamboozle me with facts, figures, pistons, crankshafts, thrust, horsepower. I nodded my head in admiration and wonderment, not understanding a word but loving the sound of her lilting voice.

"Tea's ready, they're having stand-easy," I said.

"Okay," she said, and I unashamedly watched her beautiful body encased in a tight-fitting black one-piece costume ascend the ladder. I followed her up. There was no time to relieve myself, although it would not have taken long. When these situations arose as they frequently did, I resorted to a plan that never failed me. I would imagine horrible things, happenings. Falling from an aeroplane without a parachute. Forced to drink milk. It's for calves I would tell my teachers, or having an arithmetic lesson with Wackford Squeers clone at Dr Radcliffe's. Passion abated, heart rate down, all at rest, I climbed the ladder, one hand gripping my trunks, not an easy task. Without any interference from the Sub-Lt who appeared quite content to leave things to us, it was decided by popular vote that the theme for the week would be piratical. This first day being a Tuesday left only three days to prepare before the gates were opened to the public. The girls were confident that they would be able to purloin enough material for us to resemble marauders of the high seas, and with the Chief Petty Officer designated as Blackbeard, this was not a difficult task. There was a Captain Hook, Captain Kidd, but no one fancied hopping around on one leg so no Long John Silver, besides, we had no parrot.

Next day after pillaging the stores, the girls had secured a large quantity of old uniforms, work clothes and some of their personal apparel, plus a borrowed sewing machine and set to make Corsairs of us all. As we had all fantasised about losing an eye whilst sailing under the Jolly Roger, eyepatches gave us additional authenticity. Not one of us had lost a limb of course, but we made up for that by livid lipstick scars on our cheeks and all other visible parts of our torsos. The older men had been given permission to discontinue shaving and were already quite stubbly. I cursed my youth and my luck when the bloody Glaswegian tart made me a ridiculously looking red beard which the malicious Chief Petty Officer ordered me to don. There followed fits of howling laughter except from Tess who said I looked stunning. I wore it all times then, even on the bus. I wonder now how she could have kept a straight face. The remainder of the week was taken up by more rehearsals and devising absorbing ways to interest kids, ensuring certain parts of the old tub were safe for visitors and battening down hazardous compartments. I personally thought that the wreck should be out of bounds, but this was a long time ago before the age of litigation.

Saturday came, with us eagerly assembled before dawn. At 0800 Hours, the dockyard gates swung wide and began ingesting a huge holiday crowd that surged over the ground as unstoppable as a rip tide. Naturally, there was scant interest in us and the old hulk, and I began to feel sorry for the ancient warrior. People were keen to see Nelson's Flagship and the modern ships of the line. The carriers, cruisers, destroyers and frigates.

The Sub-Lt then spoke for the first time in days, suggesting that we drum up some interest. We all thought that the best way to achieve this was to begin fooling about with the Jack Stay that had provided much fun during rehearsals. Normally at sea, a canvas chair is used and the occupant strapped in. However, being young and super fit and regarding the chair as an encumbrance, we dispensed with it unanimously. Very soon, passers-by began stopping, and in a short span of time, we had an audience of at least a thousand watching us zooming back and forth, cardboard cutlasses clenched between our teeth.

The Sub-Lt, swollen with importance that his idea had paid off, then suggested that a volunteer be called upon to ferry an injured crewmember to an imaginary larger ship for surgery. A few seconds elapsed whilst we looked vacantly at each other when I was shoved from behind by the hefty Glaswegian Wren, roaring, "Three cheers for Erik the Red!" I could have murdered the bitch. Ready for take-off, one hand clutching my trunks, the dreaded woman had my arm in a grip of iron when she was pushed aside by an injured beautiful Tess who clasped me around the neck, gripped me strongly with her thighs and with a bemused, adorable countenance we sped off with my uncomfortable member digging into her navel. Using two hands to support the extra weight, confident that Tess's thighs plus my rampant condition would ensure my wayward trunks remained in place. We had reached two thirds of the way when I began to ejaculate in mid-air. The thought then struck me with horror as to what would happen at journey's end amongst the cheering throng. Cooling off was the obvious solution.

"Sorry, Tess," I said to that understanding face, so near and yet so far, and we plunged into the basin.

Tess, with a couple of quick strokes and supple undulations of her body which reminded me of an otter, was halfway up the ladder. She looked back and saw me dog paddling with one paw while my other hand was desperately holding up my trunks. She back dived into the water to retrieve my beard, put it on herself and assisted me with my cursed trunks. We somehow scaled the ladder amidst a laughing jolly mass of humanity. I have never forgotten what that sweet girl did for me that day. She was fully aware of my feelings for her. She never mocked me or led me to believe that she had anything other than friendship to offer me. I knew this. She was a woman and I was just a boy.

Our efforts during Navy Week were mentioned in despatches and congratulations kept flowing in. For most crewmen on a ship in commission, being open to the public is considered a pain in the arse. Only the duty watch, men under punishment and stoppage of leave remain on board to conduct folk around and patiently answer the inanest questions imaginable. Whenever I was called upon to perform this duty, I revelled in it and with my inventiveness sent visitors on the way with some pretty weird ideas about the Navy and the running of a ship.

Back on Mercury and the dull refresher course, I was beginning to feel restless. I had not seen Tess for a couple of days. One dinner hour, I went to Transport in the hope of seeing her. A young Wren in the office looked at me strangely and handed me an envelope. I had never seen her handwriting but I knew it was hers. 'Hugh' was all that was written on the envelope. Just my name but it had a sound of a hammer when it strikes a horseshoe on an anvil. I took the envelope and with the strength leaving my legs, made it to the stand of oak and fell trembling to the grass. I knew at that moment without reading the letter that she was gone from my life forever.

She had requested a transfer to Scotland some months before to be nearer her family. She had left the day before and begged me to forgive her for her cowardice in not telling me herself as she could not bear to see my reaction. She thanked me for making her life pleasurable so far from home during the few weeks we were acquainted. She had been promoted to a Leading Wren and intended making the Navy her career.

"You've a long way ahead of you, Hugh. Be brave, be happy and go for it, Tess."

That afternoon, I scrubbed pots and pans in the galley, the steam disguising my misery, skipped tea and got paralytic drunk in the canteen. Apparently, I was conveyed to my quarters by 'Piss in Boots' who must have dropped me several times enroute so bruised and lacerated was my body the next morning, but what did that matter compared to the pain inside. Somehow I got through that desolate day. I knew the difference between being alone and loneliness. It was the first time I had experienced the latter. I counted the hours down to opening time in the canteen. I needed a bracer, that's all. After tea, I watched 'Piss in Boots' quench his Falstaffian thirst, played cribbage and nearly broke down when a kindly old Geordie said, "I see your lassie's left, boy."

I had to grow up, I told myself, with or without whiskers. I thought of Grampy who didn't see his wife for four years and his daughter, my mother was nearly five years old when he returned from the Somme, a stranger. I was under orders. Be brave, be happy and go for it. I knew I had to leave this place where I had experienced love for the first time, so I spoke to Odin as I had been doing since I was twelve years of age whenever confronted with a dilemma. I had read a book on Norse mythology. Odin, the God of victory and the dead. He never replied to my pleas but I felt His guidance and endorsement when making decisions. At mid-morning, the next day, the Tannoy blared for me to report to admin. I bolted from the signalling course and was ordered by a Regulating Petty Officer to, "Pack your gear, Rose and get back here as quick as Christ'll let you." I was well used to these polite directives eliciting haste from our Lord, so I sped off to my mess, excitement mounting, something was happening. Kit bag, hammock and overnight bag. I scribbled a note to 'Piss in Boots' thanking him for being him and arrived at admin in Christ's allotted time, puffing and ready for anything. Stunned, I was driven to Portsmouth and dumped at the gangway of a brand-new minesweeper. Everything a blur, my gear was stowed below for me, the Coxswain shoved five pounds and a return ticket to Banbury and said, "Say ta ta to your mum, we sail Saturday morning at 0900."

With that, I was driven to the station where I spied a lorry slowly passing in the traffic with Stratford painted on the side. I flagged the driver down, hopped on board, taking it for granted that he was going via Banbury. Not only was he but he turned off at the Duns-Tew sign post and let me off at No. 5. I thanked the driver, asking him if he could make use of the railway ticket; he could and he would, he said, "Glad of your company, mate." And he was gone.

During subsequent leaves from Portsmouth, I would invariably retain my rail voucher and make for the main road to the north to wait for the many trucks passing by. In uniform, one never had long to wait with outstretched thumb before a knight of the road pulled up. "Where you heading, whacker?" If the accent was Brummie or anywhere further north, I was assured of being dropped off a mile from the village. If the wait exceeded two minutes, a fantasy would take over, of a stunning chinchilla cocooned brewery heiress who would beckon enticingly from the plushness of a chauffeured Bentley Continental. The reverie being shattered by the breaking of a haulier, then the hurrying to clamber aboard, fifty yards down the road. The furious heiress incensed at rejection.

The few hours at home went quickly, but I made the most of them. The Navy could be tough, but they were considerate and fair also. The farewell at the White Horse was noisy and jolly with me unable to say how long I would be away. I knew as much as they did. My mother noticed an absence of my usual optimistic mien but put it down to my possible long absence. She would never know of the love that lingered. Up at dawn on Saturday, I hugged my mother and a wriggling Bobby, and I was on my way. Pop drove me to new horizons and talked his way past the dockyard police. I boarded my ship in time for breakfast and left Pop standing at the quay for a couple of hours until we cast off and slipped down the Solent. We had not spoken much on the drive down; we never did. When driving to Brecon as kids, we would record the inn signs, ever a source of interest for Pop. Not that he was a toper by any means, he just loved talking with a pint in his fist. Within minutes of walking into a pub for the first time, he held the floor and the clientele spellbound. Pint drained, he left leaving his audience wondering who the hell he was. Now he was watching his son sail away, as he had done as a boy, on the battleship 'Royal Sovereign'.

# Chapter 5
# Minesweeper

My previous ship, the Urchin, had a crew of about one hundred and eighty. My new ship's complement numbered twenty-eight, with the Captain having the rank of Lieutenant. She was a quarter of the size of the Urchin, and I very soon felt her very different motion. As soon as we entered the channel, I became violently seasick for the first time. As is or was the custom, I was left where I lay. Everything I had eaten that day sluicing over the side, with the sea we were shipping. Soaking wet, retching the green stomach lining, I lay until dark until someone put me below where I remained until dawn. The smell of breakfast cooking in the galley had me clambering on deck for the much-needed fresh air. I clung to a railing for hours wishing I was slashing thistles in Frank Brough's orchard and glad that Tess could not witness the cockiness knocked out of me. We passed Ushant in the grey of dawn, the sea rising.

"We're heading for Brest, laddie," said the cook, handing me a crust of bread and cold water in a bottle.
"There is a storm warning, but we're made of timber, we're unsinkable," he said confidently and went back to his cooking.

Whether Brest was a scheduled visit or one of the proverbial ports in a storm, I never knew or cared. After a few more hours of hanging on for dear life, we came under the shelter of land and soon came alongside the Port of Brest where I sheepishly reported to the First Officer who had patiently awaited my recovery. The First Officer or the 'Jimmy' as he is known on the lower deck was the second in command, the equivalent to the first mate on a merchant vessel. The 'Jimmy' made a few points clear to me, then took me to see the Captain who greeted me with the words, "Welcome aboard, Rose." I was in the company of gentlemen. I was so used to being bellowed at, that I was temporarily in a state of disbelief.

The Captain told me that I was an integral part of the ship's complement and that the entire crew would gradually gain experience in everyone else's job. This was later to prove very useful and made life more interesting and exciting. In case I had not made it clear, on 'Ganges' I had decided to specialise in signals, semaphore, morse flashing and flags. I had been told that in signals, one's place of duty was mostly on the flag deck or the bridge, right in the thick of things. Pop had suggested I do this as he had taught me to splice rope and wire, as well as every knot, hitch and bend in existence. On the lavatory door at No. 5 were pasted the flags of all nations, the semaphore, morse code and a length of rope. Defecation accompanied by education was one of his mottos.

We spent two days in Brest, where I built up my starved body by eating like a wolverine, the ship's provender and quite a few baguettes. The storm having blown itself out, we prepared for sea. The thought of seasickness did not worry me as I had decided to not allow mal de mer to take command of my body ever again, and apart for mild queasiness running before a storm south of Crete, I never suffered from it again.

Out to sea once more and thinking of the ships of the British Navy during the Napoleonic Wars, who spent years blockading the port. Sailors never getting ashore, ship bound forever until their rum-pickled corpses were released to the deep. Sailing south towards the Bay of Biscay, bracing my shoulders and mind against any negative thoughts about the legendary stretch at sea, we came upon it at first light.

I had the morning watch, 0400–0800 Hours and was expecting a tempest or at the very least, a rough passage. The helmsman, an ancient three-badge man of about forty summers or more, exclaimed, "*Oive niver seed the loiks.*"

Descartes whispered in my ear, "Chance favours the prepared mind." We saw the bay as a puddle of molten lead, which we were slicing through as a scalpel cuts through flesh, the snow-white wake burbling into the Stygian blackness. To the east, the sun darting shafts of light banished the sinisterness, and I awoke from my reverie with breakfast wafting from the galley. A little after 0800 Hours, I broke my fast for the first time in the notorious Bay of Biscay, with not a ripple for miles. I now had another God, Poseidon. Odin would not object. Like me, he was not the jealous type.

It was so good having my sea legs returned to me that when we left France and Portugal astern with the sea rising once more, I was more focussed on what lay ahead rather than the vagaries of the weather because we would soon be

71

altering course. We approached Cape Trafalgar, a historical location where on October 21, 1805, Nelson's ships stunned the combined French and Spanish battle fleet under the command of Admiral Charles Villeneuve by splitting it in half and enfilading it with all guns ablaze. Gunners and powder monkeys in a frenzy, in the deafening, choking gun decks while the deck crew ignoring the battle, obeyed the bosun's call and manoeuvred their ships with an alacrity that had been flogged into them years before. The French flagship Redoubtable, abeam of the Victory, afforded an opportunist marksman to mortally wound Lord Nelson. There is a cemetery at Gibraltar where men having died of their injuries were buried. In the heat of the battle, the dead were unceremoniously dropped overboard.

Not Lord Nelson of course, and here we have one of the many legends as to how his remains were taken back to England. The voyage taking six weeks, what better method of preservation would there be than to immerse His Lordship in a barrique of rum. When the Admiral reached England, he was laid to rest in St Paul's Cathedral, leaving his loyal crew to ponder on the fate of the embalming fluid. They did not ponder long however, hence the term for rum in the Navy is 'Nelson's blood'. This legend has been retold a thousand times down the decades. Who can disprove it? I, for one, would not, even if I could.


## The **Mediterranean**

My first thought on seeing Gibraltar was of Captain Ahab exhorting Moby Dick to, "Breach your last to the sun, Moby." I had seen pictures of the rock from all angles but nothing prepared me for its uniqueness and impregnability. Yet, taken it was, by Admiral George Rooke in 1693 and ceded to Britain by Spain at Utrecht in 1713.

Sent to collect messages and mail, I was soon lost in the Labyrinthine interior of the rock. Traffic, road signs, workshops, offices, living quarters, lifts, it was a city inside. High up inside, cannon ports had been cut to menace Spain who have been unceasing in their attempts to regain sovereignty. In fact, the nearest thing to an invasion occurs every morning during the week when the border is open for hundreds of Spanish workers to cross into the fortress. It is a duty-free port where cheap and shoddy goods of every description from Asia are sold to green-as-grass visitors like me. I often wondered what my mother thought would arrive next, when her letter thanked me for the bone China tea set made in Formosa or some junk from the back alleys of Alexandria. But Bobby did get his Japanese fishing rod in a beautiful plywood box, lots of fly hooks and with his name inscribed in calligraphic lettering. I did not post this but hung on to it for months. I just had to see his face on opening it.

The night life was uproarious as you would expect. Bars packed with matelots from the United States, France and Italy, and a troopship load of the Highland Light Infantry on their way home from Cyprus. With no EOKA terrorists to terrorise, they fell upon each other with boots, belts and beer bottles, undoubtedly in training for Sauchiehall Street.

On top of the rock, accessed by a steep, narrow winding road are a colony of macaque, a long faced, pouch-cheeked monkey mistakenly referred to as apes. The story goes that if the macaques leave the rock, it will mark the end of British rule, and as a consequence, an old sweat-cum-historian relates tales and legends to visitors whilst keeping a paternal eye on his troop. The macaques appear to have a fondness for him also, or is it the bag of peanuts he has stowed away in his battle dress? He told me that during his tour of duty several of his kids, as he called them, disappeared occasionally only to reappear months after. There are macaques over the strait near Tangiers; could it be that there are subterranean tunnels in existence? We will leave that conundrum to the macaques.

Leaving harbour, the thought came to me that Gibraltar was a pretty good run ashore though some of my messmates were less impressed due to the absence of brothels, overt ones anyway. Brothel was an unheard-of word that I picked up on Ganges. With all my voracious reading, I had never come across it. My mates were of the opinion that I had led a very cloistered existence. I probably had in this respect. The idea of a brothel intrigued me, not that I intended availing myself of their services, as I had heard too many yarns of the consequences of doing so. Atrophy of the penis being the major horror. Testicles swelling to the size of watermelons meant not only a dishonourable discharge but a lifetime of having to convey them in a pushcart for all to see. Was voyeurism the lure? Definitely not; merely a social scientific observation expanding mind and horizons.

A smooth passage to heroic Malta that Pop knew well. Our course took us past Pantelleria to port. Pantelleria was used by the Axis powers during WWII to harry convoys striving to relieve Malta and the forces in North Africa. In 1943 after heavy bombardment from sea and air, the Allies secured the island prior to the invasion of Sicily; an imperative undertaking.

Then Gozo and tiny Comino appeared on the horizon, and soon after, Malta, which we approached from the eastern side, sailing past the great portals of Grand Harbour and moored bow to stern to buoys in Sliema Creek, which was to be our base between our regular tours of duty at the other end of the Mediterranean.

We were moored in the middle of the suburb of Sliema, less than a hundred yards from shore where shops, bars and cafes beckoned invitingly. Getting to and from shore turned out to be the responsibility of a gentleman called Spiro. While navigating his dghajsa alongside, he claimed us before we had properly secured the ship. It was the custom to hire one of these boats on a semi-permanent basis, and very useful and convenient they were. Spiro would always be there, looming out of the dark soon after a whistle from shore, to ferry one back to the ship drunk or sober, whatever the hour of the clock. He must have slept vertically. At sea, all garbage (gash) was ditched overboard for fish and gulls to dispose of. In harbour, this duty was carried out by Spiro, and if he had kept pigs, they would have fared very well. Spiro had the run of the ship. He and his family, whenever he managed to see them, would have lived well on his gleanings from the galley. A destroyer once took Spiro and his dghajsa back to England for a couple of months. I saw photographs later of him propelling back and forth in Plymouth Harbour. He was very proud of his association with the Royal Navy and equally proud of being an English 'object'. The rules could be bent a little back then, when we laughed every day.

The first time ashore at Sliema most matelots used Shank's pony as a means of investigating the delights. There were doss houses for the completely sozzled where for two shillings you got a bed and a wake-up call at six in the morning for Spiro to convey you back in time for breakfast and duty. To venture further afield, horse-drawn carriages could be hired. These were phonetically known as 'garris', spelt 'karozzin' in that impossible language gleaned from every country in the Mediterranean from Morocco to Lebanon. They were slow, cheap and dependable. Should you be in hurry but not caring whether you lived or died, you could brave a ride on rattletrap aged buses that horn honked their terrifying way through the streets; pedestrians scattering like chickens on an autobahn; the driver relying solely on the icons that festooned the windscreen. Wooden figures of Christ, the Virgin Mary and the Baby Jesus dangled impeding his vision even further. Old widows clothed in crow black crossed themselves thrice when he deigned to stop for them. My first experience of Malta's public transport was soon after mooring, to collect mail and messages from the cavernous workings beneath Valetta. I survived the trip uninjured and unbaptised. From that day and thereafter, I availed myself of the ship's motorboat for the short run out of Sliema Creek and hard to starboard into Grand Harbour. Idyllic mostly but exercising great caution in a blow. Leaving harbour, a frigate lost a crewman from the foredeck in inclement weather some months later.

Tying up alongside a dozen dghajsa, I clambered over them and as directed, entered a tunnel the size of the underground in London. There were locations and offices to discover the whereabouts of and getting wonderfully lost in the labyrinth and hoping that the rosary-beaded populace found safety here while the city was being pounded up above by the Luftwaffe and the Italian Air Force. The main tunnel rose steadily and pinprick light got bigger and brighter until I found myself blinking in blazing sunshine again in the middle of the city. I had been away a considerable time by now on the expedition of discovery; the much-expected mail must be delivered. Thirstily eyeing the bars, I dutifully and responsibly drank half a gallon of orange juice. I had no intention of breaking the rules. No stoppage of leave for me. I needed to explore this history-packed, citadel-studded island.

As it turned out, there was only time for two runs ashore, one to Valetta and the other, a trip to Medina, which I believe was the capital centuries ago. A Naval Chaplain organised this excursion and I was the sole heathen in the group but genuflected with God-fearing pilgrims in the numerous churches and shrines we muttered devotions in. I would pray all day to visit places of interest with knowledgeable folk to enlighten me.

Gratis excursions, called Grippos, were on offer in most foreign ports when showing the flag. Blank sheets of paper were pinned to the noticeboard inviting those wishing to attend educational visits to breweries, distilleries and vineyards. These sheets were swiftly blackened with autographs of the topers and drunkards. Sheets offering hairy veterans all they ever wished to learn about glove making or quilting remained unblemished as a nun's veil. In order not to offend or fracture diplomatic relations, the Master-at-Arms and his regulating staff forged the signatures of those under punishment and stoppage of leave. During my time at sea, I had occasion to fall into the latter category regularly. But ever keen to get ashore, no one had to forge my signature. Perfume or lace-making factories, I always had my hand up. Get ashore at all costs. With my positive mind, I never failed to gain something.

Leaving Spiro with a small retainer and a couple of hundred cigarettes, we took our leave of the amiable old pilot fish and sailed east, destination Famagusta on the island of Cyprus.

The day after leaving Malta, requests were made by most of the crew to discontinue shaving. Permission granted, those who chose to participate were given three weeks to prove that they were capable of producing a reasonable-looking hirsute appendage which did not resemble a moth-eaten beaver. I had been shaving my bumfluff daily with a diligence that bordered on mania. It was really only necessary weekly but daily, there was a slight chance I could stimulate some growth. When granting my request, the First Lieutenant, with contrived seriousness, gave me twenty-one days to leave boyhood behind.

After an uneventful three days' voyage, passing a few merchant ships, we sailed under mountainous Crete. A day later, the southern coast of Cyprus came in sight. We passed Limasol and Larnaca, where there was an air base and a large military presence. At the eastern extremity of the south coast, we turned due north and soon entered the only harbour at the time where it was possible to berth alongside terra-firma. Famagusta.

Our deployment to Cyprus plus the military presence was due to a political situation, which I am still not fully conversant with to this day. Apparently, the Greek Cypriots wanted liberation from the British and union with Greece. I don't know what the Turkish Cypriots thought about it, and I don't suppose anyone bothered to ask them. One faction called EOKA (Ethniki Organosis Kyprion Agoniston) were considered terrorists by the British and patriots by whoever was in favour of them. The spiritual head of this organisation was Archbishop Makarios, who was in exile in Athens. The man with his boots on the ground was Colonel Georgios Grivas, who had a sizeable bounty on his head. The EOKA were in the habit of tossing bombs into the backs of passing troop lorries and other nefarious deeds of havoc. Politics has never interested me and the same goes for politicians. A fair-minded statesman I can admire, but they are thinly scattered. I never had the desire to be a leader nor did I particularly like being led, preferring to stay in the slipstream until required to buffet into the wind at the head of a gaggle of geese. I have always been there whenever the occasion arose, rather like a stand-off half.

Our engines had scarcely shut down before a Turkish policeman-cum-interpreter installed himself on board. His named was Mustapha, and I am not making that up. Mustapha was the size, weight and configuration of a drum of diesel. He was very willing and useful when storing ship. With a one-hundred-pound sack of oranges in each hand, he would remove a cigarette from his lips, spit and carry on regardless. Mr Papadopoulos, and I am not making that up either, was our ship's chandler and a brave man indeed. He had been shot and fire bombed but picked up the pieces and lived on. Business comes first. "I like pounds with Queen Elizabeth, not Drachma," he mused Homerically.

There were merchant ships of several nations in the port, which appeared quite narrow. We had entered from the north between the battlements of a fort and a breakwater. The entrance was so narrow and shallow that the seabed of rocks and seaweed was clearly visible through the crystalline water. How the large merchant vessels docked, I never discovered as we were under orders not to stray, but there could have been another entrance to the south. Our berth was at the fortress end of the harbour, where beneath the massive walls prefabricated sheds stood incongruously, with two patrol boats floating idly nearby; their generators humming faintly below. Security appeared not to be a priority as the harbour gates were open and unmanned all day. Folk were wandering continuously back and forth, some seemingly with a purpose; the remainder flaneuring up and down.

Under the wall of the fort, I saw a man doing what I surmised was his dhobeying. On closer inspection, I saw him flogging the daylights out of an octopus on a rock with the hapless cephalopod changing colour with each pounding. Seeing my interest, he told me that this process was to soften the flesh as he had killed it by biting it between the eyes, which was the swiftest method. Fraternising with the Greek Cypriots was not encouraged, neither was it forbidden so we became acquainted. He returned the next day, bringing a tentacle for me. On and off for about two years, I got to know George well. I gave him cigarettes, and in return, I enjoyed occasional morsels of his wife's cooking. Strange but delicious.

I wrote a long letter to my mother that night about Cyprus, George and the octopus, then realising that I had only been here forty-eight hours and what could lie ahead. She wrote back saying that the swallows were packing their bags and the pheasant season was about to commence. The following year in the spring, on a passage back to Cyprus in a pitch-black storm, our steaming and navigation lights had attracted thousands of migrating swallows to their doom; some possibly heading for Duns-Tew to their mud and spittle nests under the eaves of No. 5. At dawn, we found them lying thickly dead and with brooms pushed them over the side, sodden, dead but still beautiful. They were returning to their place of birth. Thousands of swallows had no need to build that year; there were empty nests all over Europe. Mother was realistic about the cruelties of nature, but I spared her this.

Two days after our arrival, we took over from a sister ship that had been patrolling for two weeks. We sailed north east to Cape Andreas, rounded the Cape and sailed slowly west. Our mission was to stop and search any small vessels, fishing boats and caiques that may be smuggling munitions into the island, either by sympathisers to the cause or mercenaries in the gun running business. We worked at night, occasionally boarding the same vessel two or three times, especially the fishing boats who could have been hauling something other than fish from the depths. In two years, we found nothing. Two fishing boats – caiques, we got to know very well. They were the 'Ayia Eleni' and the 'Maid of Verdala'. We were on first name terms with the hard-working crew who were clearly not interested in anything but fishing. At no time was there any violence or animosity perpetrated towards the Navy. Mutual respect and empathy between sea farers, I suppose. This was tiring, sleepless work compensated when the sun rose, and we anchored off a small cove or inlet in complete isolation to the troubles on the island. We swam in the turquoise sea and slept for hours on warm soft sand, waking to pick oranges and grapes from deserted groves and vines, the only sound other than the sea lopping onto the sand, a faint tinkle of a distant goat bell.

A favourite spot on the chart was 'Fontana Amarosa'. Paradise, one felt Jesus Christ would appear through the trees at any moment. How did it get that name? There was no one around for miles. During these broken nights and idyllic days, I began to think of Tess less and less, at first with a pang of guilt which subsided to lengthy periods of equanimity. Was this the sign that I was growing up? It was only six weeks since I saw her last. Maybe Odin was releasing me from her sirens allure. There was still a couple of weeks before the down on my face came up for inspection, constantly stroking my chin narcissistically for any sign of a few bristling follicles. Just for once, I was not feeling very optimistic.

A day later, we came upon the beautiful town of Kyrenia. The area is quite mountainous, and on top of one of these mountains lies a castle built during the Crusades. Some months later, we were lucky enough to get a ride up there in an Army lorry. St Hilarion Castle is a well-preserved ruin of that barbaric time. There is a road up to the castle where the final approach is very narrow and although prone to a lengthy siege, as most castles were, would have successfully repelled any sudden attacks. The sheer walls of the castle and the rocky descent supporting it, still showed signs of the boiling pitch that was poured on attackers. Looking north and a long way down, you can see Kyrenia and its small harbour accommodating caiques and sundry small vessels. Larger vessels would anchor and use a motorboat to land, as we did on the morning the Captain and I landed to collect the mail from the region's Army HQ. In full uniform, webbing, boots and gaiters, each with a service revolver; I couldn't think of a surer way of committing suicide. The only thing missing was a yellow patch pinned over our hearts.

We headed towards a quayside stone building with barred apertures where detainees shrieked threats and curses. Startling for me, but those walls had been hearing it since the Crusades. Walking further, we came upon shops and a café. The Captain spied army vehicles about two hundred yards off. He ordered me to wait while he went ahead; I never found out why. It was very warm, and we were wearing winter uniform. There were tables outside the café where several Orthodox priests with black chimney-shaped hats and majestic jet beards sat drinking coffee and eating cakes dripping with honey. The Captain had not returned after an uncomfortable half an hour, so I risked sitting at a spare chair with the 'enemy'. I took the heavy webbing and the idiotic revolver off, in order to sit. Sitting down, a kindly looking priest with cornflower blue eyes offered me a glass of coffee, another of raki and a plate of cakes. I fell upon them not caring that the coffee mug may have been laced with cyanide and the cakes booby trapped. I said, "Thank you, Vicar," for want of something else to say. He didn't say anything else, neither did I; we just looked at each other; I, a callow youth and he, of unimaginable knowledge. I recall thinking that if they kidnap me and carry me off to their monastery, I would learn Classical Greek. A useless accomplishment, but it had a strong appeal. I had been impressed by Eddy Clack, a boy on 'Ganges', whose useless accomplishment was his ability to consecutively fart fifty-two times and often irreligiously accompanied the Last Post with flatulence and flair.

I had no recollection of dozing off; the raki, the sun and my trusting nature had put me in mortal danger. The cool barrel of my revolver against my forehead awoke me. "You should go, English boy," said the priest, towering over me.

If he hadn't been smiling, I think shit would have run down my legs. Frozen with fright, with Bobby playing with his puppy flashing before my eyes, I uttered the most-inane words of my seventeen years.

"Oh, thanks, how remiss of me," Then I gently grasped the revolver's barrel, which was pointed at my head.

Still smiling, he released the revolver and handed me the webbing and smiled with his eyes. Someone had removed the revolver from the holster in those few seconds; the priest had intervened. From that moment on, I determined never to question a man's belief. Despite my narrow escape, I still found time to regret not having met Laurence Durrell who lived in the nearby village of Bellapais.

We spent another two weeks circumnavigating the island and got to know the coastline intimately. When having a break from patrolling, we exercised extensively at minesweeping. Towards the end of 1955, we headed back to Malta for a much-anticipated break. Requests were made to shave off beards and I, who had been given an extension, reluctantly shaved off an inch of angora wool. Three days later, nearing Malta, I had to shave once more. I had got my wish, no more baby arse cheeks; they had a sandpapery feel to them.

During the return passage to Malta, we did gunnery practice. The ship was armed with a Bofors on the fo'c'sle and a large calibre cannon abaft the funnel. There were no targets to aim at, so I guess this was an opportunity to see if they worked or not. They did; and I had a shot at dropping clips of shells into the Bofors. A deafening procedure. Revolver practice ensued on the Quarter deck aimed at released balloons. Under the very casual supervision of a Midshipman, we, the sharp shooters, some firing from the hip, soon had the deck littered with spent ammunition while the balloons happily bobbed away and up into the ether. "God save England," I heard Frank Brough say once more.

Ships invariably entered harbour in the early morning, and we were no exception to this rule. All signs of the voyage and solid sea time needed to be swept away, bright work had to gleam, a sod of a task. Bright work had a tendency to turn green due to exposure to the elements at sea, and ours was as green as a piece of Stilton. The ship's bell had been stowed away; a master stroke of genius. Spiro tied up alongside as usual, while fumes still hissed from the funnel. Straight to the galley he rolled, returning with two slabs of bread, bacon rashers sprouting from the edges. I cleaned nothing, put on my gaiters and webbing minus the revolver of course and took the motorboat for the mail and messages. A happy postman.

The crew were divided into four watches in port and not being in the duty watch, I was aboard Spiro's liberty boat as soon as free gangway was piped. Cold bottles of beer flowed at the first bar. Elvis and Bill Haley and the Comets on the Jukebox. We lustful lads appraised the talent promenading in the balmy evening, sternly chaperoned by mothers and aunts who forbade their leveret eyes to wander.

I got on with most messmates of mine on the various ships I served but never sought their companionship as a matter of course. Invariably, I bumped into someone or even a group. My policy was that flying solo for however long gave chance its opportunity to guide me somewhere other than the inevitable bars. It always worked, not that I didn't have some great times with others, even though we had been living together for months. And that was how I came across the 'Gut'. Strait Street was the official name of the Gut; a narrow thoroughfare that ran from the heart of Valetta steeply down to Grand Harbour. Shops, chop houses and bars operated on both sides of this fascinating and noisy alley. The bars offered good cheap beer and legend had it that when it was announced that the price of a bottle would increase by a penny, the Commander in Chief of the Mediterranean fleet threatened to take all ships to sea indefinitely. Consequence, no price rise. The bars also stocked henna-haired and heavily made up grand-mothers who made a living by cajoling drinks from semi-inebriated matelots, soldiers, marines or airmen, receiving tokens from the bar owner in return. These 'drinks' would have been nothing more than coloured water or the poor old girls would have been under the table if the number of tokens they had managed to wheedle were taken into account. They told interesting but tragic stories of the war, of family killed, hunger and constant fear. Most of it must have been true, and if it wasn't, so much the better. We empathised with them.

Those eager to get ashore would miss out on the evening meal onboard, so as the night wore on, hunger set in and the numerous chop houses became the main focus. Their proprietors would spruik their culinary achievements with urgent cries of, "Inside Navy, two bob only, steak egg and chips or Spaghetti Bollocknaked (as that famous dish was dubbed)." If selecting the chef's signature dish, a steak, it was mandatory to first eat the egg and chips in order to build up the necessary strength needed to bite through and masticate mouthfuls of pensioned-off karozzin horse that had been euthanised in the local knackery or had recently dropped dead betwixt the shafts. If you weren't up to this formidable task, the spaghetti and minced horse slid down fairly easily.

On weekends, we would often make up a quartet and hire a karozzin for the day, visiting small towns and seaside villages within the range and the capacity of the horse who we fed regularly on carrots, apples and boiled sweets. We also fed the driver, stopping at wine bars and cafes and stuffing ourselves with pasta and delicious rabbit dishes. Were the rabbits wild or farmed? I never found out, the latter I would think. Very unwise to let rabbits loose on such a small island. Occasionally, a larger group would take a Naval tender, which had bunks, heads and other facilities to Gozo and Comina for the weekend. We didn't see many people there, but plenty of goats, donkeys, priests and places of worship. The priests made their own wine; excellent and very strong, and they were very helpful in assisting those who over-indulged back on board. Rationing my intake, I was avoiding trouble very well and enjoying myself just as much. I particularly appreciated rising the next morning recalling everything that had happened. I endeavoured to get ashore three days out of four. At my age and rating, my pay would just stretch out the fortnight, but I could keep up the high life due to the many weeks seabound, where I spent next to nothing. I had also made an allotment of two pounds per month to my mother for her to spoil herself and Bobby with something special whenever she wished. She now had two mouths less to feed as Gordon who had attended Banbury Grammar School and apparently learned something, was sailing the seven seas as a cadet with British Petroleum. I was never broke; just not rich. But with a comfortable bunk, three meals a day, not a care in the world, who needed to be rich? I knew what a hedonist was, and as it harmed no one, I went for it, as instructed by Tess.

There was nothing in particular to do on duty watch. In case of an emergency, someone had to remain onboard. Alongside at Famagusta, it was different altogether. Patrolling the deck all night long with a Lanchester, a cumbersome inaccurate machine gun, keeping a watch-out for frogmen who might stick a limpet mine on our wooden hull. I beseeched Odin to prevent this. I didn't wish to kill anyone, especially a Greek. I liked Greeks.

While on duty watch in Malta, I could catch up on my reading and writing; always enjoyable. On one duty watch, an aberration in the normal routine took place. There was to be a cocktail party, a frequent event for the officer class and their wives. Our lucky ship was the venue, and I, the lucky dogsbody, was shanghaied into assisting the Maltese steward in the diminutive pantry. The wardroom was small as was everything else on the ship, so things soon became stuffy and crowded. The guests began wandering around looking for fresh air and space. This was the steward's baptism of fire as far as cocktails went, and he was getting flustered remembering what he had been taught. I knew nothing about them and still don't. Gin was plentiful along with Vermouth and a few other potent-looking bottles. No beer of course, so it was going to be a dry night for me. At my suggestion, the steward stowed away a couple of slugs of gin to fortify himself as I could see that he was petrified. I readily took to the task of ferrying trays of gin and tonics and canapés around without any fortification. Gin always smelt like mother's nail polish remover. I could never face it. The steward, not normally an imbiber of repute, had taken on a silly smile and appeared dangerously relaxed; in fact, he was sitting down, not a wise thing considering the circumstances. Black coffee was all I could come up with to revive him from his stupor, and closing the servery sliding door seemed a bright idea also. But I had no sooner done this when a woman lurched into the pantry and declared the drinks rather weak, grabbed a bottle of mother's ruin and topped her glass up. She was an awesome sight, Slavic possibly. Lupine eyed, the nose on her broad face was as bulbous as the prow of an ice breaker. She then lurched out. Pouring boiling water onto a shovel of coffee grounds, I stirred it, added ice cubes and managed to rouse the sad-looking steward who quaffed it greedily and gratefully. Seeing him vertical at last, I opened the hatch door to see if anyone was suffering from dehydration and found all was well. I took more canapés around and asked if any more drinks were required. I received a negative response. The steward was correct; cocktail hour was exactly what it meant.

Returning to the pantry, I attempted to shut the door not knowing that the same woman, now inebriated, had brazenly followed me in. She poured more gin into her glass, bit my left earlobe, squeezed my testicles and hiccupped. "We must get together, handsome," she purred. Where was her bloody husband? Miles away I hoped. I very nearly fouled my underpants. She left quickly, and I turned to see the steward wagging his finger at me and mouthing, "Naughty, naughty." Why me? What had I done? I had nothing to worry about, she wouldn't remember a thing in the morning I reassured myself. I left the ungrateful steward to clean up the shit and went to the fo'c'sle for some fresh air. Boats were ferrying guests ashore and to other ships. There was no sign of Mrs Genghis Khan, and I hoped I would never see her again. But as usual, you don't always get what you want.

For the next couple of weeks, we did minesweeping exercises and an operation called 'Swinging the compass'. I never understood what that was about, but as it concerned our finding our way across vast distances of the ocean, let's say it was important. Another dull activity was degaussing; it was to do with magnetic fields and electronic currents and this also had to do with the compass. We would leave harbour at first light and return at sunset, too late for me to collect the all-important mail, a fact that was the cause of much grumbling.

I cheekily suggested to the Cox'n that I remain behind one day to collect the mail as there was clearly nothing onboard that required my attention and that I was prepared to spend the day alone in order to get the crew their longed-for letters from wives, sweethearts and mums. I was stunned when he put it to the First Lieutenant who gave it the thumbs up. Fortune favours the bold. I could scarcely believe my luck. The next day, with ten shillings out of the ship's fund for expenses, I was put ashore by Spiro. Marooned on Sliema Creek while my trusty motorboat sat in the davits on the disappearing minesweeper. My home. I watched her out of sight then flagged a karozzin for the slow plod to Valetta. Sun shining. Money in my pocket. I sat back and sighed. What could go wrong?

I got to thinking idle thoughts, daydreaming, could it rain? Surely not. In fact, I don't recall breaking out my oilskin once during all my time in the Mediterranean Sea. How did Malta get its water? There were no wild rivers, snow melt was impossible. I must enquire of the driver at journey's end. It was still very early in Valetta. Shop shutters were going up and sun shades down. A fruiterer, busy stacking oranges into a pyramid, reminded me of water. I put the question of Malta's water supply to the driver as I paid him. "From tap," he said, looking at me as if I was retarded.

"No, no, where does the whole of Malta get their water?"

"From lots and lots of taps," he spluttered, fidgeting with the reins and reaching for his whip in case a speedy getaway was needed from this British lunatic. I don't usually give up easily when attempting to understand and be understood in a foreign tongue, but as we were conversing in fractured English and getting nowhere, I considered that the wisest option was to curtail the conversation forthwith in order that we both retain our sanity. The man was well used to the behaviour of sailors at night when they were in their cups, but sober and not long after sunrise, he found a trifle unsettling. Sitting at a café with a cup of coffee, I pondered how to fill the day in; a luxury I was unaccustomed to and loathed to waste. I entered a bookshop, always exciting and read the first and last pages of about twenty books. I could feel the proprietor's eyes boring into my back and left flourishing the empty mail bag to indicate no larceny had taken place. Next came a record shop where younger members of the crew with money from the ship's fund bought cacophonous pop music to play on the ship's radio early in the morning, much to the annoyance of the thirty years plus old hands who hated it. There were cubicles where would-be purchasers could listen to their record prior to buying it. On my own, I could indulge. Never would I allow my shipmates to discover about me and Beethoven, Dvorak and Chopin. I heard the *Pathetique* right through, beautiful. I thought of my mother. Shamelessly, I informed the eager shop owner that I preferred Arthur Rubinstein's rendition. I felt his eyes also. Would he have empathised if I had explained how starved I was of this music and what sublime pleasure it had given me. Maybe I should have tried.

It was 1100 Hours now; the city centre was alive, smells more acute in the sun. The tunnel lay just ahead. A vehicle slowed down dangerously close to the kerb. A mudguard of an MG sports car brushed dangerously close. A voice I had fervently hoped I would never hear again said, "Hello, darling, had lunch?" I felt my sphincter muscle go into spasms of indecision.

"Yes," I said lamely, "and the crew are waiting for the mail," I babbled.

"Don't tell naughty fibs, darling boy, it doesn't become you. Your ship's playing war games and they simply won't be back for hours, so don't be tiresome, my love, hop in and we'll go for a drive."

Christ, the day had augured so well, too well. This fucking Tarantula knew everything about me. An order from an officer's wife must be obeyed, or so I thought. I was as green as grass on these matters, so I hopped in reluctantly. What would she have done had I refused? I did not dare think.

The MG purred its way to the outskirts of the city, then picked up speed and began growling at the open road. She was a very good driver, going through the gears smoothly and taking her hand from the gear stick once only in order to put my hand on her bare crotch. Anticipating my startled reaction, she applied pressure daring me to remove my hand while she changed gear. I had never felt or seen a woman's vagina before and here it was at eighty miles an hour. The woman's hair was wiry and springy resembling wire wool. Lust overcame fear and I delved deeper until my index finger entered the soft wet pulsating interior, and with the speedometer needle creeping closer to 90 mph, for the second time in my life I ejaculated with my trousers on at speed. Expecting a crash at any moment, I pulled my hand free from her vicelike thighs. I didn't want our bodies pulled from the mangled wreckage with my finger inside her. There would be photographers. What would my mother think; Bobby too and Tess up there in Dumfries? She was looking quite mad with her hair blowing wildly in the wind, when she expertly changed down through the gears and turned into a cul-de-sac in a pretty hamlet. Not a soul stirred in the noon heat. She was breathing heavily, got out of the car and towed me by the wrist to one of the mews-like houses. I felt uncomfortable with the stickiness in my trousers. Noticing my plight, she said, "Do hurry, darling, I'll clean you up." She just knew everything. The door opened onto a very large room, baronial, almost. Sparsely but adequately furnished, ceiling at least 12 foot high. Walls an apricot shade. A small painting seemed to be growing out of the far wall; a woman's head. A Chagall. Was it a print? A grey cat sprawled in the sunny recess of a window. Walls 18 inches thick cooled the house. In nano seconds, I took this in. I turned to her; she was stark naked. I stared at it. It was as if it had been added as an afterthought, a rosette. Were they all like this one? Surely, Tess's would be prettier. She threw a thick eiderdown on the floor, undid the buttons of my trousers where they fell to earth in a crumpled heap. Alas, my gaiters interfered with the removal of my trousers and boots. I took charge of this encumbrance while she was busy whipping off my white front like a topman changing sails. She then pushed me down on my back and stood over me with a leg either side of my head. All I could see at the top of the suntanned Doric pillars was a tussock of hair descending slowly and purposely until arachnid-like she covered my body. Her broad face was a wanton mask of lust; saliva dribbled from her lips. I thought of weaning Frank Brough's calves with a bucket of milk and managed to turn a suicidal laugh into a coughing fit. I only lasted about four seconds, which didn't seem to surprise or disappoint her as she smiled and said, "Let's get you cleaned up, my darling." And she led me by the wrist once more to the shower, where we bathed each other all over. Places I had never touched before were offered for washing and my knees nearly buckled with shock when she thrust a Howitzer breast in my hungry mouth. Bolder now, I asked her where her clitoris was, and taking my hand, she guided me to it, saying that it was of paramount importance for me to know. Afterwards, still naked she sponged my trousers and underpants and placed them in the sun with the cat.

It was now an hour past midday when at the point of starvation, she produced chicken and salad with a bottle of white wine for lunch. Together, naked we ate as eagerly as piglets and guzzled the wine from mugs. The animal in her appealed to me. She asked me my name. There was something she didn't know about me.

I asked what her name was. She didn't reply. Her husband was a Naval Officer at sea somewhere; the Pacific, I hoped. She just kept talking and touching. She was born in Germany of Hungarian parents who were both doctors of medicine. They were living in Munich but shrewdly decamped to England when Hitler began his Beer Hall ranting. She talked on constantly, touching me until I was ready again and in a moment was on her back, knees drawn up to her chin, I beheld the great wound for the first time. She beckoned, "Come to Mummy, darling." And I, Oedipus, came.

We lay resting for a short while then she leapt up, retrieved my clothes from the window, tossed them to me and disappeared in the bathroom. I dressed quickly, and before she returned, I approached the painting. It was signed 'Marc Chagall' and it was not a print. It was 1500 Hours and we left quickly as though expecting a sudden intrusive caller. We drove back steadily and calmly, both of us deep in thoughts. She squeezed my knee just once as if to say, another trophy. Stopping a few yards short of the tunnel, she said, "Goodbye, sailor," in a voice that told me I was released from bondage. Overwhelmed with relief, I ran down the black tunnel with the mail bag.

Dawdling back to Sliema, I drank cold beer in several bars. I felt guilty and slightly unclean. I could tell no one. It would take a while to unburden myself of this albatross. Then I saw Spiro and we sat together until our ship rounded the point.

Even though I felt assured that I would not cross paths with the woman who had initiated me, fear of retribution from a cuckolded husband had me looking over my shoulder for the short time remaining before departing for Cyprus once more. The fact that he could have been a thousand miles away did nothing to steady my nerves.

We now had a new Commanding Officer, a tall pleasant-looking man who didn't look as if he would abandon me with a sanctum of Greek Orthodox priests, if that is the correct collective term. His wife had recently joined him to set up home in Malta. She was an artist and appeared at least ten years his junior. She was very pretty, shapely, very approachable, and we were all madly in love with her. The usual salacious comments whenever a woman was aboard were not expressed; she was treated as a little sister; carnal thoughts were kept to oneself. The older hands had never known an officer's wife coming to the mess deck for a cup of cocoa or a serious game of Uckers, a Naval version of Ludo.

Enroute to Cyprus, we were to spend four days in Sicily at Messina. The Captain's wife didn't wave us off which we thought odd, but we were relieved the next morning when she was on the jetty at Messina.

I had read lots about the Mafia, particularly about the bandits that lived in the mountains and were heroes to the peasantry, but I didn't expect to meet any, and I didn't. Mount Etna refused to erupt which was rather a disappointment. We chugged up a creek in the motorboat for a picnic with little sister at the tiller. The creek narrowing, bushes brushing our outstretched hands, we came upon a potter treadling away outside his stone and timber abode. We bought wine from him, straining it through our teeth and broke bread and ate fat black olives and goat cheese with his wife and almond-eyed brood. We gave cigarettes, which they puffed on happily, kids included.

A cracked amphora stood by the doorway, with nasturtiums hanging down the sides. The potter's great grandfather had hauled it from the deep whilst netting fish in 1887. My mother would have loved it. She would have half hidden it in the shrubbery to be discovered anew when hanging the washing out or going to pick peas. She had far too much taste and sensitivity to place it at the portals of our council house. She would have loved the Chagall also, but that woman in the frame had seen too much and would be a constant reminder of that partly terrifying day that I was complicit in.

At sea once more, to beautiful Cyprus where we ran before a storm south of Crete. Huge following seas picking our cockleshell ship up and dumping us fifteen to twenty degrees off course. We hurried for shelter in a bay at the eastern extremity of the island at night, with the benevolence of a full moon. At dawn, the sparse population had taken to the water in a variety of craft to investigate the strange vessel that had turned up; the likes of which they had never seen before. Cigarettes, the ever welcome and powerful currency, were freely distributed. We came as friends seeking a break in the weather. Not like Francisco Pizarro with evil intentions in the name of gold and God.

Farewelling the flotilla of well-wishers, we sailed in a boisterous sea to Cyprus, Famagusta, musclebound Mustapha and hopefully George the octopus catcher. Alongside at Famagusta, there was no sign of George, but the brave and mercenary Mr Papadopoulos was. He stood next to his truck, which was packed with crates of oranges and vegetables. Mustapha, our Turkish Cypriot policeman, wheeled his bicycle up the gangway just as we were leaving to rendezvous with the fleet oiler and thence once more to sunny coves to sleep the days through.

The nocturnal boarding commenced, in search of possible gunrunners and to renew acquaintances with the fishermen of the Ayia Eleni and the Maid of Verdala. Using torchlight, they willingly helped us rummage through piles of fish and seaweed for the non-existent weapons.

During the first few days of the patrol, I turned eighteen years of age. I, who had spent sleepless nights on patrol, was now entitled to all night leave. No one wished me Happy Birthday. No one knew this important milestone had been reached. I had no idea when our next run ashore would be, but I resolved then that wherever it was I would spend the night ashore even if I sat on a bollard on the jetty until 0700 Hours. A couple of days later as dawn broke, we contacted a platoon of the Highland Light Infantry who had mail for us. Slipping ashore as quietly as the motorboat would allow, I and a midshipman were met by two unshaven temporary expatriates from the city of Glasgow who, smelling like goats, handed us a bag of mail in the surf. There followed a handshake, a few Jimmy's this and a few Jimmy's that, which I interpreted for the uncomprehending midshipman, then they vanished into the scrub, sten guns cocked. We were to meet them in more congenial circumstances on the first day of the following year. The day was spent as usual, swimming in Elysian waters, sleeping on warm December sands. I searched the faces of the contented men reading and writing their letters, and fervently hoped I hadn't delivered a 'Dear John'. A letter from mother came, along with a card autographed by all at No. 5; my nose pressed to Bobby's grubby hieroglyphics redolent of puppies, dirt and love.

A couple of days later, we were back in Famagusta for a break and to re-provision, and where I caught up with friend George once more. He had been busy catching octopus for Christmas as he was expecting an invasion of relatives. With bitter disappointment, I had to refuse his invitation to join them. It would have been wonderful, the Ouzo, Retsina, Moussaka, the Bouzouki melodiously accompanying the callipygian girls dancing together. I nearly blubbered. Two days before Christmas, we were on patrol again with our fisher friends off the radar, obviously having a holiday. We still had to be up all night.

For Christmas dinner, the Jimmy decided that we would roast a goat at Fontana Amorosa. On a previous visit, I and Kelso, a Scottish electrician from Aviemore, in answer to faint tinkling of goat bells, had ventured uphill and inland about half a mile to see what was afoot. We came upon a girl of about ten years old, carrying a newborn kid. Unafraid, she led us to a stone hut of two rooms, her home. Her father and mother shyly welcomed us. The man's English was limited but adequate. The mother and girl spoke only Greek and a crawling baby gurgled happily in its own language. We had nothing to give them as neither of us smoked but promised to return one day soon.

In order to prevent the Jimmy from shooting willy-nilly any goats he was so set on roasting, we decided to let our secret out of the bag and mentioned the goat herder we had befriended, who would probably sell us a goat. Luckily, he seemed to agree that this suggestion had merit and a crowd of us set off to secure Christmas dinner. The deal was done swiftly with the man, receiving five pounds for a protesting young goat, which was more money than I received in a fortnight; also, they were given 100 cigarettes and chocolate for all. I was so pleased with their delight. The goat was then secured with a length of cod line, and we all stood around wondering what to do next when someone suggested we kill it. As we had no intention of roasting it alive, this proposal was received with much nodding of heads. The animal looked as though it would tip the scales at around thirty pounds, and I proposed that the goat walk to its place of execution half a mile back to the beach. I was slapped on the back for this stroke of genius. By now, the goat herder had a fair inkling that we didn't have the remotest idea of what to do with the bleating animal. He and his family joined us on a slow meander back to the beach, baby and all. During this pleasant walk, we took turns in leading the young goat, sometimes it led the way and very quickly became part of the group. Arriving at the beach, a driftwood fire was blazing, big enough for a bullock, a stark reminder of the eminent execution of the young goat. The only good thing about what ensued in the next ten minutes was the swiftness of the goat's demise. The goat herder's knife flashed in the sun; blood spurted; the midshipman gagged in the bushes. None of us wanted to eat any goat as we had made friends with it. All too late. The midshipman knew he'd fucked the day up, so gave the bewildered goat herder another quid and told him to eat the goat themselves. God knows what that happy family must have thought of us, but the midshipman rose a little in my estimation of him. We returned to our ship for an improvised dinner of corn beef, egg and chips and two cans of beer. We enjoyed a proper Christmas dinner on Boxing Day, complete with pudding and rum sauce. The memory of the unnecessary slaughter of the goat remained; the goat which should be still browsing and following the tinkling bell. I had no vision of vegetarianism as I had not experienced Asian cuisine then and what a revelation that was when I eventually did.

As a boy, we were taught to shoot for the pot. "After all," I had heard Pop say with what sounded like an acknowledgement of guilt and shame, "we are human, the greatest predators the world has ever seen." 'Shoot them on the rise' was the law of the moors and the heather. Duns-Tew was a long way from the moors. We had a law of our own. The pot.

On New Year's Eve, still on patrol, I, being the youngest member of the crew, dressed up in the Captain's uniform to ring the old year out and the New Year in; 16 bells in all. In the six-foot seven-inch Captain's jacket covering my knees, his hat several sizes too small, I performed the ceremony looking like a clown, but with an extra two bottles of beer, I was past caring.

The next day, sailing west past Kyrenia and the ever-watchful, waiting castle of St Hilarion, we rendezvoused with a company of the Highland Light Infantry who had invited us to a Hogmanay lunch at their camp in the scrub where we were regaled with roast turkey and tatties. This was of course preceded by the Sonsie Haggis piped in to a great cheer by a rubicund Pipe Major. I had never been called Jimmy so often until this day. I was impressed to see that the officers acted as waiters and servers and dispensed beer with humour and camaraderie that I was unaccustomed to. The only thing conspicuously absent from this highland welcome was whiskey, but it was not too difficult to reason why.

Mid-afternoon, we wandered back to the beach. I, clutching the mail bag which I courageously and stubbornly refused to broach. Splashing in the shallows, we awaited the motorboat, to venture any deeper after the feast would have been risky. I have been to many Hogmanays since in various climes and locations, most forgotten but not New Year's Day 1956.

We circumnavigated the island on this patrol, calling in at Paphos for mail. Ships were at anchor taking on cargoes of oranges, limes and lemons by lighter; we passed by, inhaling a citrusy zephyr. We were becoming used to venturing ashore in isolated locations and had fun guessing whether the village was Greek or Turkish by the aromaticity of the cooking. If in doubt, there was always Mustapha, so adept at breaking the ice that we had some very interesting times without being shot at. We were unarmed at all times. We posed no threat. The people knew this.

There were cliffs as we passed along the south coast; somewhere here Aphrodite was born, washed ashore in the foam. At Limassol on Akrotiri Bay, we were allowed shore leave where the cheapest drink was a brandy that tasted of paint stripper and creosote. After the first sip in an act of disloyalty and cowardice, I tipped my glass into a large pot plant, which showed signs of withering almost immediately. The boys, determined to finish the bottle to the last drop, began to look quite bilious and stupid and behaving like idiots. Being sober, I seriously thought about giving up the grog for good. Did I really look like this when in my cups, I asked myself? The Red Caps were summoned and that terminated that run ashore. Next day, of course I was quizzed why I had not been tossed in the guard house with them. I bragged that I could hold my liquor; didn't I drink with them glass for glass? The feeling of shame took weeks to dissipate. But it finally did and I didn't give any more thought to taking the pledge. The fickleness of youth.

George was on the wharf at Famagusta; he had heard from Mr Papadopoulos that we would be arriving. He gave me a large box of confectionary and what I supposed was a huge chunk of Greek Christmas cake that weighed several pounds; leftovers from the happy family gathering. Most of our crew were young and had missed the usual Yuletide fare, so they willingly chipped in with all the cigarettes they could muster. George was very pleased. A consignment of films was waiting for us along with the mail. That evening, we rigged up a screen on the wall of the fort and held a film show from sundown till late for the next three nights. They were well attended by the crews of merchant ships in port and were a regular event whenever we were in Famagusta. George never came. Night time was for fishing. I was warned on several occasions that George could be an EOKA sympathiser and to watch him. I ignored this advice. I would have trusted him with my life. There are some things that you just know.

Over the next couple of months, life was pretty much the same on patrol. The fishermen were still fishing; days were spent idling on the beach. At Fontana Amarosa, I went to check on the goat herd. There was no one there. Gone. Moved to the high life of Nicosia with the fiver they had received for the goat! Their solid stone dwelling looked forlorn but also expectant, patiently awaiting the family to refill it with laughter, tears and tinkling bells.


## 1956

Things are a bit hazy as far as the dates of occurrences and sequence of events are concerned. For example, as a boy in England if a meteorite had demolished my school and a subsequent blizzard had completely buried the wreckage under sixteen feet of snow, thereby precluding any restoration or rebuilding to take place for a considerable time, I would indelibly recall that the celestial blessing had happened sometime during the months of December, January or February. Not so in the Mediterranean, where the climate, from my experience, never differed from nice, making it difficult to pinpoint accurately any event. Our first run ashore in the New Year was to Beirut, an overnight run and very welcome. We tied up alongside an American destroyer. The only memories I have of the Lebanon and Beirut was the bus trip through the fertile Bekaa Valley to snow-capped mountains covered with majestic cedar trees, and that most foreign currency, both notes and coins, were negotiable. New Guinea boar tusks being one of the exceptions. The American warship showed 'movies' every night on the 'fantail' and dished out Coca Cola, popcorn and ice cream. One 'movie' was titled *Mr Roberts*, which hadn't yet been released in the United States. The Yanks really did pamper their boys.

From Beirut, we met the peregrinating oil tanker, thence to Mr Papadopoulos and the anticipated mail. As expected, a letter from mother, and to my surprise and delight, another envelope smudged with Duns-Tew and boy dirt again, address just legible, guided by mother's hand. I read mother's usual informative letter, caught up with the latest village gossip; recent births, fathers unknown, learned that the broad beans were already poking through a light frost. Then to the task at hand, the deciphering of the hieroglyphical missive from my little brother Bobby. He had been attending the village primary school for some time as the law required, but what chance of success does a teacher have with a student who leaves his fishing rod in the lobby. My mother had taken a job at the US Airbase at Upper Heyford as she had more time on her hands. Pop was working away from home a lot, sometimes abroad, Ireland and for a period in Malta whilst I was in Cyprus. He was disappointed, but I was secretly pleased as I knew he would be mixing with brass hats and the thought of being in his company and possibly bumping into the Tarantula, I found unnerving, to put it mildly. I think my mother by then had decided to hold on to Bobby and not lose him to the uncertainty of the sea. So, she allowed him a loose rein. On leaving school, he was apprenticed to a carpenter under whose guidance he excelled and from there to stone masonry. Fishing, shooting and poaching were his other cherished pursuits. I still love hearing from him at Christmas, writing as he speaks.

Less than two weeks later, out of the blue we were ordered to sail for Malta. No one knew why, except the Captain and the Jimmy of course, and they seemed reluctant to divulge anything. There were plenty of rumours as usual, from the imaginative to the absurd, but we were all eager for a run ashore, so were happy to wait and see. Well, surprise was not the right word when instead of Sliema Creek we slipped into Grand Harbour and into dry dock. I don't recall what the problem was exactly, but it was something to do with the screw and drive shaft. I can only presume that the reason for the secrecy was due to the age of some of the crew, which included National Servicemen. If this measure was undertaken to prevent anxiety amongst the crew, it was quite unnecessary. We were so gung-ho, that breaking down and drifting at sea, sparking a massive rescue operation, would have been a welcome diversion to most of us. Our ship, emblazoned on the front page of the newspapers; we would be on TV waving to our girlfriends and mums. What fun. Once in dry dock, we were billeted at Fort Ricasoli, which reeked of centuries of strife and intrigue. The fort was built by the Order of the Knights of St John. We slept in recesses carved out of the rock, which had graffiti etched into it from the present time down to centuries past. I was enthralled. I would drink beer after the evening meal at an area previously unknown to me called the 'Barbary Coast', then sleepy with the beer warm inside me, I fantasised about the knight with sword and buckler by his side who had slept here, possibly after jousting with Saladin or sacking Jerusalem; my reverie accompanied by Radio Malta blaring on the Tannoy, Bill Haley and Rock around the Clock. Pure Monty Python. Later, I was to find that Fort Ricasoli had been built in the seventeenth century, quite new. The discovery failed to erase my fantasy.

We stayed at Ricasoli for about a week, working on our ship during the day. So obsessed with the centuries old chiselled graffiti, that I remained 'on board' for three nights in a row, to enable me to document as much of the often-lewd legend that I could, while the sleeping berths' present occupants were ashore drinking. I was getting drunk on history; it was difficult to comprehend. Was I going around the bend? I don't think so, I had always loved history. I loved its smell. I had slept where Nelson died and given a chance, I would sleep on the tomb of the Black Prince.

Out of dry dock, we spent a few days working up, doing speed trials and minesweeping exercises and mooring in the evening at Sliema once more with our old retainer Spiro ferrying us ashore sober, and taking great care to return us safely on board whether still sober, half pissed or well over the eight. The man was a treasure. We were soon to part again but under such joyous circumstances that Spiro was happy too. We were to fly to the UK for a week's leave and then bring another minesweeper out to the Mediterranean. One and all were euphoric. No time to write home, I would get there before the letter, and barge in on them whatever the hour. Maybe Bobby would be in bed, if so, I would wake him to see his face when I gave him the fishing rod.

Two days later, we flew from Luqa airport in a DC3, I think, refuelling at Lyon in France then landing at an airport not far from London. From there, we were bussed to Portsmouth where we stowed our gear aboard our new ship. Then we were paid, received return rail tickets and sent on our way rejoicing. I just loved being alive.

The train picked up and left off passengers on its way north. At Reading, where Oscar Wilde resided for two years, a boisterous family of five burst into the compartment. We recognised one another; they were from the village a couple of miles south of Duns-Tew. A boy the same age as I offered his hand. I took it. Smiles all around, we had both changed from the two boys who at school frequently came to blows over nothing in particular. Disembarking at Oxford, I was invited to join the family in their Bedford van and they kindly dropped me off at No. 5. It was 1100 Hours. If not for their generosity, I would not have got home until much later.

There was no one at home. Of course, mother was at work, brothers at school. I was locked out. Whenever the house was emptied for trips to Wales of wherever, the back door was bolted and the last person out shut the front door. This was the sole time anyone in the household used the front portal. The only others who had the temerity to blemish the knocker with their fingerprints were the Avon Lady and the bold weather-beaten gypsy women carrying baskets of clothes pegs, which they sold to the superstitious villagers, who feared being cursed if they refused. My mother, well supplied with pegs, having bought hundreds over the years pre-empted any haggling by sending the women away with a cabbage or whatever she had an abundance of. This tactic could easily have merited a curse because if the gypsies were wanting a cabbage, they knew where they grew.

The back door had a lobby where muddied boots and wellies were kicked off before venturing onto the polished red tiles. The butcher, baker, greengrocer and rent man all knocked here. I had never needed a key before so I looked in the usual safe spots that folk are hiding secrete keys. Under mats, pot plants, etc. Bob the dog who was leaping around trying to remember when he had seen me before, let me check under his bowl. He looked also in case a morsel had been overlooked from his last meal. I tried the windows in the back garden, trying to avoid mother's flowerbeds, peered in the kitchen window, and as I expected, there was the loaf of bread alongside the carving knife and two tins, one of golden syrup and the other of black treacle. No butter. You don't have both. Memories of Huntly and Aunt Mary flooded back. The loaf would be demolished soon after school was out as a preliminary to dinner in a couple of hours. Mrs Jenkins called over the hedge, said mother would be back at five, then asked the first question I was always asked when coming home, "When are you going back?" Murray was at Steeple Aston School where they had hot dinners, so Bobby must have taken his lunch to the village school. Not yet midday, the kids were still trapped inside.

I stowed my bag and Bobby's new fishing rod in the laundry, then walked to the school and knocked on the door. The formidable Mrs Barwick wrenched open the door with such force, that the vortex almost dragged me over the threshold. She smiled on recognising me and invited me in. I bravely accepted. Bobby jumped up, excited. Did he have a key? Not on him, he said, then informed me and the entire class plus the village and any would be burglar for miles that the key was suspended on a piece of string in the apple tree.

I had never experienced tutelage under the old kestrel-eyed battle axe and neither had she known the frustration of attempting to drill arithmetic into my unresponsive and completely disinterested brain and I was pleased she hadn't. She was a good teacher having had success in assisting several students to pass their 11-Plus; brother Gordon being one who benefited. The bus to Steeple Aston picked up at the village school. Whilst waiting, boys and girls that wished to, kicked a ball up and down the road. At the arrival of Mrs Barwick, the infants ceased trying to get a kick of the ball and scampered into the playground and lined up to greet their mentor. Her house was visible a hundred yards away and at her appearance at her front door, ball kicking stopped; the battered tennis ball was quickly stuffed into a farm boy's jacket pocket in company with a wood pigeon or possibly a pheasant for Mr Fulton, the worshipped woodwork teacher. Fashions come and go, so farm boys' jacket pockets with the capacity of kitbags are no longer in vogue, along with the piquancy of ferret or rabbit. Playing in the road was considered dangerous. "You might get run over." Run over by what? A plodding milk cart?

Did I detect a glimpse of amusement in her face at Bobby's security breach? During the clamour for temporary freedom as she rang the dinner bell, she said that Bobby could have the afternoon off. She was probably thinking also that if he had six months off, it would have little effect on the end result.

The key was swinging in the breeze, for the last time; a board meeting would convene later to decide upon another depository. Lunch and the tins of syrup and treacle were put on hold. What had I brought home? He knew what the plywood box contained but pretended he didn't. Just to please me. The pseudo-Japanese calligraphy that a fellow shipmate painted on with the name Robert John Wynne invited Bobby to open the box with gasps of astonishment. The fibre glass three-part rod lay shining, multifarious coloured flies with exciting names: Red Zulu, Black Dragon and Kamikaze; he was speechless. I suggested that it would not be appropriate to be seen fishing while school was still in session. I could see he was having difficulty identifying any logic in my proposal, and to be frank, so was I. I changed the subject. I dreaded being moralistic. Nature intervened, it began to rain and our attention turned to the cottage loaf. We had intended saving a crust for Murray, but it looked so lonely that we polished that off too. Naval training had to be adhered to. The kitchen table was spotless. I had a gift for Murray, it wasn't edible, he would have to wait for dinner.

The rain had stopped; Bobby was practising casting on the lawn. I hung my uniform up and found that most of my civvies no longer fitted. I had muscled up and grown taller. I had to make do as I had no intention of renewing my wardrobe for just a few days. I joined Bobby on the lawn; he was bragging to Mrs Jenkins that his teacher had given him the afternoon off.

Mrs Jenkins and my mother were on good terms from the start. A friendly woman with a large adult family. They were over the hedge friends, hanging the washing out friends, keeping up a conversation with a mouthful of pegs each. They were not flower garden friends as the Jenkins grew spuds right up to the back door. Mrs Jenkins rarely left her premises for longer than was necessary, and my mother had nothing in common with the village women. All the inhabitants of the council houses were blow-ins, with infestations of kids, which certainly livened things up.

Mrs Jenkins had three sons still living at home. Derek was a 12-year-old boy with Down Syndrome, a term not in regular use at the time. Sufferers were offensively referred to as Mongols. I had no idea what the Mongolians felt about this. Derek was as powerful and energetic as a yearling, who, that first spring of 1950, broke the as yet untilled frozen ground, solo, with a spade and in all weathers. This was before the privet hedge was planted and only my mother's fair-mindedness prevented him from cultivating our back yard also, much to

Pop's annoyance. "Keep the lad occupied, fit and healthy," he reasoned. I worked in tandem with Derek on a few occasions but could not keep up.

I often wondered what happened to Derek. He would join us boys and girls at cricket and football at 'Warlands' paddock, adjacent to the houses. He never once kicked the ball, only making contact with it when a stray punt ricocheted off him. At cricket on the rare occasion, he fielded the ball on the boundary. It was quite difficult getting him to part with it, allowing the batsmen to score two or three dozen runs, due to our rules being proclaimed without taking Derek into account. When my family moved to South Wales some years later, all contact was lost, as is so often the case.

Murray was the first to kick his boots off at the back door. I shoved his present in his hands hoping it would interest him enough to not notice the absence of the afternoon snack. It didn't, but he seemed not to mind. Mother's mini-van rolled up next and soon after, Pop putt-putted up astride an auto cycle. His loathed, but the only mode of transport at the time; a temporary conveyance I was assured. Mayhem ensued for the next hour; cider, ginger beer and parsnip wine flowed from the larder whilst mother cooked dinner. Presents were handed out to oohs and aahs, mostly cheap but fascinating junk that I had picked up in Gibraltar, Malta and Beirut, some of which had been made in the renamed city of USA in Japan. Duty-free cigarettes for Pop with 'H.M. Ships Only' printed on each and everyone. How proud he was to flash them around the 'White Horse' and wherever he went.

Pop was about forty-eight at the time and a fairly heavy smoker. He had not taken up the practice until he was thirty as he was still playing rugby and swimming until then. He had medals for lifesaving and a special gong for swimming twenty-eight miles down the Bosphorus whilst serving on the battleship 'Ramiles'. These medals gradually disappeared years ago, and I acknowledge guilt regarding the loss of one of them while on shore leave in Belize, British Honduras, where the rum was exceedingly cheap. Twelve bore shotgun and fishing rod aside, Pop cared little for possessions. His solid silver half hunter watch-and-chain was a plaything for Murray as a toddler, and when it gave up the ghost with the rough handling, Murray mended it with a hammer. I have always treasured my books but have very little else I value. As a profit-making concern, I could not run a second-hand book shop. As there would be a permanent sign on the door, 'Back in Five Years'.

As it was not holiday time, no one suggested we go to Wales. The Beacons had brooded over Brecon for a million years. They would await my return. Duns-Tew was enough for me knowing that the week would flash by.

Bobby tried his rod and flies in Sow Brook. Nothing doing, he would have to wait for Wales. It then rained for four days, and I enjoyed the luxury of reading and listening to music. Evenings were spent visiting favourite pubs, and greeting as well as fare-welling old friends, some of whom I probably wouldn't see again. Towards the end of the week, guilt consumed me once more. Lovely to be with the people I loved, yet eager to slip the moorings and sail to whatever lay ahead.

Come the day, up at sparrow fart, gigantic breakfast, boys to school, mother and Pop to work. We all left together, leaving the bread and the two tins on the table. Bob the dog tagged along to the bus stop. The Oxford-bound double-decker groaned up the hill from Deddington, stopping for a breather to let me board. "Go home, Bob," I said and he galloped off. Diesel fumes coughed from the exhaust; first gear engaged. We were off.

The platform at Oxford station was deserted except for me, and a man and a woman with a teenage girl, about eighteen years old I would guess. They were conspiratorially whispering so urgently that I heard every word they said. Would the girl dare to? I braced myself for the light timid touch on my collar. A few seconds later, there it was. I turned and saw the most gorgeous face beginning to blush as she skipped back to her parents like a lamb that had strayed too far. I approached them, took the girl's hand and pressed it gently on my shoulder. The poor girl was crimson now. "I need all the luck you can spare, miss. Thank you." The train arrived seconds later. They were first class, I was steerage.

I got back on board with hours to spare. Quite a few of my crewmates had reported their return. A chap from the Outer Hebrides had arrived the day before in case rough weather in the Minch delayed his ferry.

A two-tonne van was parked on the wharf. It was full of 'Wagon Wheels', a wheatmeal biscuit roughly the size and density of a railway refreshment room saucer. They were covered heads and tails in chocolate. They were very much in vogue and larger ships stocked them in the canteen. We didn't have a canteen. It transpired that one of the midshipmen was well connected with the manufacturers of this popular snack and had generously donated a ton of them. They must have thought we were an aircraft carrier. The question was what to jettison in order to stow this feast onboard. Hardly ammunition, we may need to defend ourselves. Minesweeping gear! No, we were a minesweeper. The

Coxswain with permission from the Captain via the First Lieutenant solved the dilemma; the biscuits were to be distributed evenly to avoid listing, in any available space. Before a week had lapsed, we were sick of the sight of Wagon Wheels and the pervading smell. In Malta, we would offload more than half of them. I would never eat another Wagon Wheel again.

The voyage to Malta was uneventful. We called at Gibraltar for forty-eight hours where I picked up the mail from somewhere in the interior of the majestic monolith, returning in time to hear the pipe for shore leave. Discarding my webbing and distributing the mail, I then turned about and joined the eager crewmembers, bent on a carouse. Remembering my promise to myself, I managed to veer off on my own, bought more interesting baubles and gimcracks from Formosa and returned onboard relatively sober, which didn't go unnoticed by the Officer of the watch and the bosun's mate. "Something wrong, Rose?" the Officer enquired, a worried frown forming on his brow.

"No, sir, just ensuring you don't sail without me," I said with all the seriousness I could muster. Historic Malta awaited, I needed to be set ashore in Spiro's dghajsa on the first evening, instead of under punishment for some misdemeanour in Gibraltar. I still didn't trust myself.

We arrived at Malta a few days later; here was Sliema Creek once more, and Spiro was there with his trusty dghajsa. I took the brand-new motorboat for its maiden voyage to Valetta for the mail. In the evening, I was indeed set ashore by Spiro. Scrutinising the passing traffic, lest an MG should be patrolling the creek. I ducked across the street with fugitive strides and reached the sanctuary of the first bar, swallowed two bottles of beer for the courage to venture further afield. Then slunk along the pavement like an escapee and hailed the first karozzin available. The Gut beckoned; she wouldn't dare be seen down there.

It was Friday. It was Malta; that meant fish for dinner. Flushed with money, I bought dinner in a proper restaurant and drunk a whole bottle of white wine. I had remembered the label on the Tarantula's bottle. The waiter was quite impressed; he would expect a tip. He had served me as he would a gentleman. I felt like a big shot so I left him five bob. I had a habit of doing daft things like that on the spur of the moment.

Stepping boldly out into the street with wine undergoing a secondary fermentation, not caring if she was around or not. I would show her. It is amazing how wine can erase blue funk. Strangely, I felt the need for the company of my own kind. I had enjoyed the posh restaurant and knew it was not me. That would come later.

Sliema-bound, the karozzin was at a fast clip for a change. Must have been a young horse or maybe an old one bent on proving that he is not quite ready to be made into Bolognaise sauce. I needed the wisdom and years of Aviemore Kelso, and I knew where he would be. We booked in at a two-shilling doss house, with early morning wake up call, then drank beer until we had to prop one another up. We knew we would be incapable of climbing the steps to get on board, and Spiro would probably refuse to take us for fear of our drowning. The old boy really cared.

Next day, both Kelso and I were on duty watch. I would write letters and read, also plan my secret Sabbath adventure. And secret it had to be, except for one person. There wasn't the remotest chance of anyone going to Medina but Kelso had to be let in on it. Kelso was a Catholic, very much lapsed but not lapsed enough to have forsaken his crucifix. I told him of my plan. "Yer fucking mad yer daft cunt ye," he spluttered. "But I'll lend you it, only because you're a weird kind of daft cunt," he said kindly. I didn't know what he meant by that but decided not to ask him to elaborate. Genuflection was the first lesson and took ages to perfect, and Kelso wanted it right. So much for lapsed Catholicism. Next followed Latin incantations and pious utterances, but it was impossible to sustain an air of solemnity and also I didn't wish to insult the church so Plan B would be put into operation; I would feign an attack of laryngitis. This ploy would preclude an error on my part such as referring to the place of worship as a Kirk. Kelso was still nursing a sore head from the previous evening's imbibition (I was never afflicted with this menace to most topers) and was eager to catch Spiro's dghajsa at a respectable hour the next morning. As I knew that Kelso was practically penniless, I gladly donated the price of a few beers until I caught up with him later in the day. I thought I detected moist eyes of gratitude, daft that I was. Kelso then turned in to suffer the night through, clutching the ten-shilling note as if it were a fragment of the Turin shroud, and I took over as bosun's mate on the gangway until midnight. The next morning, Spiro put me ashore at 0900 Hours; he wondered why so early on Sunday. I didn't tell him the reason of course; he would have thought that I was taking the piss, so I thought of something else hastily. Kelso would go ashore when the bars opened at a respectable Sabbath hour. He had suggested that I endeavour to get to Medina by midday when praying began in earnest. As my mission was of a religious nature, I felt it would be safe to risk a bus ride. Sitting behind the driver and his icon-festooned windscreen, I prayed for a safe journey. With no thanks to the maniacal driver, I arrived shaken but intact, at Medina. Not since the end of WWII had I heard such a frantic pealing of bells. Pulling the crucifix from beneath my white front, I shuffled pilgrim-like after the cathedral-bound throng with the crucifix dangling ostentatiously like an Olympic gold medal.

Following every move made by a middle-aged couple; he with double medicine balls for buttocks and wearing socks with sandals, an English affectation and utterly ridiculous. She, the antithesis, tall and thin, on flamingo stilts. She stumbled on a step and fell forward. The gentleman, encumbered in front by a corporation that must have cost thousands of pounds was unable to assist her. So, Errol Flynn stepped into the breach and not forgetting that I was suffering from laryngitis, helped her silently to a pew. She thanked me in an Oxford accent, which made me break out in goose bumps. I imbecilically nodded my head and beat a hasty retreat whilst concerned onlookers clamoured about her. I stood out like an Imam at a Bar Mitzvah so found sanctuary behind a pillar and a little subdued, awaited the show to commence. The startling sound of the thin woman's accent had unnerved me somewhat. Furtively scanning the congregation from the rear for any sign of the Tarantula, the thought occurred to me that my conspicuousness needn't be. In future, I would adopt mufti; all I would need were a pair of trousers, shirt and sandals, problem solved. Why hadn't I thought of it before? Getting a bee in my bonnet always meant a single train of thought taking over my brain to the exclusion of almost everything else. All interest in the purpose of my educational pilgrimage vanished. From behind the pillar, I could see most of what was taking place but saw, heard and understood little of the service. There appeared to be more than one priest, possibly three, who continuously passed a goblet of Christ's blood back and forth.

Waiting until the pious and mesmerised believers had ceased praying and crossing themselves, then burst into the roof-raising hymn, I backed out of the great doors genuflecting whilst going astern. Not an easy task. Out of the shadow of the great dome and into the sun-baked street, I walked self-consciously on the shady side of the road until I passed out of the edge of the town for about a mile. Finding a quiet spot out of the sun, I awaited the first bus. I reasoned that this would not be until all devotions were done with. I saw no one after leaving the cathedral, but gradually, after an hour had elapsed and my thirst had increased, folk were beginning to appear in the distance with the happy laughter of children chasing one another. Medina was coming alive and ready for lunch. I quenched my parched throat at one of the taps that the karozzin driver had boasted of and soon after a belching bus rumbled out of a sirocco of dust and shuddered to a halt. The driver was the same lunatic who had delivered me to Medina. He was grinning maliciously, inviting and challenging me once more to test my faith which didn't desert me.

Soon I would be discussing the matter with Kelso who would be punishing his liver in the usual haunt. He smiled at me through an alcoholic haze; I had come to his rescue, a Saint Bernard in the Tyrol. He had been supping on the dregs of a warm beer for the previous hour. "I thought ye'd deserted and taken Holy Orders, ye mad fucker," he gibbered with obvious relief. I was well used to these terms of endearment from Kelso; I don't remember him ever calling me Hugh. I bought two cold beers and put my idea about getting civvies to change into once ashore. He peered at me as if I had just announced that I had invented the wheel. Leaning forward, purporting to whisper a confidence in my ear he said, "It's about time for yez to buck up, ye fucking wanker, it's been going on for years." I pulled a couple of quid out and fondled them idly. His eyes sparkled and he called me mate and fellow countrymen, followed by a temporary cessation of the insults. Apparently for an extra two shillings, the proprietor of the Doss house would not only look after the mufti or uniform but have it laundered and ironed. Unless the shirt and trousers had been torn to shreds due to riotous behaviour, his wife was very willing to mend any superficial damage.

Buying more beer, I asked if he agreed that a white shirt and grey pair of trousers was a rather drab ensemble. Not a good question considering his condition. "I thought that was the idea for fuck's sake, if yer wanting every cunt in Malta to ogle yer, wear a deerstalker and smoke a fucking pipe, a fucking Meershaum pipe maybe." Kelso's sarcasm could be merciless as well as enlightening. Thanking him for his enthusiasm and encouragement, I left him with two bottles of beer and two shillings for the Doss house and departed leaving him looking philosophically at the two bottles. I had bought him two different brands. Which to drink first, I hoped it was a tough decision. Crossing the street where the Sunday evening betrothal market was well underway, I hailed Spiro who carried me safely to my bunk and fantasies.

As it turned out, the purchase of my incognito disguise did not eventuate, as we were leaving for Cyprus in three days and were busy taking on supplies.

Shops had closed by the time I had got ashore in the late afternoon. The thought had occurred to me about buying the clothes in Valetta during the mail run but decided against it. I was becoming cautious in my advancing age. 'He who hesitates is lost' was being superseded by 'Look before you leap'. Was I wise, I wondered? My impulsive compulsive nature had dumped me in a lot of shit at times, but they were far outweighed by the opportunistic occurrences that I had enjoyed. As well as taking on supplies, we easily disposed of a hundred weight of Wagon Wheels to grateful recipients. A day's minesweeping exercise followed, when I was left ashore to collect the mail for the last time before it was redirected to Cyprus. The usual jitters descended upon me at Valetta, but my gods were looking over me. I felt reassured that I was free of the arachnid at last.

We set sail in the afternoon. Good bye, Spiro, good bye, Sliema, good riddance, Tarantula. We were off to the same old beautiful routine, but instinct told me that it would be a little different this time. It was a smooth passage interrupted only by the testing of all ordnance, revolvers exempt, much to the disappointment of the Gary Cooper and Glen Ford fans.

The usual greetings at Famagusta, Mr Papadopoulos, Mustapha and friend George, who looked up from his octopus flailing as we slowly passed the corner of the fort about thirty yards away. I waved, but he didn't look up as he was unaware that we had a new ship. While the ship was being secured, I hopped ashore, collected and thanked the squaddie who was sitting smoking in a lorry with the mail. I distributed the mail to the loved and the lovelorn, then I took off to see my old mate. When I gave him the promised pipe and tobacco, I thought he would burst into tears. I told him that some of Mrs George's tentacles would be ample, thanks. He asked where the other ship was. I mentioned casually that we had sunk after striking a WWII mine. I immediately regretted saying it. George's sense of humour was not in synch with my dark, impulsive and sometimes twisted mind. It took a while to convince him that I was pulling his leg, but I don't think that he really understood, so we began loading the bloody expensive briar pipe that I had bought at Banbury Cross. Setting the pipe on fire, I left him to his smouldering pleasure and trusting that he would soon forget about my unthinking flippant remark. Another lesson learned the hard way.

We left for patrol the following day, rounding Cape Andreas and during the next three days proceeded along the north coast as far as Paphos, then turned about to retrace our course. One night during the middle watch just off Kyrenia, which I recall, because the town lights were the sole illuminations of any consequence on the entire north coast, we received a coded signal to immediately break off patrol and rendezvous with the auxiliary tanker off Cape Andreas. We were to refuel and take on fresh water. My premonition of something happening out of the norm on leaving Malta, was palpable. At 0400 Hours, at the end of the middle watch, the much looked-forward-to couple of hours in the bunk were forgotten. We were at full speed heading to meet the oiler. My excitement was volcanic as I roused the crew with Elvis' *Hound Dog* over the tannoy. "Get up, you lazy bastards, something was up." We hadn't gone this fast since speed trials in the Solent. What the fuck was happening? We were then informed that there would be a general muster of all hands once we had disengaged and were free of the oiler but still in the dark as to what was up. We made our own enquiries. The wheelhouse binnacle confirmed that we were racing in a south-southeast direction, plus it was obvious to all that the sun was not in its usual position. The muster of all hands was called at 1100 Hours when we were told that we were headed for Egypt. By the course we were steering, only a 180-degree alteration off course could have prevented it. The question was why? Later that day, we learned that the president of Egypt Gamal Abdel Nasser had closed the Suez Canal and scuttled ships in it, much to the annoyance of Britain, France and Israel; all of these nations had decided to do something about it.

However, before the last bulletin, older hands were busy stirring the cauldron of intrigue. Tales of Bag Shanties (brothels), unimaginative yarns were spun of girls performing unbelievable congress with donkeys, exotically named drinks such as Red Biddy, Screech and Arrack. Bum Boats. Warnings, don't trust the cunts. Dirty postcards, offers to fuck their virgin sisters and graphic depictions of the consequences of 'Dipping one's wick'. The Marquis de Sade and Caligula would have stowed away with us. Clichés, rumour and legends. Would it ever end? Was this all they knew of Egypt? Stupidly, I mentioned the Valley of the Kings. They stared; I had to be careful but tried once more with Tutankhamen, then risking my life bunged in Luxor and the ruins of Amanhotep III temple. "What would you know about Two Ton Carmen?" demanded a three-badge AB. "Runs a brothel at 'Alex'. Gigantic lesbian. Makes a football disappear sitting on it. Cunt like a horse collar." I gave up but laughed with the rest. I lived in two different worlds. How could I see humour in that brief crude monologue and think of Tess without shame?

It was the distribution of the tin hats and the opening of the magazine, plus the issue of anti-flash clothing that brought reality back to the table. There was change in the air, young men, some excited, some down-right scared, all anxious. I qualified in every category. Older members of the crew, several veterans of the Korean campaign and a few who had served in the last years of WWII, realised the seriousness of the moment and did well in calming the situation but not without plenty of light-hearted banter.

In answer to questions on being sunk, such as,

"What will happen to the money I have saved?"

"Stuff it in a French letter, tie a knot in it and hang it around your neck (which appeared to be the method widely in use)."

"What about my sock of two bobs?"

"You can stuff them up your arse."

"What if the Carley Floats (life rafts) get blown up?"

"The ship's built of timber, laddie, there'll be plenty of slabs of the hull to cling to."

"What about sharks?"

"Don't worry the crocodiles have eaten them all." It went on and on. Some couldn't make up their mind whether to laugh or cry.

On course for Suez, all guns and minesweeping gear were uncovered and readied for action. As promised by our previous Captain, all hands had been initiated in experiencing other duties. I had not had a trick on the wheel for some weeks and eagerly took it up again. I loved it. I knew I was a good helmsman. It was a nice feeling. I was a natural; I could anticipate the ship's next move. Years later, steering an oil tanker through the Bitter Lakes with a Russian pilot who had no English, only sign language, I was about to be relieved on the wheel when the pilot baulked at the idea. I remained on the wheel another three hours, being served sandwiches and tea by the Captain's steward and pissing in a bucket. I felt so proud but no desire to live in Russia. On voyages in mid ocean, ships of the Merchant Marine usually activated the automatic pilot (iron mike) during daylight hours, which was welcome as being on the wheel could be very dull unless one was a moron. However, steering through ice in the Gulf of Finland or navigating the St Lawrence Seaway and the Great Lakes right down to Duluth in Minnesota added another dimension to the word happiness. Adventures that never crossed my mind when steering Frank Brough's horse and turning new mown hay to the sun, but that is where it all began.

We had acquired a new cook, an English one this time. The previous Maltese cook, the one with the cocktail party phobia, had been put on shore duty because of a mental breakdown. I don't suppose he was used to the sight of a drunken officer's spouse squeezing an innocent boy's testicles, but who was? I felt sorry for him but realised that being with his wife and four children would undoubtedly help restore his health.

I became great friends with the replacement cook, an utter clown and brilliantly funny. He had been on the wheel a few times under the supervision of the Cox'n, with a couple of tough Able Seamen standing by in case he needed to be wrestled away. He handled the wheel as if driving a tractor; the ship only on course occasionally as the bow swayed ten to twenty degrees either side of the lubbers' line. We were all thankful when he returned to the galley for good. The very thought of him with his finger on the trigger of the Oerlikon engendered an instant cold sweat.

On the open bridge, my eyrie, I had an opportune moment to scan the covered chart table for clues as to how long before we came under the anticipated baptism of fire. Shifting the parallel ruler out of the way, it did not appear to be very long before we donned tin hats. I didn't have the remotest idea about celestial navigation, which involved numbers but manifested a keen interest in something that a knowledgeable person could offer, which is an excellent method of advancing one's understanding. I would write down the readings as the midshipmen were fixing our position with the sextant, using the sun, moon and stars. My reward was being taught coastal navigation to a degree that we were all pleased with.

The morning dragged on. We must be nearing our destination or destiny I thought. A faint glow off the port bow. Was it Omar's hunter of the east or something more ominous? Why weren't we at action stations? The Bofor's crew were standing by voluntarily. They couldn't wait to blast away at the first thing they saw.

We had sent a bag of mail off with the oiler. The bag had been sealed prior to advising us of our destination. I had not sent one. I felt a lump in my throat, so began thinking of other pressing matters. I felt the French letter around my neck stuffed with Cypriot pounds. I remember they were brown. Where would Mr Papadopoulos have kept his? He was as rich as Croesus. "I like English with Queen Elizabeth, not Drachma." He would be frantic, I know, they didn't make French letters that big. Mr Papadopoulos was an accumulator of pound notes; I was a circulator.

Pop's mother, Nanny Wynne, a wonderful, large big-hearted woman stowed hundreds of pounds in her corsets. No bank interest; no robberies either. She had had a hard life. Pop's father had been gassed at Passchendaele and was an invalid for the rest of his days. They lived in Hastings where during WWII to escape the bombing she scooped all her grandchildren up, travelled to London and thence as far as the train was going in Wales, which turned out to be Brecon. She rented a cottage halfway up the Beacons, sans power or running water, until it was safe to return the children home. She remained in Wales for some years, delivering mountain babies in the snow and nursing the sick and was much loved by the locals who could be quite difficult to get to know. Weekly, she walked down into Brecon to shop and rest in the Blue Boar with a pint. Should the pub be full of soldiers, she would somehow retrieve a fiver from her impregnable bank, give it to the publican and request that he let the ale flow free. At the completion of her shopping, she was driven back to her cottage in a police car, on orders from the Sergeant of whom she had made it a priority to befriend.

As the sun rose behind thick clouds and in a dead calm sea, the horizon was no longer flat but breaking into lumps, soon the lumps turned into black palls of smoke with sporadic flashes from explosions. Without warning, two Israeli jets buzzed us at no more than a hundred feet, their thunderous roar scaring the shit out of all of us. They must have enjoyed that.

We slowed down upon receiving an order to sweep an area to the east as quickly as possible to allow supply ships to approach with safety. The operation took two days and nights. During the day, we kept an eye out for any mine we may have cut free of its mooring during the night. We sighted what we thought was one. Approaching it, it was obvious that it had been lying in wait for decades, as it was encrusted with barnacles and seaweed. Moving off about a quarter of a mile, the Oerlikon farewelled it with two bursts. I had my Box Brownie at the ready, expecting an explosion, but it sank without a whimper after filling with water. Just a little bang would have been appreciated.

Minesweeping gear recovered and secured, we approached Port Said and found a berth alongside chaos and the stench of burning rubber. Royal Navy and French ships looked as if they had turned up for a courtesy visit. Not a scratch on them. Jets rocketed overhead and the superstructure and masts of merchant vessels were sticking out of the water. The area had been secured, so we took a stroll ashore. The statue of Ferdinand de Lessops lay prone and headless in the rubble.

Someone had brought a football along and in a rare clear piece of ground boys began kicking it around. An aimless punt sent the ball over a low shattered wall, coming to rest between the legs of a man sitting with his back to another wall. He was the sole local inhabitant we had seen so far. Calls of 'Kick the ball back, Wacker', were soon replaced with 'Fucking deaf wog cunt'. Dogsbody was sent to recover the ball. I scrambled over the wall and approached the man in a friendly smiling manner and discovered the reason for his uncooperativeness. He was dead. I raced back feeling quite shaken. "Where's the fucking ball?" demanded a Leading Seaman.

"The man's dead," I whispered weakly.

"So the ball's no fucking use to him, is it? Go and fetch the fucking thing."

Someone chimed in with, "I saw the cunt climb over the wall and sit down."

Kelso, who had just bowled up in time to get the general drift of the problem said, "Let's go, Jock", buoying me up instantly, and together we went over the top. Nearing our goal, Kelso who had seen plenty of dead cunts in Korea, said, "I think you are right, mate; I think he's snuffed it", and gave the ball an almighty drop kick sending it back from whence it came. As a teenager, Kelso had trialled with Raith Rovers of which he was justifiably proud. Turning to go, Kelso looked back and said, "Better make sure." He took the man's still limp arm and checked for a pulse. Negative. Diagnosis: heart attack. The man then slid on his side and from under his shirt cascaded thick wads of postcards that would have given the Pope a heart attack too, according to Kelso. "Waste not, want not," said Kelso, stuffing them in his shirt. "I take it you'll not be wanting any, laddie," he said patronisingly. I nodded in the affirmative. Still stuffing his bulging shirt, he found it necessary to adjust his crucifix. He looked at me and then at the crucifix, shrugged and returned it to keep company with the filth but not without a little prick on his conscience.

It was quiet during the next couple of days. Marines patrolled the area allowing us to wander further afield with safety, where we witnessed demolition crews breaking up ships and pumping others out. One vessel that remained afloat was ex-King Farouk's yacht. Why it was referred to as a yacht was beyond me. It had no sails. It sat and sulked, kingless, crewless and useless. He had to go; no one has the right to live like that when thousands of his countrymen lived on the pickings of garbage dumps. Stories abound about Farouk's life, apocryphal mostly. As a boy, he had an English nanny who instilled in the young glutton that it was the custom in England to always leave something on one's plate after a meal. I thought that I was up to speed on most English customs, but this was a new one on me. Not in the Cotswolds anyway. Apparently later in life and fond of his nanny's memory, he would regularly order twenty lambchops for lunch but ate only nineteen. Some Nanny! He was found dead doing what he liked best. Face down in his dinner.

I fail to recall how long we were at the Canal Zone. It was only a few days. The night before we left, there was a picture show held on a tank landing craft. The house was packed; we all stood as at the Henry Wood Promenade concerts. There was a news reel revealing events that had taken place a month previously, cartoons, followed by a Fred Astaire and Ginger Rogers romp. I couldn't concentrate on anything but Ginger's legs as I fully expected to be blown up by a limpet mine at any moment. The next day, we left for Famagusta where we would no longer feel in danger.

I had really appreciated Kelso backing me up back at the canal. He was about thirty years old and an electrician. I was beginning to detect that there was something more to him than being just a foul-mouthed pisspot. He was beginning to be less harsh and treating me more like a grown up instead of a boy who had his head in the clouds and who was prone to acts of idiocy. I had my thoughts on the matter confirmed some days later when on patrol. Anchored as usual throughout the days with most of the crew ashore, swimming and sleeping, except the duty watch of which I was a member. It was afternoon, I was keeping watch on the bridge and occasionally wandering about the ship to keep from falling asleep. Between decks and for'ard, I came across Kelso and the POME (Petty Officer Mechanical Engineer) attending to the showers which were malfunctioning. The usual cursing and swearing at having to miss out on the beach party, I heard the POME exclaim how he loathed showers and always enjoyed a bath when available. Kelso vehemently disagreed. "Yer never get properly clean wallowing in yer ain shite and dangerous too, look what happened to Marat." The shower loathing POME politely enquired who the fuck Marat was, and there followed a few joyous moments with Kelso filling the mesmerised POME with a swift but detailed account of the bloody events of the French Revolution. Girondists, Robespierre, Charlotte Corday. Stunned, I returned to the bridge realising that I did not know Kelso at all.

Somehow I had to find a way to breach the subject of Kelso's knowledge of France and the revolution. I couldn't ask him straight out because aspiring to any knowledge way and above how many pints of beer did a firkin contain or which ports bints removed their pants the quickest, was leaving one exposed to ridicule. Not that Kelso was incapable of looking after himself. Far from it. But experience had shown me that it was unwise to sit too high on one's horse on the lower deck.

After much cogitation, I decided on an underhand method. I would wait until we were back in Malta, which was scheduled in about a fortnight, where I could be sure that on the blank week Kelso would be in a state of pecuniary deficiency. Hung over and looking quite dejected, I would casually flash my wad of Maltese pounds at him. Kelso, without sixpence for Spiro even, would spill the beans. Patience was required on my part as he would be in ample funds for the first few days, but I was confident that it would not take long for him to do his bit for the local economy.

This was how I discovered that Kelso spoke French, had a French mother and had spent some years in Pondicherry. Fascinating. Kelso loved Asia with a passion, spoke of the people, especially the women, with such tenderness there were tears in his eyes and mine too, almost. I could have listened for hours. He spoke so kindly without uttering any profanities. Then he nearly spoiled it by telling me not to listen to the cunts back on board. "Asian girls dinna have horizontal vaginas." Vaginas! Kelso had said vaginas. I asked him to repeat what he had said. He told me to fuck off as I knew he would, so I bought two more beers and didn't pursue it. He had paid his dues and left me very impressed indeed.

We patrolled for another five days and then did a day's minesweeping exercise with the C in C. Cyprus, Admiral Myers VC on board for the day. With the Captain and First Officer and the two midshipmen busy controlling operations, it was left to me to entertain the estimable submariner who showed little enthusiasm in the sweeping, which was usually fairly dull. Had we been in a thickly sown minefield with cut mines popping up all over the place like a mad woman's shit, as Kelso would have said, no doubt he would have soon lost interest in what I had to say, which was plenty. He questioned me on diverse subjects, from 'did I think St Angelo would win the racing whalers trophy yet again at the Fleet Regatta?' to 'what was my favourite dog?', to which I replied, 'Borzois'. We had a succession of Border Collies since my mother had parted with Boris, Kish and Nan prior to my birth so that was a bit of bullshit. I think he believed me, especially when I reeled off their pedigree names. They were a pleasant few hours with an interesting man who despite his rank put me at ease immediately. Ludovic Kennedy, another interesting man accused the Admiral of war crimes, which I have chosen to ignore.

Two days later, after taking on fuel and water, we left for Malta. I could not tell George that I would not be coming back. I gave him cigarettes, a couple of Cypriot Pounds, one English ten-shilling note and a handful of Lebanese shrapnel. A poltroon's farewell.

Once a week the midshipmen would join us as we crowded around the radio for the *Goon Show*. This was then followed by a couple of days of insanity. A midshipman would order an alteration of course down the voice pipe to the wheelhouse in the persona of Eccles. Major Bloodnock, the helmsman would acknowledge. Our cook was able to memorise and imitate the entire performance and had you been on watch and missed the show and did not mind being addressed by Blue Bottle, Gryptypethynne, Minnie Bannister, Henry Crumm and the hero Neddy Seagoon, the cook was your man. Another popular radio broadcast was *Voice of America* from Wheelers-Field Airbase in Tripoli, Libya, when it was possible to tune in to Humphrey Bogart and Lauren Bacall in *Bold Venture*, a serial thriller not to be missed, provided you were still in your teens.

A few days after arriving in Malta where I successfully got Francophile Kelso to relate his life story thus far, we learned that we would be paying off and returning to the UK by troopship but not before being rewarded with a cruise for our service in Cyprus. I thought of those idyllic days on the sands of Fontana Amorosa, the turquoise water, the tang of oranges and the tinkle of goat bells. Who needed a reward? This, however, I was eager to accept. It was the visit to Livorno that had my pulse racing due to its close proximity to Florence and Pisa. My God, I thought, people pay through the nose to visit these fabled cities and here I was having them thrust upon me.

We visited Syracuse in Sicily on the way north, where it rained for the three days we were there. I went ashore two days out of the three. I don't remember much about the scenery, just the interiors of several wine bars. I know I behaved and so did Kelso, because he stunned us all by remaining onboard. It wasn't the weather that kept him ship bound; he was from Scotland after all. Kelso had spent the last two days in Malta onboard, something was up. He got quite annoyed when we offered to take his temperature and check his pulse. "Away and fuck ya'sels ya cunts," he growled. Kelso still had funds aplenty from his last pay, and we were due another one on arrival in Livorno. He had plans, and from what I learned about him, it wasn't about getting legless in the first bar he happened upon. Could it be he intended travelling further afield, a train journey possibly? I said nothing. I'd bide my time. If he meant to go where I thought he was going, he would expect me to hold my 'whisht'. I remained hopeful.

The rain had ceased by the time we had slipped our moorings, and we sailed the Strait of Messina to the Tyrrhenian Sea, then set course for Livorno. Adjusting our rate of knots, we tied up at our destination on a Friday after a smooth passage and found the port busy, bright and smelling of Italy.

Shore leave on week days was granted from 1600 Hours and at the appointed hour I saluted the quarter deck. Kelso had remained on board. I, bent on a reconnaissance sortie, marched purposefully past the sleazy bars outside the dockyard. Bars that doubled as brothels where girls and women beckoned and cajoled, and as success came their way would glance over their shoulders at the parasites who 'protected' them. Girls, some had been beautiful but now aged and worn, they plied their trade with a frightened desperation and aware that to step out of line would mean a beating and or a razor.

Leaving the ugly and disturbing scene behind, I drank red wine that had been tapped from a barrel in a better type of wine taverna. I enquired of the friendly proprietor of the location of the railway station and the best way of getting there. Of all the wine bars in the street what made me pick this one? The man had been a prisoner of war and had worked on a farm in Gloucestershire and still pined for the taste of scrumpy. When he discovered that I was born not far from Gloucester and knew it well our camaraderie was cemented.

The station was not far and a horse-drawn conveyance (like the Malta karozzin) would be awaiting me outside the bar the next morning at midday. I would be ferried to the station in time to catch the 12.22 to Florence, returning to Livorno at 20.10. As for Pisa, there were plenty of trains back and forth between the cities. I could have hugged him. He had fond memories of his POW years in Gloucester, and felt lucky that he had been captured in North Africa and that Mussolini had got the trains running on time. On the way to Wales some months later, I sent a postcard of Gloucester Cathedral and received a reply of undying gratitude. It would be framed and join Jesus and the Virgin Mary over the rack of barrels.

Naturally by this time, I was bursting to tell Kelso the news and to see whether they coincided with his plans. After my first tantalising taste of pizza, cooked by the man's dumpling wife and sluiced down with a litre of red, I thanked them both profusely. Happy to have been able to improve Anglo Italian relations I ran the gauntlet of the sleazy bars and returned on board to the puzzled looks of the Office of the Watch and the bosun's mate.

Kelso, deeply engrossed in what he was reading, ignored my return, so I sat opposite him at the mess table. He was studying two phrase books; English-Italian and French-Italian very seriously. I said nothing. I would have to wear him down. I had patience. He did not. A minute elapsed silently. I cleared my throat. He put the book down slowly and deliberately and said, "What?" Invited to speak, I scrambled for a reply and said that I thought that French would be understood by a large percentage of the population up here and in the north west of the country. "Thanks for the advice, but that point had occurred to me, now what is it that is really fucking your brains at the moment?" I took the bull by the horns and waded straight in saying that I had met a chap who spoke excellent English who will have a karozzin waiting at midday to convey me to the train station from where I plan to head to Florence and Pisa, and unless he had anything better to do, he would be welcome company. "Actually," he said, "I have a date with Gina Lollobrigida, but in view of your kind offer, I will decline the horny bitch's promise of an unforgettable night of unbridled passion and gratefully accept a seat in your carriage." Waxing lyrical was a forte Kelso rejoiced in.

I made myself a mug of Ky, which didn't sit very well on top of the vino rosso and pizza, and combined with my excitement, I made it to the heads in time and regurgitated the lot. Feeling better but still in a state of euphoria, I borrowed the English-Italian phrase book, read half a page then fell asleep until about 0200 Hours when a couple of inebriates tumbled down the hatch.

Despite the punka louvres, which operated permanently below decks, allowing constant fresh air, on awakening at 0600 Hours the mess stank of stale beer, wine and a thousand farts. Kelso, already up, passed the metal container of breakfast down to me and making as much unnecessary racket as possible, began serving it up. He had wet the tea and placed the urn on the table. We both dug in to break our fast with a dish called devilled kidneys. This powerful smelling delight, consisted of chopped and sautéed kidneys wallowing in a glutinous gravy and piled on a thick slice of deep-fried bread which had the density and resilience of a fire brick, was fondly known throughout the Navy as 'Shit on a raft'. It tasted quite nice to be fair and was very popular. However, few of the late-night revellers were in a fit state to appreciate the dish so Kelso and I stoked ourselves ready for what lay ahead.

114

Breakfast over, all hands repaired to their parts of ship; me to the bridge, Kelso to wherever he was required. Halfway through the forenoon, the order to secure was piped and free gangway would be open at 1100 Hours. The survivors of the night before would once more be turned loose on Levorno. Kelso and I were in no rush, so we attended the queen's uniform with extra care. What condition the uniform would be in upon returning was never given a thought. No one imagined that far ahead. If you were going to worry about that, you may as well spend the day sitting on a bollard on the jetty. The day was there to be faced whatever the outcome. It was the general rule in the Navy that one could return onboard after carousing in practically any state of intoxication. Politely tight, tottering and gibbering, stinking drunk or paralytic but under assistance. Provided one hit the sack without causing a disturbance, returning onboard under the influence was not a punishable offence.

Kelso and I had barely spoken a word since his ungallant decision to leave Miss Lollobrigida in the lurch. There was nothing to say. Time to go; we crossed the quarter deck, saluted as we crossed the gangway under the scrutiny of the 'Jimmy' who was probably thinking, *I wonder what that pair of bastards have in mind?* Kelso had a camera which I had not seen before. It dwarfed my Box Brownie and had a detachable barrel about a foot long. I supposed it to be telescopic, but I never did find out because he left it on the train to Florence and my Box Brownie had to carry the day.

Eyes to the front, ignoring the catcalls and whistles from the orgiastic bars, we marched business-like to the wine shop. I introduced Carlo to Kelso who tried a few phrases of Italian to no effect. He then tried French with moderate success. With a glass of wine, he finally broke into English, well, Scottish English, which caused further bewilderment to Carlo. "He speak funny English, this Kelso," he said, turning to me. Kelso visibly stiffened at the unintended slight. Before he began expounding the common belief that Edinburgh was the place where the English diction was spoken at its finest, I hastily interrupted. I gave Carlo a carton of cigarettes; thanked him and his wife. We clambered aboard and lay back as if travelling to Ascot in a Phaeton.

Made possible by the late but unlamented 'Il Duce', the train pulled out of the station bang on the dot and was soon diddly boom diddly dumming its way to Firenze. The correct pronunciation of Firenze was acquired from Carlo, who caressed the name like an operatic tenor pledging undying love to the heroine. I don't recall the cost of the return tickets, but they were not expensive. Not that it mattered, as we both had rolls of Lire the size of bofor shells. The tickets were for Pisa but allowed us to alight at Florence and to carry on to Pisa later. A very convenient arrangement. We stood in the corridor all the way to get a better view of the passing countryside. Gradually, the endless cultivation gave way to suburbia, and soon after, we slowed smoothly and came to a halt in the city that was once the domain of the Medicis, Lucrezia Borgia and Dante.

Alighting from the train, we both thought that the best thing to do to steady our minds was a tumbler or two of the local grape juice. We had not to look far. While saluting each other with a generous glass of vino, we watched the train speed away with Kelso's camera. He blasphemed once and never mentioned his loss again. The man had so many traits that I admired. We took a taxi to the Ponte Vecchio, which was the first place I could think of and gazed at the Arno with the wine warming in our bellies. We began walking to walk off the 'Devilled Kidneys' in order for our stomachs to accommodate the lunch we had planned. I referred to the meal as lunch because at the moment I was feeling socially superior to the yobbos who ate dinner at that hour. It was getting a bit past the hour of lunch, but I was confident that with our wealth we could order and be served lunch at midnight had we so wished.

Strolling along, we tried the phrase book on a few uncomprehending boulevardiers who were all tourists; British, French, German and an American couple who spoke to us in Italian. We had begun to enjoy ourselves immensely because we had suddenly realised that we were an oddity. Two British sailors in uniform was not a sight often seen in Florence. Kelso was engaged in a fluent conversation with a middle-aged French couple, prompting the New York American to ask, "How come you have French guys in your Navy?"

"We don't," I said, "he's Scottish where everyone speaks French; do you remember the Auld Alliance?" He did not. The stuffy British couple asked if we had been drinking, causing Kelso to interrupt interlocution with his newfound friends, telling the despised Sassenachs to meet us here in a few hours and repeat the question. I thought he was going to tell them to fuck off. It was the first time he had shown restraint to morons that I had witnessed. The English pair tut-tutted and scurried out of our presence. The New Yorkers then suggested we go 'chow down' but Kelso advised them that we had a table booked for four with the French couple. The American and his honey went in search of presumably a hamburger or a hot dog. I would not have minded inviting them along; they were as naïve as I was. But Kelso had made the call. As far back as I can recall, I entertained the idea that the sole purpose of my life was to enjoy it and have fun, though not at the expense of others. Yet, I felt comfortable that I was not guilty of selfishness.

We had struck it lucky with the French couple. I was not taught French at school, so understood nothing of the earnest conversation taking place. Apart from Deauville, St Cloud and Chantilly; major race courses, and Hugo; Proust and Voltaire and numerous famous and infamous figures, the sole French word I was sure of was 'Oui'. I could manage counting up to ten, an accomplishment which came in handy when ordering drinks or placing a wager on the tote, resorting to fingers when the counting exceeded dix.

Kelso's new friends were both teachers. They could not get enough of Florence and visited every year. They had travelled to many countries including Scotland and both were aficionados of Burns. Kelso must have conveyed to them that there was a fair chance that we may never pass this way again and that we were pressed for time if we wished to get to Pisa, which was an hour away, so action stations were sounded.

First, a delightful small restaurant in an alley where Botticelli may have passed by. It was run by a Florentine gent and his French wife, old friends of the teachers. I remember little of the repast except to say that it was delicious and speedily partaken of. This solecism was kindly forgiven in view of the situation. In unseemly haste, we were soon gaping at Fresco's by Giotto in the Podesta Chapel, ushered under and into the Duomo; Kelso's crucifix prominent but tangled somewhat in his black, thick chest hair that poked over his white front. We passed over the restored Ponte Santa Trinita that the Germans had destroyed in WWII. Apparently, the German Commander-in-chief had disobeyed orders by refusing to blow up the Ponte Vecchio for which we are eternally grateful. There followed a lightening visit to the Uffizi Gallery where I could have happily spent a month.

Extending deepest thanks to our hosts for their kindness, a taxi was hailed. The train was boarded; we sat back and sipped from our skin bags of wine as we dozed our way to Pisa where we made a dash for the tower arriving with twenty minutes to spare before closing time.

We were both quite tight by now, and our condition made it extremely difficult to form an opinion as to exactly which way the tower was leaning. Ascending to the top up the spiral steps, a procedure that further unsettled our equilibrium, we reeled out on to the balcony gripping whatever was to be grabbed at the tower. As we crept to the leaning side, an acute attack of vertigo hit us. I was beginning to wish the tower had been closed. Holding hands like Romeo and Juliet, we prepared ourselves for the descent.

We bought postcards at the desk on the way out, where we were immediately besieged by several vendors of previously unknown art works, unknown even to the artist that is. As our intoxication increased, so too did our deluded belief in their authenticity and our confidence that Sotheby's could be swindled. I spent most of my remaining lire on a Caravaggio that had recently been discovered in a Venetian palazzo with Kelso snapping up a Tintoretto, slightly soiled by the grime of centuries in the wine cellar where it had been chanced upon only a week before.

Triumphant and pissed, we were speeded to the station by two massive blue-chinned carabinieri who assisted us aboard the Levorno-bound train. We fell asleep clutching our treasures. The train tarried a while on arrival at Levorno to allow the cleaners to carry out their periodic duties, which was fortunate for we had to be aroused from our slumbers. It was 2100 Hours. It had been a hectic and unforgettable day.

Having significantly boosted the Italian economy, we had very little Lire left with a lot of time to spend it in, so more excursions were out of the question. At the cinema, we caught up with La Lollo in a film called *Trapeze*. The soundtrack was in Italian of course but could have been in Swahili for all it mattered. Gina was attired (if that is not an overstatement) in a leopard skin-patterned outfit fashioned from a handkerchief that had been cut into three pieces which failed to conceal her tits and the other place entirely. If there was a plot, I don't recall it; I just sat watching her swinging and somersaulting in my usual state of unrest. Nocturnal activities were confined to Carlo's wine shop where we practised our Italian while pleasantly and quietly getting drunk; enjoying the good wife's pizza and a variety of pasta dishes.

The evening before our departure, after farewelling a tearful Carlo with all the cigarettes we could scrounge, we drained our wine bags sitting sated on bollards but with a feeling of having achieved something, and I knew that whatever port I was in, there would always be locations of great interest, provided I eschewed the waterfront, as I had just proved I could. I had merely to catch a train to anywhere. South, back down the Tyrrhenian Sea, in the black of night, Stromboli fired a twenty-one-gun salute. An unforgettable sight. My first exploding volcano. Etna hadn't counted. Etna's smoke wispily recollecting

Grampy's stinking, sulky allotment bonfire. Stromboli's midnight salutation never to be forgotten.

Then once again, Sliema Creek and dear old Spiro. One run ashore to farewell bar and doss house owners and friendly tarts some as old as my grandmother who cried their eyes out. We packed our kit bags and stowed them with lashed hammocks in the tender for our transfer to the troopship moored fore and aft to buoys in Grand Harbour. The vessel had already taken on board a couple of hundred Highland Light Infantry at Cyprus and there was no way the authorities were about to let them loose in Malta. Imagine Sauchiehall Street on a Saturday night.

Slipping through the portals of Grand Harbour, Sliema Creek to port. Spiro, out of sight on the other side of Manoel Island, would be doing what he had been engaged in all his life. When bombs were dropping around him, waves causing near capsize, keep going Spiro. I couldn't say goodbye. I did not know how to. Excitement mounting at the idea of going home. I struggled to put out of my mind the siren call of the beautiful island and stared straight ahead, not daring to turn around. It would be fair to say that Kelso and I were sort of mates by now, but with Kelso, you never took anything for granted. We mostly did our own thing. We didn't piss in each other's pockets is the phrase of his which comes readily to mind. He came in handy on the passage to Gibraltar though. A RAF Corporal had latched on to me and beagle-like followed me everywhere. He would magically appear next to me at meal times, tombola and the cinema. I ignored him to the best of my ability when suddenly he lost interest to my immense relief. Found a prettier boy, I supposed. The fellow's behaviour had not gone unobserved, however. Bumping into Kelso later, he said, "I threatened to toss the fucking deviant cunt over the side." Not one to mince words, our Kelso.

That evening, I developed a painful swelling on my right cheekbone. So rapidly did the swelling increase that the next morning I could see my breakfast with only one eye. Kelso naturally suspected that I had been assaulted and enquired who the perpetrator had been, which rather annoyed me. I weighed a little over twelve stone and could look after myself. I ungratefully told Kelso that I didn't need him to protect me. It was the first occasion I had adopted that tone with Kelso, and I instantly regretted it. He didn't reply. He didn't have to. He understood the situation. Maturity versus callowness. Attending the sick bay, a sick berth attendant casually diagnosed a boil which I knew it was not. "The curse of puberty," he said. The insulting bastard, I thought. I would be drawing my tot in two years' time. I had been in action; well, sort of. Experienced jet fighters screaming overhead; friendly ones, I'll admit. I helped dispose of a possible WWII mine; a dud one. I had seen a dead man. Bloody puberty!

We were due in Gibraltar the next morning, so I requested permission to visit the Naval Surgeon. After docking with a painful night behind me and a 'boil' the size of an egg, I squinted my way through the now familiar dockyard like Cyclops groping for Odysseus to the Naval Hospital where a kindly Scottish Surgeon Commander took one look and exclaimed, "You are harbouring a foreign body in your cheek, laddie." I didn't know whether he was congratulating me or accusing me of theft, but with the agony I was undergoing, I pitifully asked if there was anything short of decapitation he could do, adding 'please, sir', to hopefully soften the flippant remark.

There was no answer; he shoved me in a chair and with the assisting SBA, holding an enamel dish alongside my head, squirted some frozen substance on my 'boil' and lanced it with instant relief. The mucus that spilled into the dish resembled addled duck's eggs. The entire operation had taken a whole thirty seconds and poking among the slime with long tweezers he fished out a minute splinter of steel he immediately and positively identified as a fragment of shrapnel. Where had I got it? He said it could have been dormant for some time, which had me thinking it may have happened whilst shooting Frank Brough's pigeons or while staying with my grandparents during the bombing. He then enquired where I had been recently. I mentioned Cyprus and Suez, insisting that we had not come under fire, although I would have much preferred to have related how we single-handedly fought off a large Egyptian task force. "There you have it," he trumpeted. "A war wound at your age. In the American Navy, you would have earned a Purple Heart." I felt that I should have been up for a DSO, Distinguished Service Order. At the very least, considering what I had endured. I was very grateful however, so I remained silent. The relief of the intense pain that has assailed the right half of my head had brought tears to my eyes. I politely asked if I could keep the splinter. "Not only keep it but with a seal of authenticity, laddie," the jovial doctor boomed and handed me a small capsule with the practically sacred projectile inside. With a band aid over my war wound, I thanked and saluted without my cap and stepped out into the fresh Gibraltan morning, the sun not having shown its warmth to the western half of the monolith. I had instructions to have the dressing changed the next day. I would show that bloody SBA. I had also been told to take things easy. By that, I assumed the good doctor meant to allow one hundred Highland Light Infantry to have the town to themselves that night. But I had more Formosan gifts to buy and unless Kelso expressly wished the pleasure of my company, I would shop, down a few beers on my own, if that was possible, then return onboard to plot my course to Portsmouth.

Amazingly, we sailed on time the next morning. All the Caledonian combatants being accounted for, but with a mob congregating outside the sick bay resembling the aftermath of Culloden Moor with bandaged walking wounded staggering here and there, I didn't think there would be a band aid left to spare, so I gingerly pulled the post operational one off and let the Atlantic wind and the sun heal my face.

I was going home to quiet little Duns-Tew, where nothing ever happened. I was not yet nineteen years old. How would I handle six-weeks of pastoral tranquillity?

# Chapter 6
# Back to Barracks

A rustic six weeks' leave followed the memorable period in the Mediterranean. Gordon was a cadet on a BP (British Petroleum) oil tanker. Murray had joined the Royal Navy and was enjoying the rigorous induction, I hoped. My mother, Pop, Bobby and Bob the dog declared a lengthy camping trip to the Brecon Beacons was well deserved. We lived on trout, rabbits and anaesthetised ourselves nightly on the contents of a nine-gallon keg of cider, which remained cool wedged between smooth boulders in the rushing mountain stream. Wading out with a quart jug, turning the spigot, the heady aroma tantalising the brain. We would walk to the inn at Llanfrynach on a Saturday lunchtime. The inn was filled with sheep farmers discussing wool and lamb prices, and anglers debated which flies were being taken by the salmon. Hikers spilled outside in the sunshine after scaling a Beacon or two; animated conversation as if they had conquered the North face of the Eiger.

It was all over too soon as is the case when one is having a good time. There was something different about returning to Victory barracks this time. What lay ahead? Anything but doing time in a Royal Naval Barracks. After three days of keeping my nose clean and dodging the brass and the regulating staff, I was sprung once more and drafted to a frigate of the same class as my first ship. Soon we sailed for the Med, Malta and Cyprus; so unsettling this time. I was merely a number; no longer special as I had felt on the minesweeper. Someone had usurped my coveted role of postman. Resentment joined forces with my innate recalcitrance. As it turned out, the time spent in the Med was not all bad. Great runs ashore on the North African coast. Learned a lot and behaved myself, although drinking with some legionnaires in Algiers, I was rescued by a vigilant shore patrol from being trucked to Sidi bel Abbes and God knows what. I neither saw George again nor got ashore in Cyprus. On night watch, I witnessed my caiques boarded by others, and in daylight, the distant familiar coastline evoked pleasant memories and a little sadness. How was the goatherd and his brood? And the priest with the tall black hat? They swam before my eyes.

The remainder of our deployment in the Med I found humdrum and déjà vu but with the exuberance of youth, made the best of it. When we left for home waters, I turned my back both physically and mentally on that warm sea. The cradle of civilisation. Cooler breezes welcomed as we neared England's South Western Peninsular, and on entering Plymouth Harbour, I saluted Sir Francis Drake's bowling green with my mind on scrumpy, Oggies (Pasties) and home. A joyful period of leave followed by an immediate drafting to a destroyer where we took part in important NATO exercises with American, Canadian and French ships. On the first day, we witnessed a jet come to grief on take-off. A swift response enabled us to retrieve the freezing pilot and several lifebuoys which had been enthusiastically hurled overboard. A day he would never forget.

Naval life had at last become interesting. I had come of age. 20 years old. Drawing my rum ration on my birthday 'The Queen God Bless Her' emblazoned in brass on the half barrique. 'Up spirits' was at midday and after downing my tot and the customary 'sippers', offered by my messmates, my legs gave out and I was laid to rest on the hammock rack. I came to six hours later, none the worse for wear.

A few nights later during heavy weather, we lost a boy overboard. He was the lifebuoy sentry who was stationed aft, usually safe, unless one strayed when the ship shipped hundreds of tons of water on one side, when altering course at speed. The reality of the boy's loss was felt by all. His kit was auctioned on returning to port, the proceeds given to his mother. I thought she would have preferred his kit.

My next ship was a 'Daring' class destroyer. Following a few exercises, we left for a much-anticipated voyage to the West Indies, the Bahamas, Windward Islands, Belize (at the time British Honduras) and Port of Spain. I leave it to the imagination of any reader of this book as to what took place in these exotic ports. Steel drum music, sun, surf, cheap rum and beautiful girls. Cyprus not forgotten but fading into the past. Leaving the Windward Islands, reluctantly, we visited Hamilton in Bermuda then sailed in the warm Northerly current to Nova Scotia and the Port of Halifax, changing into more suitable apparel as we left the tropics astern.

During the voyage home, quite a lot of gunnery practice and other performance enhancing activities took place including nuclear decontamination drill. I was fervently hoping that we would not need to put it to the test. Once more in Plymouth and leave. Before I had finished packing my bag, my locker was searched by an RPO (Regulating Petty Officer) and a bottle of 'Appleton Estate' rum that I had smuggled aboard was seized. I had been dobbed in. There was only one suspect. A persistently objectionable national serviceman. I had previously brought into question the validity of his parents' marriage certificate; a commonly used adjective, not intended to be an insult. I regretted my words immediately on seeing how hurt and angry he was as he hurled his puny body upon me. Luckily, a couple of mates pulled him from me before he had rearranged my looks beyond recognition. I apologised and meant it and thought I had allowed him enough satisfaction. I know I felt atonement for my insensitive remark. But he obviously did not.

I sat in the Regulatory Office for about an hour while the ship's complement streamed over the gangway and dispersed to all points of the compass. Accepting my fate, I filled in time by appraising myself of all the rules, regulations and the various BUMF adorning the noticeboards. Eventually, a very pissed off CPO manhandled me to the Captain's cabin, knocked and left. I heard permission to enter and shaking a little, entered. The Captain, a Scottish Laird whom I admired, stood silently peering out of a scuttle, my crime sheet in his hand. He turned, glanced at me, then pointed to his desk where my bottle of rum reposed, "Report to the master at arms, Rose. Get out of my sight and try to behave like an adult." Not having been asked a question, I had not uttered a word. I was stunned and in the grip of disbelief. I had been prepared to accept my fate. I recall stammering 'Yes, sir' and backing humbly out of his cabin.

The standard procedure of being 'run in' was to appear before the First Lieutenant's defaulters. Charges being read and the appropriate punishment handed out: stoppage of shore leave, which included extra work. A more serious offence would be referred to the Captain. Those facing anything more heinous could expect Detention Quarters, or possible imprisonment. None of this had happened. I had been let off. I have wondered why to this day. The Master at Arms was waiting, bags packed in his office. He would have loved to have punched my head judging by his ferocious countenance. He shoved my pay, pay book and return rail pass at me and hissed, "Now piss off, you useless bastard." Maybe he had missed his train.

A Petty Officer, a member of the skeleton crew remaining on board, called out, "You lucky sod," as I saluted the gangway and quick marched to the dockyard gates.

Catching the train bound for London in the nick of time, I caught up with several shipmates on board. They were amazed and equally puzzled, as I was in the leniency I had been shown. I was amazed also at the bottle of 'Appleton Estate' they were passing around. I partook of a swig but not without a little guilt. I went to Grampy and Nanny's place that evening. After taking them to the pub for a few drinks, I spent the night in the familiar bed that I used between voyages and where I had slept with my brother Gordon during World War II. I left early the next morning for home.

About this time, things were noticeably changing in the Royal Navy. We were putting the age of Jellicoe and Beatty rapidly behind, leaving the dilemma of what to do with the uneducated dunderheads like myself. Rumours of discharge by purchase were being bandied around. Notices began appearing confirming that certain branches could begin releasing personnel who could stump up with the required purchase fee of one hundred and seventy-five pounds sterling. I was fully aware that any advancement in the Navy was beyond me. I did not wish to lead nor did I particularly like being led. I enjoyed going through life like a wild duck, sometimes breaking the wind during a migratory flight, then when the need for rest arose, ease back into the slip stream. The purchase price presented a slight problem as there was no indication of an instalment plan. Two days into my leave, sufficiently primed with Dutch courage, I broached the sensitive subject with my mother, tentatively enquiring as to the health of the family treasure chest. Without hesitation, she produced her budget box and handed me a bank book with every two pounds per month I had allotted her since joining the training ship. I felt a lump in my throat. I didn't know what to say. "It's yours to do what you like with," she said.

I had completed the application form and submitted it while I was in the West Indies. A letter of approval arrived whilst I was on leave, and I was to report to Victory Barracks Portsmouth at the end of my leave. I had never wished my leave to pass as speedily as this one. At the barracks, on entering the imposing gates, roll of pound notes gripped firmly, I still felt like a recidivist. The date was 9th November 1959.

# Part II

# Merchant Navy – Tankers, Freighters and Coasters

That afternoon at Grampy's once more, he asked me what I intended doing now. "Go back to sea in a different capacity," I told him. He looked at me with puzzlement in his eyes, as I suppose any sane person would. Having spent numerous Christmases away from home, I was keen to have one at Duns-Tew, so I postponed my intended foray to the shipping offices at Leadenhall Street, Aldgate in the Eastend of London. Yuletide with all the trimmings and trappings flew by. It snowed. Brother Murray was home. Bob the dog died one night. We buried him at the bottom of the garden, the snow quickly obliterating all trace of Bobby's lifelong companion. His absence was noted at the White Horse. A friend excused himself, leaving his beer. We supposed he had gone for a pee, instead he returned with a pup, a doppelganger of Bob. We learned that the resemblance was not a freak of nature. "The randy old bugger was hanging around my bitch a few weeks past. His last throw of the dice." We rejoiced and drank to Bob's health several times. Mother was making the gravy, her back to the dining table. Pulling the pup from inside my coat, I placed the shivering wee hound in the middle of the table where he promptly peed. Mother and Bobby were delighted with the new addition to the family and between them intended to name him something other than Bob.

Early in the New Year, I joined the Seaman's Union and signed on an oil tanker as a Deck Hand Utility, DHU, at 32 pounds per month. Notwithstanding my extensive knowledge of seamanship, I was unable to gain Able Seaman status. I would sit the exam at a later date. The oil tanker lay at anchor miles down the estuary. Night was falling. Mournful foghorns sounded hauntingly together with the knelling of bells from hidden fo'c'sles. How we located the tanker in the murk I'll never know. No sooner had we boarded and been shown to our cabins, the bosun ordered me to relieve the bell ringer who had been freezing at this post on the fo'c'sle for some time. Relieved after an hour, expecting every minute to be rammed, I partook of a welcome late supper and turned in. My cabin was roughly the same dimensions as the mess I had shared with 11 shipmates on the minesweeper. The cabin was equipped with a desk, chair, chest of drawers plus a spacious wardrobe to hang my oilskin and spare pair of jeans in. The next morning, the fog had cleared. Many ships remained at anchor, but several had formed a convoy which began working its way up river. Breakfast over, the bosun divided us into three watches, 8 to 12, 12 to 4, 4 to 8. Several hours later, we weighed anchor and slipped down the estuary and into the North Sea and so on to the channel bound for the Persian Gulf via the Cape of Good Hope, before tying up at Durban for bunkers (fuel and water). I recall clearly the few hours spent there. Time to taste the 'Lion' beer and bear witness to a gang of prisoners chained together clinking past the pub. The guard, a 20 stone behemoth, glared threateningly whilst gripping a vicious looking sjambok. The men appeared to be resigned to their plight. Not a glimmer of hope in their countenance. What on earth had they done to deserve this treatment? What on earth had the guard done to be put in charge?

Life on a tanker between ports could have been exceedingly dull but for the overtime, which was mandatory and welcome in spite of the work being stupefyingly monotonous. Chipping rust patches of which there were hundreds of them, daubing red paint on the bare steel prior to several top coats. When in port, the purser would open his coffers for spending money; most men budgeted their expenditure according to their overtime earnings, leaving their regular wage intact, ensuring a decent pay off eventually. Some men drew enough money for a couple of beers, some to get drunk. There was very little time for anything else as the crude was pumped speedily into the ship and quickly syphoned off at the port of discharge. Cargo ships often spent a week unloading and taking on cargo. I looked forward to that.

Steering north, each day adding one pound-sterling to my pay off, we passed the Horn of Africa before entering the Persian Gulf. I don't know what I had expected but the oil terminal came as a pleasant surprise. Having secured fore and aft to buoys, work began on hauling a pipeline of at least 12 inches in diameter which had been floating not far from a long jetty. The sole sign of human habitation was a concrete building at the end of the jetty. The atmosphere was so hot and dry that perspiration evaporated instantly. Due to leave in under eight hours, I followed a platoon of seasoned tanker men to the building, with high hopes as they were not out for a stroll in the country. There appeared a sense of eagerness in their gait. American-owned and with a special licence in that arid land – arid on two counts – ice cold beer could be obtained accompanied by bowls of pretzels and peanuts. The port was a moonscape of mountainous sand dunes. A lone camel stood in the shade of a telephone pole. Motionless, it could have been stuffed and possibly was, in that Daliesque setting known as 'Umm Said'.

I was asleep when we slipped our moorings, and by the time of my watch, we were well on our way to clearing the Gulf, entering the Indian Ocean, destination Kwinana, Western Australia. As a small boy, Australia had held a magnetic fascination for me. It had an aura. Its siren-like lure, its beckoning palpable. I would not jump ship. I would return to its weird animals and equally interesting citizens I had encountered in my travels. One night in the Indian Ocean, in a calm sea, the only surrounding sounds were the snorts and splashes of porpoise. My lookout watch on the fo'c's'le was about to end when something electrical seemed to charge the air around me. At the same time, a bright amber light appeared to starboard for a few seconds and vanished just as quickly. I determined not to mention what I had seen, as it was not the first time I had witnessed what I believed was a galactic phenomenon and being subjected to ridicule. Arriving at the bridge for my trick at the wheel, the Officer of the Watch met me on the starboard wing and asked me if I had seen anything, in a rather challenging manner, I thought. I said I had. He told me not to mention it as he was to sit for his extra master's ticket and had no wish to be placed in a straitjacket. I promised my fellow believer that I would remain silent. Arriving at our destination, discharging of cargo began immediately as fresh provisions were taken on board. Knocking off, taxis were called for the drive through the eucalyptus-drenched evening to a pub in a place called Rockingham, where a long awaiting skinful of cold beer was enjoyed. Returning to the ship around midnight, an overwhelming feeling of déjà vu enveloped me. I had come home. Here my destiny awaited.

In ballast, we left for the Gulf, this time performing the odious task of freeing the holds of gas, the vessel being at its most vulnerable until mission accomplished. The bosun, a colossal Maori who had served on the ship for several years, injured his leg badly during the operation. Confined to his cabin, drinking rum and blackcurrant juice, he would recount how he volunteered at the outbreak of World War I; he was sent to Egypt and thence to Gallipoli. Surviving the landing, he was repatriated soon after, when he was discovered distraught over the injured body of his 15-year-old twin brother. He would boast of his tattooed grandfather who ate long pig and bemoaned the banishment of the practice. It was intended to put the stoic old man ashore at Bahrain rather than one of the Arabian ports. Bahrain being a British protectorate, prompt treatment could be expected and if necessary, a flight to the UK. However, an unexpected delay caused a brief deferment of the plan. In a glass smooth night with a pilot onboard, a ship named Baluchistan rammed us for'ard of the bridge leaving ten feet of its bow on our foredeck, snapping off huge bollards, rivets popping and spraying the bridge. She then continued to slide the entire length of the starboard side, disengaging and vanishing into the night. I had vaulted out of my bunk on impact and saw our aggressor's steel side grating past my scuttle. Thankful that my cabin was not the point of contact, the reality of what could have occurred hit me later. The ship had healed slightly and a lifeboat was lowered as a precaution. The impact had caused a large fissure from the foredeck to the water line. A few hours later at a very low rate of knots, we limped into Bahrain. Heartfelt wishes were expressed to the bosun who appeared to have deteriorated physically while steadfastly retaining his humour. Stop gap repairs began in earnest over the next few days. Salvage crews armed with acetylene cutters were busy dissecting the bow of the Baluchistan, lowering segments into a lighter. A ton of miscellaneous steel debris also needed clearing away but not before I had souvenired one of the dozens of rivets, which would have maimed or instantly killed anyone unfortunate enough to be in the line of fire. Company and insurance officials arrived to assess the damage. The outcome being that we would sail the ship back to the UK, Newcastle upon Tyne to be exact.

The trip took the best part of a month, as speed was constantly adjusted in respect of the vagaries of the weather. The ship had an excellent library. As spare time was limited due to keeping watch and the overtime, I could not afford the luxury of browsing, as in a second-hand bookshop where I would often spend hours. I adopted an excellent method of selection, with my eyes closed taking the first book I touched upon, not looking at the title until returning to my cabin. Occasionally, I picked a dud one, but I also enjoyed many books by unfamiliar authors and genre that normally would have passed me by. Eight books were read on the journey home. Lying in the sun, reading and earning one pound per day; suntan becoming deeper, haystack-coloured hair until the Bay of Biscay put an end to it. Docking in Newcastle, we were immediately paid off, and I caught the first train going south rather than get involved in the Newcastle brown ale booze up that had been planned. I had already decided that a change from tankers would be a good idea. Constantly discharging cargo at refineries miles from anywhere and the swift turnarounds afforded little opportunity to reconnoitre. I wished to linger in ports, explore, see the sights and meet the people. I spent a couple of weeks at home with my pounds sterling once again changed into ten-shilling notes. An affectation I could not resist.

In the Merchant Navy, unless one were a company-man you could pick and choose. Not having a clue in the selection process, I signed on the first ship that did not carry crude. I was assigned to join a small freighter leaving for Rotterdam, where we would load vast quantities of Heineken beer destined for North Africa, consigned to American interests. At the end of each shift, the Dutch stevedores accidentally on purpose expertly damaged a case, shattering fifty percent of the contents. The surviving bottles were shattered also, after they had been done justice to. I, and other crewmembers on duty to prevent broaching of cargo, did not finish a shift with a clear conscience. Ports previously unknown to me were visited in Morocco, Libya, Tripoli, Algeria and over to Italy. But alas not to Levorno. In one port for an hour to offload a tractor. Three ports in one day were recorded. As soon as space became available, it was filled quickly. On one occasion a thousand hessian sacks of peanuts were stowed below. With an average of four hours of overtime every day, the ten shillings notes were adding up. In some places, we stayed for forty-eight hours; enabling us to be diddled in madding souks and addled on arrack.

On returning to Europe, the ship's first port of call was Bremerhaven. It was also my last. One evening, I was witness to a shooting on board. Two firemen, one Latvian, one Irishman, had been at each other's throats for the entire trip. Having a yarn with Paddy in his cabin late one evening, we were suddenly confronted by his adversary who with an amateurish appliance fired a shotgun shell directly at my companion's face, then calmly walked away. The shot not having travelled through a barrel lacked the velocity to blow his head off. Able to walk, I assisted him to the upper deck. I propped him up against a hatch coaming, picking pellets from his bloody face while a shipmate conveyed in pigeon German to a dockyard worker to call a doctor, an ambulance and the Gestapo. Even Paddy found this amusing. Incredibly, his eyes had escaped injury. Wiping the blood that trickled from his scalp, I picked more pellets only fractions from rendering him sightless. Teutonic thoroughness sprang into action. Within minutes, wailing sirens could be heard. An ambulance skidded to a halt. The Gestapo arrived in force and swiftly winkled the assailant from the bowels of the engine room. The ship was due to leave the following day for Hamburg. I was stunned when the company agent informed me that I was required to remain behind to attend the court hearing. I asked him what hospital they had taken Paddy to. He said he would enquire. Accommodation was arranged for me plus an ample daily allowance. I slept onboard that night, packing my bag at first light. The mate and the agent were racing around organising a replacement fireman and a deckhand. I visited Paddy in the hospital. His mother would not have known him; face puffed up like a souffle with pustules where the pellets had punctured. He asked what had happened to the Latvian. I said that he had been arraigned to appear at 1000 Hours the next day on a charge of attempted murder, adding that I would call again.

The courthouse, an imposing grim stone building, conjured up visions of Jack-Booted Nazis clicking their heels in the labyrinthine corridors. I morbidly wondered where the interrogations in World War II took place. It transpired that it was only a preliminary hearing, there were just four persons present. The judge asked me to identify the accused who stood in the dock, handcuffed to a policeman. Bruises on his face indicated that he had been subjected to a tough time, but at least, I was able to recognise him, which was more than I could say about Paddy. The judge then asked me to state what I had seen, under oath, and that was that. I left and never discovered what punishment he received. I could not have cared less really; I was more concerned about Paddy. Enquiring of the staff, I was informed that Paddy's condition was not serious, and as soon as his sight improved, he was free to go. This could take a few days. Paddy was in surprisingly good spirits considering, and his good humour increased when I slipped him a bottle of Schnapps.

At the agent's office, I was handed a rail ticket to the Hook of Holland, which included the fare to Harwich on the ferry. I said I would like to wait until Paddy was fit to travel in order to escort him back to the UK. He declared this a good idea. Back at the hospital, Paddy had been told that he could leave on the following Monday, if he felt well enough; I said I would hang around and accompany him home. He took a swig from the bottle, winced as it stung his lips and squeezed my arm as I left. Down at the docks, I ran across two stevedores who had been on shift at the time of the shooting. They treated me as a celebrity and forced me into a bar with them. It was a young folks' hangout, full of happy youth. Pretty, friendly frauleins and young men who bombarded me with questions about the shooting which had been reported in the papers. I tried not to dwell on the fact that their fathers may have been members of the Hitler Youth. I spent most of the weekend at the bar sitting in hot sunshine, drinking Pilsner and stuffing myself with every kind of sausage. On Monday, Paddy was raring to go and was cleared to leave after signing out.

We collected his ticket and some cash for expenses, then headed to the railway station. The train to the Hook would leave in two hours, giving me plenty of time to buy two loaves of Pumpernickel, which I knew my mother would love, plus a few bottles of beer. Soon after, we were speeding to the Netherlands. I don't recall the duration of the journey; what with the beer and the three-quarter full bottle of Schnapps Paddy had saved. He was still very sore but had been given medication to ease things. The swelling, having subsided significantly, enabled him to see quite well. His main concern was that his success with the opposite sex would be affected. Crossing the border, we whizzed through windmill country, disembarked at the Hook, boarded the ferry and some hours later awoke to find the ferry tying up at the terminal at Harwich. I sprang to the upper deck to see my maritime Alma Mater. 'Anson' division at the bottom of the covered way, my old mess greeted in the distance. Who was sleeping in my bed? Faith, Hope and Charity. Three flights of stone steps. I had had my share of the incongruously named staircase, doubling up and down with a broomstick raised above the head for any misdemeanour however slight. Small wonder I was super fit.

In London, we were paid off at Head Office; I offered to accompany him to Liverpool to ensure that he safely boarded a ferry to Ireland. His face creased with pain as he laughed. "I'm not going to Ireland," he expostulated. "I live in Liverpool." I should not have assumed. Liverpool, the unofficial capital of Ireland. Check the telephone directory. About to board the north-bound train, we parted company. Not saying much. The way it is with seaman. One wave and he became another memory. I had posted a letter to my mother from Algiers; she expressed surprise that I had left the ship that I was obviously enjoying. I concocted a feasible story rather than the distressing facts.

A pleasant few days at home, catching up with friends and acquaintances saw me ship out once more, this time transporting blood stock to South America. Timber loose boxes had been assembled on deck. An Irish stable boy of about fifty years introduced us to the horses as they were led aboard. 'Falls of Shinn' placed second in the Irish Derby. 'Petite Contessa' a full sister to 'Petite Etoile' who had triumphed in the 'Prix de l'arc de Triomphe'. Apparently, 'Petite Contessa' was intractable and had unseated Lester Piggot, a champion jockey three times in as many minutes. Some horse. We supplemented the horse feed with additives of our own. They were particularly fond of ham sandwiches, Mars bars and roast potatoes. At Buenos Aires, a massive plate glass department store window slipped from the crane's clutches, shattering it to a million shards. The stevedores did not seem too concerned, treating it as an everyday occurrence. Up the River Plate, in some spots, the yards brushed past treetops, we docked at 'Rosario'. The horses were put ashore. The brutal treatment handed out to 'Petite Contessa' sickened me and has been impossible to erase from my memory. The sight of a slavering rabid dog lurching around the wharf being my other recollection of the port.

Crossing the River Plate to Montevideo, we passed over the grave of the German battleship 'Graf Spee', scuttled in World War II by Captain Langsdorf, rather than let it fall into the hands of the Royal Navy who had damaged her badly during the Battle of the River Plate. Remaining in the port any longer than 48 hours would have imperilled Uruguay's neutral status. The majority of the crew were put ashore, leaving a scuttling crew to open the sea cocks. Captain Langsdorf committed suicide and went down with her.

We loaded a stinking cargo of wet hides in Montevideo. The stench was all pervading, clinging to every fabric of the ship; the only temporary relief being a cross wind occasionally. Whilst ashore, everyone I spoke to had been on familiar terms with Adolph Eichmann, who was employed at the local Mercedes Benz factory prior to being traced by Mossad in 1960 and spirited away to Israel to face war crime charges. Taking advantage of the northern current, we sailed up the east coast of the Americas, turning at the appropriate time for Europe and home. Feeling sorry for the unsuspecting stevedores who had the foul task of unloading, I swore never to take a job in a tannery, no matter how destitute. I took home a variety of leather goods including a macho-looking pair of Gaucho boots, which looked ridiculous in Duns-Tew.

The Barley Mow was a delightful inn near the airbase of Upper Heyford where B52 bombers from the US Airbase flew day and night. They kept Russia under surveillance whilst still skimming the rooftops of my old school on take-off. I was playing darts with some Yanks. A Master Sergeant dwelt on his 3rd dart; another airman his shove-halfpenny un-shoved. Base alert, men scattered, leaving me as bewildered as the two old rustics who had ploughed with horses.

They left their dominoes and hobbled to the taproom door and wondered with rheumy eyes, at trucks and jeeps screeching off with men clinging to them, feet on the running boards. Lucky Strikes smouldering in ashtrays and deserted pint glasses, ale foaming down the sides. "Turn your ships around, Mr Kruschev," warned John Kennedy, and Mr Kruschev obeyed.

It was Christmas time. Restless as ever, I was constantly recalling the scent of the eucalyptus. In the wake of an ice breaker in the Gulf of Finland on Christmas Day, I decided to seek warmer climes. Arriving back in London, the ship docked upriver from Tower Bridge. I requested of the agent to be paid off, as I had other plans. I immediately rushed to Australia House to join the throng of enthusiastic emigrants. Awaiting a reply at home, I called on friends and relatives.

# Part III

# Australia

At home, I kept a vigilant eye for the postman by day, played darts and drank copious pints of Hook Norton ale in the White Horse by a blazing fire while snow settled in drifts against the stonewalls and hedgerows, and rooks froze in the elms. I lay in wait for the postman willing him to walk up the garden path. So keen was my resolve I would have done a 'Sydney Carton' with 'Abel Magwitch'.

Two agonising weeks elapsed before a letter from Australia House arrived requesting me to report to Tilbury docks where a P&O passenger liner awaited to transport me and a thousand others to the far side of the world unfettered. What the ten-pound fee was for, I could not imagine. If it was to cover the cost of feeding us, it did not sound very promising. We were also to prove solvency and not likely to resort to busking or begging in order to participate in the nightly beerfest. Ten pounds, I would have been skint before we rounded Ushant. I still had most of my pay-off from the Finnish trip so I could easily stave off dehydration until Freemantle. Our passage down the channel and the Bay of Biscay was calm. The sun smiled on us with just enough warmth to show promise of what lay ahead.

I stood alone in silence to salute Cape Trafalgar with the now familiar Mediterranean up ahead. Gibraltar in the morning sun rose like a breaching whale. Lingering until she vanished from view, on course for Piraeus, the port of Athens, where we were joined by a throng of Greeks of a type that I had not come across previously, mountain folk from the Peloponnese. It appeared that their intention was to leave for good; the grandmothers in their premature black shrouds in particular. Donkeys, dogs and goats, brayed, howled and bleated on the wharf, whilst their wildlife-infested mattresses and bedding blazed on ghat-like pyres nearby. What happened to the distressed livestock, I knew not. However, the quarantine authorities proved remiss in their duties for enroute to Suez the next day smoke began billowing from steerage, where the roasting of a kid was taking place. Occasional wafts of rosemary and other wild herbs filled the air, until extinguisher foam put an end to the anticipated feast. Henceforth, it was an assortment of English culinary delights to assault their Hellenic stomachs. It was then arbitrarily deemed unwise to allow these stoic mountain people to remain next to the bilges so accommodation was rigged up for them on the upper deck and for the rest of the voyage callipygous maidens were wooed and courted by dancing youths to the plucking and strumming of the Bouzouki.

Leaving the Bumboats of Suez astern, we entered the Bitter Lakes. Ships of the northern-bound convoy lay at anchor. The scorching heat of the Red Sea put an end to the dancing by day, with only desultory steps by the besotted to the now languid Bouzouki at night. The Indian Ocean brought welcome breezes and new life to the dancers as great armadas of dolphin and porpoise piloted us east. The vagaries of the weather had little effect on the valiant British topers who appeared welded to their bar stools since leaving Tilbury. Vladivostok could have been our destination for all they cared.

The unforgotten tang of eucalyptus on the breeze a few hours out of Freemantle brought me back to reality. All sense of time lost in the past weeks, in the course of which I had made friends and proposed to numerous girls with little success. It was considered unwise to approach the Greek maidens unless one particularly desired evisceration. At Freemantle, families who were due to settle in Western Australia were gathered on deck, packed and ready to begin a new life before the gangway was positioned. Single young men, sober now and travelling light, stood with single girls whose tears at the severing of their sea-going trysts was unbearable to behold. A few hours ashore, sampling the local brew, we cast off for Melbourne. The Greeks were beginning to become very excitable and animated although a few hours of a choppy sea in the Bight subdued them somewhat. Close to Melbourne, they broke out the Ouzo and Retsina, and danced the Zorba all night long, right up to where we entered Port Phillip Bay, not ceasing in their unbridled joy for a second until their disgorgement on the wharf, where they presumably went forth and multiplied adding further credence to that city being dubbed the Athens of the South.

We had bypassed snooty Adelaide where they are particular about who they permit to flaneur their hallowed boulevards. No South Australians can boast of convict ancestors as Victorians, New South Welshmen and Tasmanian inhabitants can and do.

## Sydney to Mount Isa

We continued to Sydney. With the absence of the Greeks, the ship seemingly lifeless, not abandoned like the Marie Celeste but soul-less, a sense of loss prevailed even among their harshest critics. The imminent parting of friendships and much stronger relationships did nothing to improve the ambience. But soon, we were through the 'Heads' with the 'coat-hanger' down harbour standing sentinel. The most magnificent harbour on earth. It was late afternoon when we tied up at the south side, the massive bridge high overhead. Farewells were said, some sad, a few with immense relief. Within minutes, the area on the wharf resembled a disturbed termite nest. Single migrants were processed quickly, young men mostly travelling light. My worldly goods were in the same bag from the Royal Navy and subsequent seagoing years.

I joined the queue of those who had chosen Queensland as their destination. We boarded a bus leaving the jostling crowd, howling babies and utter organised chaos astern. No time to look around Sydney, we were Brisbane bound within minutes. The sun was setting over the horizon as our train shot over the bridge, its last rays infusing with the thousands of lights winking on, ferries leaving and approaching Circular Quay. Fishing boats heading out for the night. All this in fleeting moments. I could have dallied for hours. Dusk and then night came, and we saw nothing of the landscape until dawn broke a few miles from Brisbane.

The sub-tropics. Different smells. I had slept like Rip van Winkle, largely due to having made the acquaintance with a chap from Cumbria. A two-bag man. One crammed to bursting point with his clobber, the other the amiable chap had filled with bottles of McEwan's brown ale, a farewell gift from friends. They were practically simmering, but we did them justice. I had not yet become addicted to the teeth-numbing beer of my new home. After pissing like Clydesdales, we alighted and were then conveyed to a hostel on Kangaroo Point, a pleasant timber building, snug among scented eucalyptus. Parrots fluttered and squawked; I craned my neck looking for a koala, but there were none in residence. The majority of my fellow pioneers had opted to remain in the city, but I could not bear the thought. The next day, I and two adventurous companions approached the head office of Mount Isa Mines and were signed on immediately and prepared for a 2000-mile rail journey to the tropical north-west of the state.

Our expedition north was due to begin in 48 hours, so we had little time to explore Brisbane but enough to take a tram to Eagle Farm racecourse and lose a few quid. It was summer, hot enough for us to soon become accustomed to the ice-cold beer served in icy glasses. They were small seven-and-ten-ounce glasses to ensure the beer did not become undrinkable by warming to two degrees above freezing point. Frozen quart jugs were available for groups to down the beer hastily in shot glasses. I quite understood why pint glasses were not in use. Hunger set in as is usual after a few drinks and here we were introduced to the Pie Cart, which dispensed a culinary delight far exceeding anything I had seen or tasted before or since. The 'floaty', a meat pie roughly the dimension of a tea plate, reposing on an inch of piping hot mushy marrow fat peas and depending on taste, adorned or assaulted by a large gout of the ubiquitous tomato sauce. The pie carts did big business then. Gradually, the sated drifted homeward, leaving Brisbane's main street so devoid of life, artillery practice may safely have taken place.

North-bound, destination Townsville. Travelling through endless miles of sugarcane, stopping from time to time at stations long since forgotten. At one small station as night fell, it was suggested that we might stretch our legs as the train would be halted for thirty minutes. Unexpectedly, a bar was open, regular passengers were taking advantage of this in the warm sultry evening. My companion and I soon followed. On our second beer, I noticed our fellow drinkers were draining theirs and returning to their seats. Anxious lest we should be left stranded, we grabbed our glasses to sink the dregs but were reassured by a gentleman who had ordered a third beer that there was ample time for another. Emboldened by the first two cold ones, we did the same and listened with interest of when once he was an engine driver. Soon nerves got the better of us. We said 'see ya' to the interesting man and rushed to board the train, where we watched our confident friend down the last of his beer, saunter to the rear of the train, produce and wave a red flag while lustily blowing his whistle.

Apart from this pleasant interlude, I only have sketchy memories of the remainder of the journey. Slept most of the night with the sugarcane blotting out the Pacific Ocean by day. My Cumbrian friend's uncle, a bricklayer by trade, met us at Townsville. A conducted tour of points of importance, mostly pubs and clubs followed. At midday at one of the pubs, 'counter-lunches' were ordered. We three perched on the bar stools quenching our thirst, plates the size of manhole covers plonked before us. No fuss. How civilised. Thumbs up to this, I thought. On time, the Mount Isa train began its long journey west, through leagues of savannah, hundreds of ant hills resolutely peppered the land.

Wildebeests would not have been out of place in that timeless beautiful panorama. I could sense the dreamtime.

## Mount Isa

Early morning, quietly approaching through the outskirts, barbers' pole smoke stack prominent. The town waking up although it never really slept as the mine operated unceasingly. Copper being the principal ore, extracted along with deposits of lead, zinc and silver. The open cut mine lay on one side of the Leichhardt River; the town on the other. It was the dry season, the river waterless. During the wet, it would transform to a torrent. We were shown our ample quarters, a large, serviced room for two in a barrack-like block, then conducted to the mess hall after which we were to report on the following day to begin a week-long induction course. Safety being the main issue, we took possession of our miners-boots and hard hat. At the course's completion, I received training as an operator, ensuring that the ore on the conveyor's belt spilt accurately into the giant silos. When one silo filled the pressing of a button moved the conveyor to the next. The shifts were of eight hours' duration; 0800–1600, 1600–2400 and 2400–0800. Up countless iron steps, my site was a hundred feet in the air. Glorious during daytime looking out over the town, red hills and spinifex surrounding. At night, one needed an imaginative mind to see the shift through, as there was little to do. Reading was the age-old panacea. Strictly against the rules of course, but there was my mental health to consider, and over the next three or four months, I devoured anything and everything in print I could lay my hands on. Partially ant eaten, age grimed tomes by Longfellow and Thackery discovered in a cupboard of an old house that a friend had rented. Keeping vigilant lest the supervisor should intrude, warmed by an empty fuel drum fire fed by tree roots that came up with the ore. The hard hat annoyed me in the warm winter days. The sole danger that my head was exposed to was the possibility of a consignment of waste matter from one of the soaring wedge tail eagles. Dirty but not dangerous. The five-day shift from 0800 to 1600 Hours equalled one day off; the 1600 Hours to midnight equalled two days off, and for the midnight to 0800 Hours the reward was four days off, giving us a great opportunity to wander. A road trip to Karumba in the Gulf of Carpentaria was of a duration I had never experienced previously and a fishing trip to the Georgina River for 'yellabelly' with a troupe of vodka-marinated Finns who preferred dynamite to regular bait. Pop would have been appalled. I kept quiet; it was a long hike back to town. I was greatly relieved when I was asked if I would mind driving the return trip. I jumped at the chance.

Mount Isa was a cosmopolitan town. Miners from many nationalities, mostly Europeans, made up the workforce and the community in general. The mess hall served imaginative healthy food, and provided one was a carnivore and not inflicted with an eccentric dietary fad, one did very well. The kitchen would have processed a bullock per week, a conservative estimate by my reckoning. Packed meals were available for night shifts. Television had not reached Mount Isa at the time, but the drive in-walk in cinema compensated. Children sprawled on the sand in front of the giant screen in their pyjamas ready for bed. There were at least two pubs to choose from. I don't remember their names; they were generally very busy, particularly on a Saturday. Football teams and various sporting clubs raised funds by holding raffles; prizes ranging from cooked chooks (devoured in situ) to vast trays of meat. I often attempted to communicate with a middle-aged Finnish miner who sat abjectly gazing at his glass of beer. He had little English, interlocuting only with his fellow countrymen. A friend confided that the man had lost his entire family during the war. I felt his pain. Passing through the town 20 years later, I thought of him, poked my head in the door and there he was staring into his beer. It was mid-morning; the bar was quiet. He looked up, and I detected a spark of recognition in his sad eyes. I said g'day and his gaze swung back to his beer. I could do nothing but abandon him to his misery.

We often boiled a billy in the dry sandy riverbed. On one occasion reaching the edge of town, we cooked lunch under the gum trees. The smell of barbequing meat lured some Aboriginal children from an unnoticed camp of derelict vehicles. Shyly, they accepted a lambchop each, then bolted. I had wondered where the few Aborigines lived that I had seen in town. As time passed, I soon learned of their plight. It angered me. I made friends with an Aboriginal family at the annual Mount Isa Rodeo, sitting on the ground with them. The man had the widest hat I had seen among a sea of wide hats. His four children dozed in the shade of its brim. He worked on a cattle station, riding gentle horses due to the multiple fractures he had incurred bull riding since his youth. He had been a champion, he proudly told me, showing dog-eared soiled snaps portraying him at prize giving events, cups raised high, wide belts with big shiny buckles. His 12-year-old son would be roping calves in a while. We moved off to watch and encourage. Meeting him in town some weeks later on a hot afternoon, I said I was going to cool off in the municipal pool. "I don't go there," he said. I thought maybe he couldn't swim. As a resident of some weeks, how could I have been so wrong?

Walking to and from town was not a great distance but loaded with bottles of beer meant flagging a taxi; the fare being the equivalent of four long necks, an unconscionable proposition. A Maori mechanic acquaintance owned two vehicles. One he intended taking home with him as new cars were not being imported at the time in New Zealand; the other he was prepared to sell me. It was a Dodge, huge, dirty and battered; cracks in the windscreen, springs poking through the fragile upholstery. To circumvent the all-invasive bull dust intruding when travelling in convoy, a hole in the floor had been cut, which also served for the disposal of beer bottles and other detritus. This behaviour seemed to be the norm. I just had to accept it. Forty pounds settled the deal. He was so pleased that I thought he was about to rub noses with me, but a handshake sufficed.

I would be required to renew my driver's licence at the police station. Avoiding a possible traffic violation, I walked the mile or so on a hot afternoon on completion of a day shift. Approaching the cop-shop, I observed a Police Sergeant about to lock the front door. I excused myself and said, "It seems I'm a little late."

"No, you're not, mate, what've ya done?" he replied.

"Nothing felonious, Sergeant, but I'd like to renew my driver's licence if you would be so helpful please," I pleaded obsequiously.

He slowly looked me up and down trying to ascertain whether or not I was taking the piss and said, "Come inside." Sitting at his desk, he asked me details such as how long since I had driven. I said it had been some time as I had been at sea. He said it was not often that he had a voluntary visitor to the station, mostly they had to be dragged there. "Lots of migrants who couldn't speak English, ne'er-do-wells, blokes on the run or hiding from their wives, all kinds. Can't all be bad though, the mines making a profit. You'll have to take another test, come on, we'll go for a drive," he ordered. He hadn't issued a driver's licence in ages, apparently no one seemed to bother about it. It was like the Wild West sometimes. A Land Rover-type vehicle was parked in the shade at the rear. One part of the building had bars in the windows, I guessed this was where he locked up any law breakers, mostly foreigners fucked from the war, was his opinion. Hardly ever an Aboriginal, as they drank on the fringe of town in their camps. The police car was festooned with aerials, spotlights, bull bar, winch and cable, only a Bren-gun in a turret on the roof was missing. "Hop in," he said. I headed for the passenger seat but was pulled up short. "How can I tell if you can drive with you sitting there; get behind the wheel." I did so and we drove down the Camooweal Road for a mile, did a three-point turn, then proceeded back to town in very dusty conditions, as hundreds of cattle were being herded through the dry bed of the Leichhardt River. The dust did not settle for hours. Obeying instructions, I pulled up at the baker's where he returned after a few minutes with a loaf of bread and a bag containing a marble cake from which he picked morsels. Next stop was the butcher. Honking, alerting a young woman who staggered out with a brown paper parcel, proving beyond all doubt that the Sergeant had not embraced vegetarianism. Stop three was a hotel. A case of beer was shoved in the back by a perspiring Goliath who was engaged in unloading a wagon load of beer kegs, tossing them around as if they were cans of baked beans. Shopping over, we returned to the station, his residence being part of the building. He signed the licence and told me that I was a pretty good driver. "Better than most," he added. I had no idea who he was comparing me with but took it as a compliment. I had been mostly honest with him, only omitting that at the last place I had driven, they drove on the right-hand side of the road. I felt sure it wouldn't have been an issue with him.

A young woman served in the mess hall. She was an Australian of Italian parentage. Anna was from the cane fields on the coast. Always of good humour and very forthright, she had every man lusting after her, pleading for a date. Some she accepted, including me. Once to the pictures and fish and chips, followed by a picnic at Lake Moondarah where she confided in me that she wanted a wedding ring on her finger prior to being deflowered. The lucky man would not be a boozer, preferably Catholic, under thirty years, plus all his teeth. This was to ensure her mother's approval. I loved her directness, and we remained friends until the call of the sea could be heard on the dry hot wind, an ocean wind, which I yearned to have whistling about my ears once more.

### Back to Sydney

I had enjoyed working on dry land for the first time, although I was aware that it couldn't last. Feeling like an Inuit in the Sahara, I gave notice of leaving, and two weeks later in the early morning, I climbed into the Dodge, pointed her east to see if the old girl could make it to Cloncurry. She did, allowing me to alter course south east. Sydney Harbour and a fishing boat seeking a deckhand was my main focus. I ignored the advice of my New Zealand friend, "Don't push her too hard, she's not used to long trips." Now he tells me, I thought at the time. Sometime later on the Longreach Road, the car developed an ominous rattle from somewhere beneath the bonnet, a no-go area for me as my mechanical expertise covered wheel changing and checking the oil level only. Amply stocked with food and beer, I decided to park for the night off the road, eating, drinking beer and reading until sundown. After a stroll in the bushes, I somehow slept until daylight on a bed of upholstery springs. Natural functions and ablutions completed, I breakfasted on water and a Dagwood Bumstead Devon sandwich, then tentatively eased the Dodge back onto the road. The rattle recommenced immediately; this time black smoke began emanating from the rear. I kept going. Every league forward was one less I'd have to walk. The chance of a lift was remote. Occasionally, a juggernaut would pass at 300 mph loaded with cattle. No use thumbing a lift as it would take about a mile before it came to a halt. By a miracle, we reached the outskirts of Longreach seemingly on fire, black smoke totally obscuring the police car behind me. Pulling over on hearing its siren, I watched the cop waiting for the smoke screen to clear in the fragment of glass remaining in the rear vision mirror. A few moments elapsed while he decided that it was safe to approach. Answering his enquiry as to whence I had come from and whither bound, a deep belly laughter of incredulity greeted the second part of the question. "Sydney!" he expostulated with a huge grin. "If youse managed to cross the border, son, they would clap you in irons." I was beginning to believe him. Instead of a ticket of un-roadworthiness, he instructed me to follow him to the wrecking yard. "Could I please go to a hotel or motel to unload my gear, officer?" I politely asked. He consented, leading me to a verandaed hotel. I checked in and stowed my bag and provisions, then dutifully followed him to a graveyard of assorted cars, trucks and sundry vehicles. The Dodge looked at home immediately. The diligent upholder of the law removed the number plates, offered me a lift back to town, wished me luck, adding, "You shouldn't have too much trouble getting a lift." I thanked him but omitted to mention that I intended treating myself to the luxury of a flight.

Lunchtime at the hotel, I met two stockmen accompanied by a young English jillaroo. They had all been at the Mount Isa Rodeo. One of the stockmen had his arm in a sling; the other sported the belt won in a bull riding event. The jillaroo was utterly ravishing, beautifully made up, upper-class accent pretentiously peppered with Australian idioms. Inviting them up to my room, we took two bags of ice to cool the ten long necks I had put in the shower recess. With exemplary restraint, we endured the twenty minutes before deciding the beer had cooled to the acceptable Australian standards, then put them to the sword. An hour later, we parted, shaking hands, thank yous and good luck. The gorgeous jillaroo kissed me on the cheek; I, a member of the lower orders. It is amazing what a belly full of beer can do for you. Stowing the empties in the wardrobe, I slept until dinnertime. The house dinner was a battered piscatorial mystery perched invitingly on a pile of delicious chips. Risking several tentative exploratory bites that revealed nothing remotely fishy, I pushed the cholesterol-infused batter to one side, prompting a semi-inebriated fellow diner to enquire whether he could relieve me of it. Giving the go ahead, he harpooned the weighty mess and offered me a slug from a large glass of sweet sherry. I declined, declaring diabetes for my refusal, to mitigate offence. "Too much sugar, mate," he cautioned, then leapt up and shuffled off in haste, as if diabetes were contagious.

Up at sunrise, I took a taxi to the airport, then a five-hour wait for an Ansett plane from Mount Isa bound for Sydney. We took off, and I felt the sea was becoming closer with every passing second. There was the 'coat-hanger' grey and obdurate. Traffic streamed over it both ways. The boiling white wakes of ferries scarred the calmness. Dozens of slack-sailed yachts prayed for a breeze. Descending over red rooftops, wheels lowered with a bump. Touch down. Engine roaring. Brakes protesting. Relaxed at last. I was never happy in the air.

### Sydney

Evening was approaching as a taxi drove me to the city via Bondi Beach. The cabbie knew a country bumpkin when he met one. He was pointing out places of interest; the lighthouse on Dover Heights, designed by Francis Greenway, who was transported for forgery; a hanging offence at the time. Fortunately, the authorities had their priorities in order. South Head overlooking the Heads, a majestic harbour entrance, then through leafy suburbs and a long winding harbourside road to a lively part of the city I had often heard spoken of: King's Cross.

Paying the informative brazen cabbie off, I thanked him for the conducted tour of New South Wales with a handsome tip. What did I care? Most of my earnings from the months at the 'Isa' were gathering interest and dust in the Bank of New South Wales.

Happy beyond words to be near the sea once more I entered a pub and called for my first schooner in Sydney. A smaller glass may have attracted unwanted attention. The pub was adjacent to where the land fell steeply away to the docks and popular withga seaman and waterside workers. A bald-headed fellow breasted the bar and ordered seven schooners in a Norwegian accent, paying with a ten-pound note. Turning to me, he said, "Cheers!" He took a gulp through his bushy red beard.

"Tirpitz," I replied, a common term in use at the time among Norse seafarers for 'bottoms up', referring to the German battleship the Royal Air Force had bombed and capsized in a fjord during World War II. Apart from a few phrases, 'Tirpitz' was the limit of my Norwegian.

"Come and join us," he boomed and beamed carrying the tray of schooners to his table. I followed with my beer and sea bag. Room was made for me to fit in and soon friendly bullshit bounced back and forth. Immediately denying England, I claimed my Scottish heritage, confident that it would seal a camaraderie. It did. They all spoke varying levels of English and understood most of what I related about Mount Isa, and how intent I was on returning to sea in some capacity. After many 'Tirpitz', heads were becoming extremely fuddled. Ludicrous suggestions were bandied about as to how soon I could get afloat. They were keen to participate in my quest. It was nearing closing time when we tumbled and lurched down where their ship was berthed. Redbeard said I could sleep with him. Fortunately, this alarming offer was overheard and swiftly corrected by one of the inebriated group with a command of English grammar far more advanced than anything I could ever hope to achieve. Where had he been educated? The sea attracts folk from all walks of life. Masefield, Melville, McLean. One can go down to the sea with them.

I did sleep in Redbeard's cabin, but on the deck with my bag as a pillow. He was still snoring when I left as the sun was rising. The nightwatchman looked me up and down with puzzlement, said something in his native tongue to which I nodded and smiled, as I sped down the gangway. The wharf was beginning to come alive as I passed into the streets of Woolloomooloo. A pub was open where nightshift workers and late-night revellers in evening wear drank on. Posh cars parked askew at the kerb. Hunger lured me to the source of bacon frying at a café patronised by taxi drivers. As the sun continued to climb, I sauntered up the side streets where Italian fishing families lived in rows of terraced houses, drying and mending their nets which lay in the bright sunny streets and old widows in black sat between doorways; sewing, telling the beads, and possibly dreaming of the village of their childhood and their first trip to Catanzaro.

Back at the wharf, I enquired at 'Red Funnel Trawlers' if they had a vacancy. Fortunately for me, there wasn't one, for just a hundred yards further on, opposite an already very rowdy pub, known as the Rockers, a fishing boat lay unloading its catch of crayfish, which were being scooped alive from the hold and stuffed into hessian bags, then swung ashore with a boom. I spoke to the chap who was stowing the bags on a truck. I asked him where the boat came from. "Tassie," he said. More questions followed. Exasperated, he said, "Why doncha jus' ask Tex?" He pointed to four men. "They're short 'anded, two blokes fucked off as soon as they docked." I didn't waste a second, leaving my bag with the truck driver I hopped onboard unasked, adopting the same method of seeking employment I had used on Farmer Brough as a boy. Apart from Anglo Saxon expletives, not a word was spoken for the next sweaty hour. A man who turned out to be Tex, the skipper, tossed me a pair of thick rubber gloves after I dropped the first crayfish I picked up. I was glad of them and had bent to the task. If they were looking for a crewman, I was their man. Soaking wet with sweat and seawater, I watched the last bag go ashore. Tex saved me the trouble of asking for a job.

"What's yer name?" I told him. "I'm Tex, get yer gear aboard; we leave this afternoon."

"Where to?" I inquired, as if it mattered.

"South," he said. "Yer wanna come?"

"I'll get my bag," I said shaking with excitement. Those were the days.

It was still daylight when we called at La Perouse in Botany Bay. The dinghy went ashore and returned with forty loaves of bread. Night had fallen when we left. There were five of us aboard; Tex, the skipper and owner; a choleric drunkard named Denny, who was under orders to abstain whilst at sea; his gentlemanly elder brother Stan, and Henrik, a very able young Dutch boy.

### Voyage to Tassie

Our next port of call was Eden, on the New South Wales south coast. I don't know if the ravages of time or the excess of progress have been kind to Eden, but back then, it was a Steinbeck dream. Cannery Row wharf, where tuna boats and trawlers nudged one another gently and rested in the sun with well-fed contented cats.

As we trudged up the hill to Tortilla Flat's dusty streets to the pub, I jokingly greeted a descending man in Spanish; his greasy hands gripped an engine component. He was an Italian fisherman from Ulladulla, in port with engine trouble.

"Where you catch crays?" he demanded.

"South," we said.

"Where south, Tasmania?"

"Further," we answered.

"How much more south?" he quizzed.

"Keep going until you hear Mawson's dogs barking," Tex countered.

"Who dis Mawson?" he persisted.

"You know, big whiskery bloke, wears a Balaclava," Tex informed him.

"Where he wear Baklava?" he beseeched us.

"On his bloody head, where everybody does," said Tex exasperatedly.

"He crazy put Baklava on head."

We continued up the hill practically in hysterics. The heat of the day enticed us to a pub. Downing a quick schooner, we then adjourned to a very well-appointed Fishermen's Club. Soap, towels and razors were available for a much-needed shower, steadfastly abjured by Henrik alone whose horror of freshwater most folk associate with sulphuric acid. Hair salt stiffened, wearing the same gear, which due to their constant exposure to the briny, remained permanently damp. Returning to the boat after a limited beer intake, a ship chandlery supplied me with oilskin, sou'wester and sea boots. I welcomed Tex's thoughtfulness as it would have been tough during the next few weeks to say the least.

An hour later, we staggered down the hill laden with provisions. Nearing the boat, Henrik veered off with me in tow, to a corrugated iron building. It housed a museum to the whaling industry, thankfully long defunct. Harpoons and flensing knives, ropes and chains bedecked the walls. I recall a whale boat, new, I think, built to scale, magnificent. But something I never forget was a skeleton of Long Tom, a killer whale that herded other species into Two-Fold Bay, to be slaughtered. No wonder he became a local hero. The drink had loosened Henrik's tongue. "Whaddaya think of that Hugh?"

"I see what was once a beautiful cetacean that has been savagely deprived of its blubber, grace and dignity."

"Speak English ya Pommy bastard," he said.

There were six berths in the fo'c'sle. I had chosen a bunk furthest from Henrik's, fortunately adjacent to the hatchway which remained open during fair weather. Utter fatigue made it possible to sleep. Denny slept in the wheelhouse, his brother Stan, I never discovered where he lay his head. Tex was in the stateroom, of which I'll explain a little later. Our boat had an interesting history. She had been a luxury steam yacht built around the turn of the century. Beautiful lines. A clipper bow, an elegant, raked stern. No longer steam of course; she was powered by twin Perkins diesel engines. To stand well for'd, and watch and feel her slicing through a swell at full speed, was a delight only lovers of the sea and ships could really appreciate. Built entirely of timber, she retained the original wheelhouse and captain's stateroom, with its carved panelling of various timber, Celery Top Pine, Kauri, Mahogany and Huon Pine. Where possible the decking ran from stem to stern uncut but proudly scarred on the starboard waist from cannon fire from a 'Zero'. She had been requisitioned during the World War II for service in the islands where she distinguished herself and survived.

By mid-afternoon of the following day, we made land fall on the Furneaux group of islands in the Bass Strait, north east of Tasmania or Van Diemen's Land, as I was to hear many an ancient say. We anchored in a small, sheltered bay at Store Island. A narrow channel separated us from mountainous Babel Island, which was but a short distance from Flinders Island, with Cape Barren Island a little further south. The islands abounded with mutton bird nesting holes. Upon their return from the Aleutians to lay their single egg the mutton birds shared these holes with the occasional snake.

We immediately set to baiting a few cray pots with chunks of frozen fish. In a fairly calm sea, Henrik and I in the dinghy dropped the pots around the rocky shore of the bay. Tired and hungry, we spent the couple of hours of daylight remaining fishing for flathead visible on the seabed three fathoms deep. Before nightfall, the pots were retrieved with some success, and with Tex's beautifully cooked flathead fillets, we stuffed ourselves to excess and turned in.

The next few days, we worked ceaselessly from first light until late afternoon. Pots were set, joined twenty feet apart, in lines of about eight to ten pots with a buoy and a flagpole at either end. On setting several lines, we would retrieve the first line, haul it in, rebait and reset it. Occasionally fish were captured, along with the despised octopus, deemed the cray fishermen's nightmare as they ate crayfish and caused them to shed their legs in fright, rendering them unsaleable. We, however, dined magnificently on these damaged crustaceans. The retribution meted out on these hapless octopods took vengeance to a new level in my eyes. A tentacle was retained for use as excellent flathead bait then they were beaten savagely, changing to multifarious colours with whatever blunt instrument came to hand, cursed, then tossed overboard. The spectacle would have appalled and mystified a Greek, Cretan or Cypriot. When the holding tank was full, we offloaded at 'Lady Baron', a small port on Flinders Islands and the catch flown to the mainland. On the island's west coast, the port of White Mark was visited for supplies and a cold beer or two. Tex had advanced us a few pounds each; in the store, I bought chocolate bars and plenty of soap. Chocolate to stave off hunger whilst fishing as we often didn't eat for hours. Henrik bought chocolate and cigarettes. He did not buy soap; he was becoming a health hazard. I beseeched my gods for fine weather, enabling me to sleep on deck.

Other boats were active in the area; one in particular regularly came alongside on calm evenings. I learned a lot from the chat and banter that occurred and became acquainted with Boyd, the boat's owner. Boyd was a horse punter of some renown and had been expounding the merits of a horse already backed into pre-post favouritism in the Melbourne Cup, the forthcoming annual horse race. Imploring all to invest heavily on the doughty thoroughbred, he announced his intention to wager two thousand pounds. Apparently, Parliament adjourned for the duration of the event.

The following week, we met as arranged at Flemington Racecourse in Melbourne. Boyd had flown over with his cargo of crayfish, while we docked near the fish markets. We all smelt like penguins. Money was good during the cray fishing season, and I had decided to trust my own luck and judgement and select a steed of my choice which offered a generous price. Most folk who punt are aware of the skulduggery that is part and parcel of the sport of kings, and I recalled Grampy's advice of years before. "Remember one thing, that in all classics and important horse races, you can be ninety-nine percent sure that every horse, jockey, trainer and strapper will be all out to win." Referring of course to the multitude of methods in use to prevent a horse from performing to the best of its ability at ordinary everyday meetings or 'creekers' as these events are known in the bush.

Boyd, the genius confident gambler, asked me how much I intended plunging on his tip, one of the fancied runners, as he could negotiate a better price with the bookies that he was well acquainted with, he assured me. I gave him a ten-pound note to shut him up. Meandering through the pulsating crowd, I approached the row of shiny suited bellowing turf accountants and presented ten tenners to a bagman, calling out boldly, "One hundred pounds on Gatum." Before I could say 'please', the money had vanished into the cavernous maw of the leather satchel. As the bookmaker wrote my ticket, he announced to all who stood around that this dishevelled, unshaven, fishy individual who looked as though he had not a pot to piss in would be collecting three thousand three hundred pounds, should Gatum Gatum greet the judge before the rest of the field.

Folk stared, some sympathetically, as I hastily disappeared into the throng. I went to the designated meeting point, which not surprisingly, served beer. Boyd handed me a ticket and confidently advised me that on completion of the race I was to present it to the bookmaker and collect twenty-five pounds. He would enjoy the schooner that I would buy him, he added. This amount exceeded a labourer's weekly wage at the time. I thanked him profusely, but as we studied the horses in the birdcage, I had eyes only for Gatum Gatum, memorising the colours of the cap and silks of the jockey, who I would be urging to ride like a Cossack, a Pony Express rider and imagining him conveying the good news to Aix with the pace and stamina of Roland.

From a vantage point selected by Boyd, we witnessed the hectic charge for positions as the field galloped past the winning post for the first time. I failed to pick out Gatum Gatum's colours among the psychedelic stampede, but Boyd seemed pleased with 'our' horse's situation, in eighth place, four horses wide at the six furlongs. Imitating the Masai and their constant habit of hopping up and down for some reason or another, I caught fleeting glimpses of the streaming field where there appeared to be a rifle shot betwixt the first and last contestant. As it transpired, I mistakenly identified Jimmy Johnson, Gatum Gatum's jockey, cantering along without a care in the world, with only two runners behind him. Things looked glum.

On average, the duration of the event is about three and a half minutes. Since the 'off', I had been ticking off the seconds whilst hopping, and I was becoming seriously out of breath. In the cacophonous, yelling and cheering, in which Boyd was not taking part, indicating that our horse was not faring as well as expected, I made a valiant effort to hop once more. At the last leap, I witnessed Gatum Gatum's gallant nose cross the line to a few roars of delight and many subdued groans. I landed trembling, knees buckling and my heart pounding. Sporting Boyd helped me to my feet, putting my collapse down entirely to my exhaustive hopping. He offered to reimburse my tenner, but I strenuously refused. There were a couple more races on the programme; Boyd had decided to remain, but Tex, being very pissed off with the result, stated his intention to cast off and make a night crossing of the Bass Strait.

Desperately wanting to keep my win from becoming public knowledge and anxious to see what three thousand three hundred pounds looked like in one big wad, I feigned a much-needed visit to the gents.

The bookie had obviously won a heap on the result of the cup, and my win was not going to spoil his humour on the day. He smiled and said, "Well done, son. How the fuck did you pick this hayburner?"

"I saw him winning in a dream," I lied.

"Turned out a fuckin' nightmare for them as backed the favourite, didn't it?" He guffawed.

"Youse can buy some soap now, eh." I did not reply.

The bagman began handing me wads of ten-pound notes, which I stuffed into various recesses of my stinking apparel.

Re-joining Boyd, I discovered that bloody Tex had gone, leaving me marooned and rich. Boyd won seven hundred pounds on the next race. He said we could sleep at a mate's place overnight, then sling a few quid to the pilot flying charter to Flinders Island the next day. He knew the ropes, did Boyd. That night, we got full of beer on someone's trawler and that's where we woke the next morning. I took a lengthy walk to a department store rather than risk being thrown off a tram, where I was trailed closely by two security men. I picked up four pairs of work trousers, shirts, underclothes and socks and headed for the checkout counter. Convinced that I was about to abscond, I could feel their hot breath on my neck. Plonking my purchases in front of the cashier, I foraged in one of my repositories, pulled out a wad, which I confidently guessed was the equivalent to a security guard's annual stipend, and nonchalantly peeled off the asking price. The pair ogled; I was certain that they were thinking my money had been obtained by nefarious means, and half expected them to alert the gendarmes. But they didn't, and I strolled out of the emporium's door leaving them wondering. They would have a tale to tell in the pub that night. I was showing off and enjoying it.

Back on the trawler, I borrowed a towel, soap and shaving tackle, took a set of new clothes which were as stiff as cardboard to the showers on the wharf. I shaved and scrubbed myself raw, dressed and stuffed a few French letters with my currency ala the Royal Navy. Boyd was waiting where I confessed to having waged five pounds on Gatum Gatum. True to his magnanimous character, he was jubilant. He had offered to cover my fare to Flinders Island, but with my big bundle of new clothes, I had to come clean. Well, partially anyway. We flew out of Melbourne on schedule and stayed at Boyd's house on Flinders that night. Up early the next morning, I had the luxury of another shower, two in two days; this was a rare occurrence in the season. His two deckhands had fuelled and watered the boat and prepared for sea. They expectantly awaited Boyd's hard luck stories, which they were well used to. Slipping the moorings, we headed for Babel Island with my toxic old clothes trailing astern attached to a heaving line.

My boat was located by radio, and sometime later, I was back on board. Tex was determined to recoup his losses before the Christmas break. He, Stan and Henrik were pleased to see me. "I apologise for pissing off, mate. I am a bad loser, I shouldn't gamble," he said with sincerity. He then proceeded to push us hard, and the more he drove us, the more we earned. And this was what we were engaged in on that fateful day in Dallas, Texas, when the world changed forever. A day we all remember where we were.

I was in a small bay trolling for salmon with Stan and Henrik. Circling in the bay for crayfish bait, we used barb-less hooks with cylindrical lead trawl net sinkers as a lure. The flowing water down the tube streamed out in bubbles causing frenzy, and with each gnashing bite, the sinker shone brighter until our wake boiled like a tub of suds. We were boating about two fish every five seconds, and we kept at it whilst we had the salmon chummed, ceasing when only six inches of freeboard remained in the dinghy. Nursing the dinghy alongside our fishing boat, a larger wickerwork creel was lowered which we began filling with gasping wriggling fish. The dinghy, safely in the davits and hosed out when Tex the skipper casually announced, "President Kennedy's been shot."

Covered in fish scales, soaking wet, it took a while for the news to sink in; was he dead? I had seen quite a few people that had been shot. They were not always dead, they just had cauterised but nevertheless interesting holes in them. Tex confirmed his death. Looking up into the evening sky, I wondered whether the missiles were already in the stratosphere.

I was keenly awaiting the Christmas break; the main reason had little to do with the festivities. Boyd had generously invited me to spend Christmas on Flinders with his family. But I cried off with a heap of outlandish lies. He also offered me a place on his boat with a bigger percentage, even that I had to decline. I often wondered what he liked about me. It could have been that we were both a bit reckless and carefree, or maybe he could recognise a good seaman when one came along.

They were all hard-working decent folk who I got on well with, but when it came to the all-important continuous search for bait, their indiscriminateness engendered disgust in me. Netting salmon, fair enough. When a beautiful seal that was basking in the sunshine on a rock was shot, and the regular murderous nocturnal excursion to club fairy penguins, as they waddled ashore to sleep, proved too much for me. I was so grateful I had the courage not to kill one, and I determined then and there to leave the idyllic life and my good companions, when we arrived at Hobart.

The wind rose for the last three days, and as we dropped the pots one by one, the waves slapped spray over the side hiding my remorse and shame as I stuffed the mangled birds in the craypots.

## Hobart

Hugging the beautiful, rugged coast to Hobart, we trolled for barracuda, which were plentiful. Tex radioed ahead and sold the lot before we docked. The crayfish were bagged in hessian sacks and flown immediately to Melbourne, after which we moved to Battery Point, our permanent berth.

I volunteered to remain onboard over the holiday period despite being offered alternative accommodation. I wanted to be alone, to meet new people and to explore the city, the countryside and learn about Tasmania's brutal convict past. Also, I wished to leave the boat ship shape and Bristol fashion. Tex jumped at this offer; ordered paint and varnish to be delivered plus a slab of beer and a bottle of overproof. "Merry Christmas," he said, giving me my pay cheque and disappeared. I never saw Tex again or the rest of the crew. They had vanished as soon as they had been paid.

First things first though; I had to bank my fortune. The water tanks were almost empty as we had not taken on water since we had syphoned off a rainwater tank attached to a mutton-birder's shed on Babel Island. Tex had completely overlooked taking on water in Melbourne, a fact he held the euphoria of the big race responsible for. There was enough to fill two buckets, one for soaping and the other for rinsing. Clean but not very well rinsed, I donned a new set of cardboard clothes; I turned to the French letters and discovered my wealth, damp, stuck together and smelling. Real filthy lucre. Leaving a hose slowly filling the tanks, I headed for the branch of the Bank of New South Wales. The bank teller's face blanched when I pushed the pile of fishy notes towards her. Refusing to touch it, she said, "Excuse me, sir," and disappeared into the manager's office, which came ajar a moment later to enable the manager to ascertain as to whether the police need be alerted. All was well though, and as the boggle-eyed manager surveyed my treasure, it was apparent that he was bursting to ask the inevitable. But in keeping with protocol, he refrained, so I thought I would ease the situation and his curiosity by lying once more and said I had been fishing for two years and had stashed away my wages under my bunk mattress for safekeeping. His eyes glazed over at that, and he set to work, with the assistance of two female tellers to painstakingly peel the notes apart. I offered them a tenner each for their trouble, but the manager refused for the three of them. This time, his eyes rolled skywards. I would have loved to have read his thoughts.

With the three hundred pounds I already had in my bankbook, I was at a loss to know what to do next. It was 1963, I could have easily bought a house large enough for a family. But that idea never occurred to me. Possessing not a vestige of business acumen, I decided that I had plenty of time to come up with a plan by staying on as watchkeeper and paying for my lodging until the boat put to sea again.

The boat was very well known in Hobart, so I quickly made the acquaintance of several folk whose work or recreation centred around the jetties and slipways. Yachtsmen, fishermen, shipwrights, slip-yard hands, loafers, drunks and derelicts. Like so many other places of its kind, it was where pensioned off seafarers gravitated to reminisce and sometimes exaggerate the facts. The flotsam and jetsam, the bladderwrack of a slowly ebbing tide.

During the holiday break, it became increasingly difficult to fulfil my promise to leave the boat in the condition I wished, because of the social whirl I had become entangled in. Barbeques, parties, booze ups and crewing in sharpies in regattas held on the Derwent and other locations. A dinner party at a posh house necessitated purchasing and being fitted into tailored clothes, something that had not occurred since my training ship ten years before. I still had two pairs of cardboard trousers, one pair that had softened a little, and the pair in use, covered in paint, grease and varnish. They were suitable for BBQs and other Bacchanalian past times, but I was about to dine with the Commodore of the

Yacht Club's family and friends. I had no idea whether they dressed for dinner, and fortunately, they did not. It was a lovely evening, with generous intelligent people, and I felt special in my new clothes, which were several times remarked upon. Looking back, it's likely they thought I was colour blind. My mother always said that I only looked smart in my Royal Naval uniform.

I did not disgrace myself with the fine wines that were on offer. So different from the plonk I had been guzzling for years. I recited poetry, Burns, Donne and was called upon to repeat *The General Elliott* by Robert Graves. Eventually, I hired a couple of out of work deckhands to get on with the boat work. They were very good, and within a week, they had it looking like the Royal Yacht Britannia. It was my way of an apology to Tex for leaving him, not that Hobart was short of deck hands, no, he was losing me and I was not any old deckhand.

One afternoon, I had showered and was sitting sartorially replete, or so I imagined, in the stateroom reading the papers when female voices called, "Ahoy there, anyone aboard?" Followed by much giggling. They obviously had not spied the two paid off deckhands who were lying on the fo'c'sle paralytic, having disposed of the case of beer and the bottle of Bundaberg rum that Tex had given me. A fire hose would not shift them for twenty-four hours at the earliest. I had been perusing the Financial Times, not that I could make head nor tail of its baffling advice. I may as well have been reading it upside down. I stuffed the paper under a cushion, not wishing to create the impression of being a mogul of the film industry. Because apart from the stacked craypots aft and the two apparent corpses on the fore deck, the boat had St Tropez and Monaco written all over her.

On deck, I immediately welcomed two gloriously callipygous Maori sisters aboard. I showed them around the vessel, pointing out the WWII battle scars and wracking my brains to come up with a plausible yarn regarding the inert bodies when we approached the foredeck. There was no need however, as the deck was littered with crushed cans and the empty rum bottle. The girls were delighted to discover two full cans, simmering in the sun, and with my say so, swiftly did them justice and drained the rum bottle. I was in love with them already. One of the unconscious drunks began peeing so we repaired to the stateroom after I had thrown a couple of buckets of seawater over the incontinent one's trousers and deck. He did not stir.

In the cool of the stateroom, we demolished half a dozen bottles of Cascade between us and made a mess of two giant crays which I purloined from Tex's freezer on the wharf, hoping he wasn't saving them for Christmas. I boiled them frozen in a large cauldron we kept for this purpose. Burping, replete and happy; what to do next? The girls were going to the pictures to see Steve McQueen in *The Great Escape*, which I had seen the evening before but did not let on. I offered to shout them a night out. A slap-up dinner first, then Steve McQueen escaping, followed by more to eat as these two lovely ladies were evidently not concerned about putting on weight.

I was outnumbered two to one so I put all lascivious thoughts aside because every man knows, one girl equals one girl, but two girls equal no girl, unless of course they were weird girls, which they were not. I would settle for their wonderful company and joie de vivre. I spent five pounds in a posh restaurant. I bought champagne; the girls drank it like lemonade and washed down several courses with it. The chef ogled through the porthole window of the kitchen whenever the two girls asked for their platters to be refilled.

At last, amid much belching and licking of fingers, the gustatory proceedings came to a halt. The girls insisted upon meeting the chef and very nearly hospitalised him with the exuberance of their hugs. Not entirely sober, but far from drunk, the girls were becoming quite motherly towards me and insisted I sit between them when we were conducted to our seats at the cinema. I could see no point in protesting.

Mr McQueen possessed a charisma that mesmerised my companions. They were purring with ecstasy with his every appearance. Erotically squirming and sighing. Folk behind us began muttering and making unflattering comments, so I begged them to behave if they wanted a big supper afterwards. Amazingly, they complied but unfortunately the cessation of activity had a soporific effect almost immediately and soon drawn-out sonorous snores drowned out the soundtrack. There was little I could do, wedged as I was between my newfound friends, and until they woke, I was as immovable as Shackleton's Endurance.

Someone alerted an usherette. The manager was called, he then sidled along the row and shook them both roughly. The girls woke up laughing and in good humour. He said nothing to me as he probably hadn't noticed me. Badly wishing to pee and making no secret of it, they stumbled up the aisle, each thumping step producing a loud staccato fart. I was crying with joy as I waited on the pavement, where I had been escorted by the manager. He made me understand that if I brought them back, he would call the law and have them deported. It was an idle threat though as he bolted when the girls emerged giggling from the ladies and ready for more. I advised them of the moronic manager's threat.

"Fuck him," they growled in unison.

"What happened to Steve, did he escape?"

"Almost," I said. "Got himself tangled up in barbed wire on the Swiss border," I added, then confessed to having seen the film.

"What happened then?" they whimpered.

"Incarceration for a month in the cooler, bouncing a baseball off the cell wall," I said. Rage and wailing followed, and I realised I should have used a simpler term than incarceration. For the first time, I saw dejection and defeat in their big brown eyes so I mentioned the supper I had promised. It had an immediate effect. At a fish and chip café, I told the girls to order what they wished. My God, I was pleased to be rich. Whilst they were having a parcel made up of about a stone of chips, prawns, scallops, squid, abalone and oysters, liberally anointed with the contents of several bottles and jars including pickled onions, I adjourned to the nearest pub and secured a case of beer. Giving the beer to Tweedledum, with Tweedledee carrying the evening's comestibles safe in her arms, we returned to the wharf and to whatever mayhem awaited us. Now was the time for the girls to meet the night owls of the waterfront. There were small rentable sheds at the water's edge for boat owners to stow whatever they wished in comparative safety.

A short rotund middle-aged man known as Sharkie was a permanent resident of one of these sheds. He had invited me to break my fast with him on the morning I met him. He was incinerating sausages on a battered Primus stove, with the mandatory bottle of tomato sauce at hand and a loaf of white bread; wholemeal bread had weevils in it apparently.

The pubs hadn't closed, so the characters who coloured the wharf by day had not yet returned to roost, so I decided Sharkie needed a change of diet from the tedious sausages. At this time of day, he had usually put paid to a flagon of sweet sherry and though remaining conscious, would be quite incapable of venturing abroad unless conveyed on a stretcher. Sharkie had a record player, a wind-up model. As we neared, I could hear for the umpteenth time, his favourite song, *500 Hundred Miles from Home*. There were a pile of records on a shelf but *500 Miles* was the only one I ever heard played. I still recall the mournful lyrics. In spite of this dismal dirge, Sharkie was a happy soul and a very generous and helpful man.

The meagre lighting on the wharf glinted on his bottle glass spectacles; he was in a sitting position and called out:

"Who goes there, friend or foe?"

"Customs and excise," I answered, stupidly.

"Shit," he cursed and staggered to his feet with a boat hook at the same time as he recognised my voice.

"Fuck, don't do that again, ya dopey Pommie bastard; ya nearly gave me a heart attack." Sharkie's thick glasses then swivelled on the two large amorphous beings who stood dark against the moonlit sky.

"Sharkie, meet my friends Tweedledum and Tweedledee who bear good tidings and Christmas cheer." He tried getting to his feet again but failed and fell back on his blow-up mattress which lay atop a bed of nets. It was fortunate that he did as the girls were in a hugging mood and a hug from the sisters may well have caused irreparable damage.

"What did you call us?" queried the girls. I had clean forgotten they were unaware of what I had secretly dubbed them. Assuming that they had not read Lewis Carroll's *Through a Looking Glass*, left me free to paint Tweedledum and Tweedledee as warrior maidens on galloping blood horses, slaying tyrants and despots who brutalised the peasantry. This desperate explanation brought forth smug smiles of approval, and we then set to making room for ourselves by shifting bundles of oars, nets, two mainsails, fathoms of rope and an outboard motor outside.

One of the girls was called Ngaio; I remember it because of the New Zealand crime novelist Ngaio Marsh. Her sister's name was Kiki or something similar. There being nothing as ostentatious as a table among the furnishings, an empty packing case was mined from the mountainous maritime junk heap. It was covered with a piece of sail cloth and the parcel of goodies dumped on top. The case of beer was unceremoniously ripped open and the feast began. Upon being broached, steam shot from the mound of chips and the various denizens of the deep, plus an unsavoury smell from the several bottled additives which had morphed into, in my opinion, a very unappetising sight. Sharkie was agog but in spite of being partly blinded by the steam clouding up his bifocals, immediately began cramming his mouth with chips, oysters and scallops; at the same time harpooning pickled onions with a meat skewer. The girls quickly caught on that they had a rival to contend with but kindly said, "Poor man, he must be starving, let him go ahead." This period of magnanimity abruptly ceased after twenty-five seconds, then they too began doing what they did best. Apart from sausages, the sole variation in Sharkie's diet was the occasional trumpeter that came in contact with the gill net he illegally set under the piers and jetties, and sometimes a permanently sunken craypot served up a nice surprise, but not often.

Slurping from a half pint mug of sherry, Sharkie was experiencing difficulty in differentiating the contents of the pile. Removing his fogged-up glasses, he was no better off; squinting as if he had been trapped down a coalmine for a month. The sisters no longer concerned about his welfare, stepped it up a notch and instinctively yet another notch when loud footsteps and raucous voices announced the return of happy waterside inhabitants. When they noticed the stack of Sharkie's goods and chattels and the puzzling aroma emanating from what remained of supper, they squeezed in and cleaned up the greasy hideous mess, with no protest from anyone. Burping, laughing and licking their fingers again, the sisters grabbed two bottles of beer each, then collapsed on a pile of nets. Ngaio had boasted to me that their great grandfather had eaten 'long pig'. I never doubted her for a second. I had not partaken of a morsel, my stomach though roomy did have a plimsoll line.

Sharkie had thrown in the towel and was snoozing like a walrus. This gave us a welcome break from *500 Miles*, and for the beery visitors, the opportunity to regale the girls and myself with bragging tales of their convict ancestry. As the beer went down so the boasting increased. I had not been in the country that long, a little under a year, so I had not enough time to gauge the amount of pride or shame among the populace appertaining to any convict ancestry. Among our guests, no sense of shame existed, only immense pride.

Bushrangers, murderers and pirates, these topped the list, especially if they had been flogged and hanged at Port Arthur or marooned on Maria Island. Pickpockets and common petty thieves were scarcely worth a mention. One, an engraver, transported for printing his own banknotes, was not considered a criminal at all but should have been elected mayor. A pillar of society; a champion of the poor. And so it went on until the beer ran out. It was about two o'clock in the morning so I told the girls to avail themselves of Tex's huge bed in the stateroom, hoping that the springs would stand the bumpy few hours that lay ahead.

The men helped me shove everything back in the shed. Sharkie was still heavily anaesthetised and would need assistance in extricating himself when he came to. Calls of nature were attended to at the rear of the shed. Moving aside an alabaster statue of a lachrymose Virgin Mary, an aperture was exposed, over which one squatted. A piece of lace, embroidered with the words 'Abide with me' was on hand to cover the Virgin Mary's head whilst one answered the call of nature. Sharkie was a considerate man; drunk or sober.

Waking up at 0600 Hours, from my bunk in the fo'c'sle head, I could hear thumps and bumps and much cursing from Sharkie's waterfront chalet. Two minutes later, I was rescuing him from entrapment. Desperate on emerging from his drunken stupor, Sharkie had cannoned into the Virgin Mary who lay prone on her face, a large chip missing from her nose. Sharkie was distraught, maudlin tears flowed down his cheeks. Tipping what remained of the sherry flagon down the hole, he swore total abstinence from then on. I fetched glue from the paint locker on my boat, retrieved the holy piece of nose and reattached it with surgical precision. The replacing of Our Lady on her plinth brought peace and serenity to Sharkie, causing him to quickly revise his oath of sobriety to one drink per day. The precise volume of this drink was never mooted. He then pumped up the Primus and began brewing a gallon of coffee, a morning ritual which normally ceased when the urge for something a little stronger could no longer be ignored.

It was two days before Christmas, one month since JFK's assassination, which was never out of the news. Time to stock up on festive provisions, fill up Tex's fridge and replace if possible, the two giant crays I had borrowed. The girls would no doubt be in search of sustenance on awakening and they would earn it by serving as my bearers on the shopping expedition. I decided to give them another hour in bed, which I prayed was still in one piece when I would risk rousing them. Meanwhile, I attempted to re-hydrate myself with a mug of Sharkie's creosote coffee and wishing I was listening to one of Johann Sebastian's *Brandenburg Concertos* or *Fingal's Cave*, instead of *500 Miles*, a lament that would remain with me should I live a thousand years.

From where I sat in one of Sharkie's self-proclaimed 'Sheraton' armchairs, which were heavily stencilled with Darjeeling, this side up, I had an excellent view of my temporary lodgings. All was quiet and calm, indicating that the girls had not yet broken their slumber, because when they eventually did, nothing, I could confidently predict, would remain quiet and calm for any longer.

A little later, laughing female voices told me something was astir.

"The toilet won't flush, Hugh," cried one of them.

"It never has in years," I said.

"Flush it with seawater, the bucket on the fo'c'sle, remember?

166

"With a heaving line attached," I instructed.

Realising the urgency of the situation, one of the girls thumped her way forward in haste as the pan would need clearing before it underwent a fresh assault. Ten minutes later, having attended to their morning ablutions, they completed the job by ducking their happy dark heads under the freshwater tap outside Sharkie's country seat, looking as though they had been asleep for twenty-four hours. I could see why the 'All Blacks' were practically invincible.

I mentioned the shopping expedition, but they surprised me with the news that they were flying to Launceston in the afternoon to spend Christmas with their father and brother who were shearing in the north of the island. I suggested a big greasy breakfast as a fail-safe bribe, and they were putty in my hands. They thanked Sharkie for his hospitality, and realising he was a little delicate, they gave him the gentlest of hugs and fogged up his glasses when they rubbed noses.

We walked into town via the beautiful Salamanca Bond Stores and headed for the Greek milk bar I knew of. They were usually open all hours and the aroma of bacon wafting in the warm summer morning had us salivating a hundred yards off. The café had a row of fragile-looking tables down one side and more substantial benches on the other, which the elderly proprietor, anticipating a possible disaster, eagerly pointed out. We sat down and looked at the gallery of blue and white villages overlooking turquoise seas shimmering in the heat. Fishing caiques jostling jealously for attention; Ouzo and Retsina palpable. A moustached bandit in knee-high leather boots, dagger in his belt, glared down at us as if daring us to eat. More like a Cretan, I thought.

I was jolted out of my reverie when in reply to the young waitress' question Ngaio ordered scrambled eggs and toast for two. Had she specified they be penguin eggs or requested a grilled leg of hairy-nosed wombat with truffle sauce, I probably would have continued absorbing the fascinating kitsch surrounding us. Something was up. What was wrong? It wasn't what they had ordered that had me concerned, but the amount. How far would these two adorable Amazons travel on scrambled eggs? Were they worried about the forthcoming flight; excess baggage? They were the quietest I had seen them. The only sound was the sipping from Coke bottles, in a desultory manner. I needed to know what had happened to the joie de vivre. I was determined to discover the cause of this sudden change of mood, although I had a pretty good idea what it was. Since we met, I had overlooked their sometimes, embarrassing ribald behaviour. In truth, I had enjoyed it immensely, taking me back to the Royal Navy days. I had treated them with respect, assuming nothing. I was well aware that I deferred to them, not that I was afraid that between them they could easily put me in traction for six months. No. I enjoyed their company; we were mates. Strongly sensing that I had all the trump cards, I decided to tell them what I thought was wrong, as there was nothing forthcoming on their part. I then leaned forward and placed my hands on theirs and said, "Listen to me, girls.

"You're broke, are you not?

"You haven't a brass razoo to get to the airport.

"You need a fucking bath and clean clothes before you see your dad."

Copious tears were flowing now. I let them bawl for a minute or so, then advised them to re-examine the menu and all would be taken care of. The sobbing subsided immediately, eyes were dried and noses sounded reveille. Smiling once more, menus tentatively examined followed by a gradual restoration of confidence, and for the next half an hour, the welcoming Babushka was run off her feet. Things were back to normal.

After the surfeit of seafood we had enjoyed in the previous twenty-four hours, the girls gave an impressive exhibition on how to eat meat and a new interpretation of the word carnivore, while I breakfasted on the cold forgotten scrambled eggs.

Keeping the pressure on, I said that I would very much like to buy them a Christmas present in the form of a new dress. I had no idea of the price of women's clothing but reasoned that as long as they didn't charge by the square foot I could easily afford it. Taking all this in, I could sense hugs coming up, so I quickly rose and settled the bill with the valiant old Greek lady, who announced that she looked forward to seeing us again soon and wished us a Merry Christmas. We returned the compliments of the season and left the old dear staring in disbelief.

The girls knew exactly where to shop having previously reconnoitred the town thoroughly. At first glance, it was evidently an off the peg establishment, not a whiff of haute couture; a welcome relief. Now for the tricky part, do I go in with them? They would probably be refused service with their food and beer-stained apparel, and what a riot that would bring about. I had visions of the three of us spending Christmas in the watch house. I quickly decided to take charge by calling a brief counsel of strategy. I would enter first, ignore the midinettes and front the Head Serang, diplomatically fondling a serious wad of currency. It worked. The woman smiled a greeting, the smile running concurrently with the wrinkling of the nose; a difficult accomplishment. I turned to see the girls with dresses in both hands and with beaming faces they waved them at me, as if seeking approval. I nodded. The dresses off the rack were very cheap, some only thirty shillings each.

"You can have two each," I said with a surge of generosity.

Slightly embarrassed, I turned to the woman who had not taken her eyes off the wad and asked her if she could demonstrate her range of whatever was worn beneath their garments. She said she could and would. Leaving them to pick and choose the lingerie, I wandered to the far end of the shop and dawdled for a few uncomfortable minutes among racks of foundation garments.

Now was the time to put a recently formed friendship to the test. I had made the acquaintance of the licensees of a nearby hotel. They had invited me to share Christmas lunch with them, an offer which I had gratefully accepted. I had also made use of their hot showers and laundry facilities. Would this be taking a step too far? I decided to take a punt as the girls couldn't be allowed to don their new dresses prior to being steeped in a tub of suds for an hour at least.

With the purchases bagged up, we sped to the emergency hot water and soap with intent. It was not only a Christmas lunch I was risking but a friendship. In we went, and taking the bull by the horns, I made a sheepish request for my friends to avail themselves of the hotel's bathroom. I needn't have worried; they were only too happy to oblige. Both he and his wife made no comment about the girls' neglected state; they probably thought that they had just crossed the Tasman in a canoe. They were very kind, giving the girls bath towels and soap saying, "Take as long as you like, ladies, use as much hot water as you wish."

I then had a yarn and quite a few laughs with the publican regarding the events of the past twenty-four hours. On enquiring of how far it was to the airport, he insisted on driving us there. I had not intended seeing them off as it would have meant a return taxi fare. I didn't mind spending money but drew the line at wasting it.

Finally, there they were, beaming and shining, smelling like bath salts, soap and shampoo, so happy and proud. Titian would have begged them to sit. I told them we were being chauffeured to the airport. After they had downed three quick glasses of beer and regaled the clientele with a ferocious, pounding Haka, we left to ensure the girls caught their flight. I had enjoyed their company, but it was time for a break. I needed to gather my thoughts and review my situation.

At the airport, Kiki whispered if could I lend them a quid. I said I never lend money to friends, but I can give you twenty quid each. They immediately began blubbering once more, rubbed their wet noses on mine and nearly suffocated me in their arms. We both watched them cross the tarmac, climb the steps, turn and wave, then their magnificent buttocks disappeared from view. Sundry topics were discussed on the way back to the hotel, but somehow the conversation always reverted to the two stupendous Maori girls. Back at the pub, the story was the same. It was unanimously agreed that wherever they were life could never be dull.

Neil the publican asked where I intended heading next, as I had previously confided in him my reasons for abjuring cray-fishing. It was a touchy subject in the fishing community, so I had been delighted when he confessed to an abhorrence of the indiscriminate practice and would have found it difficult to get a good night's sleep for a month had he clubbed a fairy penguin to death. I said I had been invited to crew on a sharpie leading up to the New Year when I would enjoy the climax of the Sydney to Hobart ocean race. After which, I wished to wander around the island, working here and there whenever there was someone needing a hand.

Thanking Neil for his generosity, I flagged a taxi outside the pub and directed the driver to a grocery store. I told him to keep the meter ticking over whilst I bought some essentials. A shadow of suspicion clouded his face which disappeared when I proffered a tenner as security. After memorising his cab licence number, I dashed inside. Returning to the wharf, I found quite a cargo to contend with. The taxi meter had not cut much out of the ten-pound note, so would the cabbie be interested in accepting what remained of it for payment for a bit of porterage. Yes, he would.

I have often wondered if it was a good idea. With two large, heavy cardboard boxes, we approached Sharkie's den. The unfit cabbie, who had the configuration of a diesel drum could scarcely see over the top of his box so had not caught sight of Sharkie but recognised his hail of welcome, as they knew each other from a long way back. After an introductory beer, there followed another, and another; with Sharkie swigging out of a bottle of malt and occasionally passing it to his mate Vernon to taste. It was not long before the taxi driver lost all interest in completing his shift.

I stowed my perishables in Tex's fridge and realised that the booze would need replenishing before the sun had set. I borrowed the taxi keys and with *500*

*Miles* serenading me, drove to the pub to fill the boot with beer. I had no idea how to operate the 'Engaged' sign, leaving would be fares waving and whistling in vain and vexation.

It took three trips of about fifty yards to stow the grog. On completion, I pondered what to do with the taxi. Parking it as far away from the road as I could, I set about locating the whereabouts of the taxi base. The two-way radio was there, but I had no idea how to operate it. After a few minutes rummaging in the glove compartment and the door pockets, I discovered the telephone number staring me in the face, on the dashboard. Luckily, his name was displayed also. Calling from a phone box two hundred yards up the street, I informed the office that Vernon was indisposed, which prompted the riposte:

"What, ya mean the fucker's pissed?"

Any friend of Sharkie's is a friend of mine I thought reluctantly. I replied that as far as I could tell there was no evidence to suggest that any bibulousness had taken place in many hours. I added that Vernon had felt a little delicate soon after breakfast that he had partaken of, a dish of scrambled eggs which had been cooked in a manner he was unaccustomed to, I lied loyally.

"Are you taking the piss out of me, ya Pommy cunt?" he spat.

I said that if he chose to see my endeavour to assist him in the retrieval of the taxi in that way, that was his prerogative. I gave the name of a street two blocks away and hung up. I then drove the taxi to the street, parked it, left the keys in the glove box and rapidly left the scene.

The enchanting plucking and strumming of the bouzouki welcomed me on returning to the wharf, leading me to believe that Sharkie had succumbed to cirrhosis at long last or that an enraged music lover had hurled *500 Miles* into the depths of the Derwent. The former had not occurred, and neither were we blessed with the latter. Sharkie and Vernon, with an arm around each other's shoulder, were somehow miraculously on their feet, giving a fair exhibition of Greek dancing in company with a very tall scruffy character. He had a plumbeous complexion and a thatch of hair of mouldy hay, reminding me of Tim the Ostler who loved Bess, the landlord's black-eyed daughter. Sweat poured down their faces, the record came to an end and puffing like perforated organ bellows, Sharkie and Vernon sank to their knees in supplication around a tin bathtub packed with ice and beer. Leaping at the opportunity of the brief silence between *500 Miles* or more Peloponnese music, I attempted to explain to Vernon about the taxi and presumably his livelihood with little success.

"Fuck the cab," said Vernon, ferociously guzzling a bottle of Cascade.

Why spoil a party by bringing up work, I thought and left it at that.

The fourth member of our little gathering turned out to be Sharkie's brother-in-law, sent on his annual errand of charity to ensure that Sharkie was in a state of relative sobriety when picked up the next day, which was Christmas Eve. His sister would transport him in whatever condition, halfway up Mount Wellington to the family seat where he would be reunited once more with kin, whose names he experienced great difficulty recalling.

Jonah the brother-in-law, saddled with the task of sobering Sharkie up, appeared unperturbed by the seemingly impossible challenge. The family were Salvation Army folk and it fell to Jonah once a year to get Sharkie up the mountain to endure twenty-four hours of complete abstinence. A kind of penance maybe? No, surely not. Why he submitted to this draconian period of torture could only have been unconditional love for his sister, but then again, there might have been a tincture of mercenariness as his sister had been the sole beneficiary of their martinetish father's huge wealth. Sharkie had been cut off due to his refusal to thump the tambourine and abjure strong drink. Jonah said that giving him money would only lead to an early death but agreed with me that he was heading that way without family donations.

Jonah intended staying with Sharkie for the night and keeping the coffee heated. It was clear that Sharkie's God-worshipping family cared about him. It had begun to rain; we dragged Vernon inside by his feet and laid him at the rear of the shed under the merciful eyes of the Virgin Mary. I bade them goodnight, took a few long necks along to a gin palace further down the jetty where it sounded as if a ceilidh was about to get underway. A prelude to the days ahead. I stayed an hour at the party, ate and drank and got excited over a very pretty girl who seemed happy to sit alongside me and I, alongside her, until I became aware that her boyfriend, with whom she had had a spat half an hour earlier, was aboard. She pointed him out; I was glad she did. He was aft, pacing up and down on the poop in an unsettled manner. He appeared to be eighteen stone at a conservative estimate with the configuration of an Easter Island statue. He turned fo'red, completely eclipsing the moon, the crowd made way for him and I could see this bonny lad eating nails with his cornflakes, so swiftly weighing up between the discretion and valour thing. I decided discretion was the wisest option. I had no intention of leaving this world with three thousand pounds in the bank so I excused myself and left to see how Jonah was faring with his charge.

With the gradual receding hubbub of the soiree, fresh sounds emerged as I neared Sharkie's shed. I heard a high-pitched cry of fright. Jonah was attempting to pacify Vernon. On being disturbed by Sharkie's urgent need to micturate, Vernon was staring bug-eyed at the lantern illuminated face of the Holy Mother, whose beneficent countenance shone with love and forgiveness. Our Lady was engaged in propping Sharkie up while he was pissing with uncanny accuracy into the Derwent. Gently manoeuvring the gibbering Vernon along the wharf, we laid him to rest in Tex's bed which had suffered badly the previous night and now resembled a weasel's nest, in appearance and effluvia. The linen which presumably had once been white badly needed laundering. Once more, I would test a friendship.

It was 2200 Hours. The evening was cool with a slight drizzle. Jonah drank coffee; I slowly drank beer and Sharkie snored for another hour, then began stirring and muttering about checking his gill net and craypot before his period of penance up the mountain began. I solved the dilemma by retreating to the rear of the shed, kneeling at Our Lady's feet and unashamedly swore that I would see that the harvesting of net and pot was carried out. I meant it and Sharkie believed me, and I remained true to Odin and Poseidon. Sharkie was not a Catholic. His family were not Catholic either; they were whatever Salvation Army personnel were. Sharkie pulled Catholicism out of a hat; anything to disassociate himself from his father. He may have chosen to be a Mormon at another time or erected a Shinto shrine where the Holy Mother now stood.

Nearing midnight, drowsy with beer; saintly Jonah at last asleep on a pile of nets, sailcloth drawn up to his chin and Sharkie hopefully comatose until sunrise, I took myself off to my bunk in the fo'c'sle where I recall little else until two cats searching for breakfast broke my slumber. Christmas Eve, I had things to do.

In Tex's stateroom, I did my best to ignore Vernon and the embarrassing state of the bed. I ducked my head under the communal tap outside Sharkie's shed. Jonah was drinking coffee and Sharkie was rummaging around in search of something, cursing quietly. The Virgin Mary was lying down; her plinth had been moved to one side of the hole, which showed signs of having suffered heavy bombardment recently. Nothing a bucket or two of water wouldn't fix. Refusing a cup of creosote, I mentioned the gill net and craypot, and Jonah, after extracting a pledge from Sharkie to stick to coffee, accompanied me in the dinghy. Paddling under the jetties, we soon located the net. One fish that neither of us could identify gasped in the morning sun. I released it and stuffed the illicit net into a hessian bag, hauled the nearby pot which contained a dead crab, removed the putrefying crustacean and returned the pot to the bottom.

Paddling back, I asked Jonah what Sharkie had mislaid that caused so much anxiety.

"Something that he won't find until he descends to sea level the day after Boxing Day," confided Jonah.

"What's that?" I said, intrigued.

"Guess," urged Jonah.

"Well, if I had a wish, I would welcome the disappearance of '500 bloody miles' for a month at least," I said.

"We have both been blessed by the Lord. I have prayed for forgiveness for the underhand method employed to ensure a few hours' peace," said Jonah humbly.

"I am sure the Lord will look upon it as a charitable act and indeed your civic duty to residents of this peaceful maritime piece of heaven," I said sincerely.

I did not wish to know what Jonah had done with the pestilent record, and he gave no sign of enlightening me. A peeved Sharkie had opened a can of corned beef and was frying the glutinous mess in a pan that by its shape indicated had performed a variety of duties over time. The two cats that had woken me were miaowing about his ankles. I gave them the prawn and two fat chips I had located under one of Tex's pillows.

I now had a large bundle of soiled linen under one arm, whilst steadying a dishevelled Vernon who had wet the bed several times, with the other. I was becoming quite concerned lest Tex called down to wish us a Merry Christmas and to pick up the two monster crayfish the girls and I had demolished. I rapidly sprang into action. Leaving Sharkie's tap running to irrigate the sheets, hopefully to partially wash away the stench, I sought Jonah's assistance to haul the mattress out of the stateroom and into the sunshine. Jonah, ever the ideas man, liberally sprinkled a bottle of aftershave which he had found among Sharkie's toiletries, over the square yard of pee. Vernon had peeled off his clinging strides and had donned a pair of Sharkie's shorts which were of a striking Taiwanese tartan.

I had tried explaining to Vernon what had become of his taxi, but he could not have been more disinterested. His money bag was hanging on a nail at the rear of the shed with a Drizabone hiding it. He said he would return it when he felt like it. He no longer would be driving a cab as it interfered with his drinking and had gladly accepted Sharkie's invitation to help him pay the rent.

I was wringing out the sheets when I noticed a gentleman in a suit approaching with a sense of urgency in his gait. Suits were a very rare sight around the wharves and jetties, so I alerted the other three to the looming phenomenon.

"Merry Christmas, Ivan," hailed Jonah.

Sharkie, still stewing over what he hoped was the temporary misplacement of *500 Miles*, acknowledged Ivan with a grunt. Vernon's sense of guilt assumed that Ivan was a detective and he disappeared inside the shed, until reassured by Sharkie that Ivan was the family chauffeur and trusted retainer. Ivan told Sharkie that his sister who waited in the car was in a hurry and did not wish to be kept waiting. Sharkie, who had changed into a clean shirt and shorts, grabbed his toothbrush, put the pan of corned beef outside for the cats, said, "See ya, mate," to Vernon, assuring him that Hugh would see him all right until his release from bondage on the 27$^{th}$.

I asked Jonah if I could get a lift to the hotel with the wet sheets. He did a double take of me and the laundry, shrugged and said, "Nothing ventured, nothing gained." I told Vernon that I'd be back shortly, when the sun had dried his trousers, after which we would venture to the hotel for a feed and a few cold ones out of the tap. I had no intention of being seen with him sporting those hideous shorts.

Outside the gate, it became immediately apparent for Jonah's initial hesitation at my request for a lift. A severe-looking woman, the image of Joan Crawford in a 1940's picture, sat stiffly in the rear of a vintage Bentley. She was dressed entirely in black, drumming her fingers impatiently on the armrest. Sharkie graciously introduced me to his sister as a great friend, a fact that did not appear to create much of an impression. I suppose she had met quite a few of her brother's friends over the years, so I understood the reason for her coldness towards me perfectly well.

I had learned earlier that the sister's name was Barbara, and on calling her by that name, I was informed witheringly that to people of my ilk, she was accustomed to being addressed as Mrs Arrowsmith. Coming from a high ranker of the Salvation Army, I thought this put down a little harsh, but as I was becoming enamoured with the frigid old cow, I let it slide. I had never minded being insulted intelligently and with style. Sharkie had previously informed me that his sister had recently returned from a literary tour of Ireland. The walls in her house were packed with books from floor to ceiling.

Jonah had surreptitiously stowed the wet laundry in the vast boot, which would have accommodated Marie Antoinette's chattels when she took a trip and possibly a brace of footmen also. The requested lift was given the nod impatiently by Mrs Arrowsmith, and I mistakenly climbed into the front passenger seat assuming that Jonah, being Mr Arrowsmith, would sit next to Mrs Arrowsmith. This was not the case. Jonah was indeed Mr Arrowsmith, but Mrs Arrowsmith steadfastly refused to sit next to him or to be seen in public with her husband due to his maverick spirit, eccentric appearance and unwillingness to conform. Promoted to the rear seat, I took full advantage of the situation by separating brother and sister as Mrs Arrowsmith had detected Sharkie's highly flammable breath, exhibiting her displeasure by fanning herself with white lace gloves.

To get her mind on to something else, I asked her if she had visited the birthplace of W.B. Yeats when she was in Ireland. She looked at me as if to say what the fuck would you know about him and replied, "Yes." Desperately attempting to come up with a single stanza from *The Tower*, I came up with half of one.

"Ran, and with the garden shears, clipped an insolent farmer's ears and brought them in a little covered dish."

I boasted that I had visited Yeats' house in Dublin as though it could have been elsewhere. She replied that she also had been there and demanded to know why we had come to a halt outside a public house. Sharkie let me out; I turned and said, "Thank you and goodbye, ma'am." There was the aroma of lavender lingering as Sharkie's dragon's breath returned to torment.

As I took the bundle of laundry from Jonah, I heard her exclaim to her brother in a high contralto. "It's a pity you haven't more friends like that nice young man. You could have invited him for Christmas," she challenged. I recognised instantly why Sharkie had not. Why would anyone of common decency and equipped with all critical faculties, invite a friend to what he considered forty-eight hours of purgatory. He could not have known the immense pleasure I would have got out of drawing the old girl out. It was not to be. A literary sojourn denied. I would have pounded the tambourine and drank tea with a smile. She glanced at me once, with less ice in her eyes as the Bentley whispered away.

Neil, ever sympathetic to my frequent request to use the hotel's facilities, unnecessarily reminded me about Christmas lunch, kick off 1300 Hours. He had received a phone call from the girls thanking him for his kindness and sending their love, hugs and nose kisses to Hugh. I imagined the rib-cracking hugs and the wet nose rubs. Their father and brother were well and had landed them employment as roustabouts and shearers' cooks. The laundry washed and tumbling in the dryer, I had a shave, showered and took a taxi uptown to buy a gift for Neil and his wife Janet. They were both keen on fly fishing so I bought them the best box of fly-tying equipment in the shop. I chose the most expensive set and though not wishing to embarrass them, thought what the heck, they had been so good to me, treating me like family.

Heading back to the wharf, clean dry linen in hand, I encountered a fellow I had met at Lady Barron on Flinders Island. Sven was a Norwegian and had docked the day before. Sven's crew were his family, wife and two children who did their schooling on board and a young Tassie deckhand named Axel. Christmas Eve was a big night for them as I knew from experience sailing with Scandinavians. I was invited along, with the instruction not to bring presents or grog. I remembered Vernon and my promise to Sharkie. Recalling Tex's crayfish, I explained my dilemma to Sven who said he had unloaded at first light yesterday but had kept some in a tank including a couple of fair-sized fish. How was it possible to be so lucky so often?

At the shed, Vernon was patiently waiting with his tongue hanging out, clad in his dried crumpled odourless trousers. Deeming it wise not to delay the reconstruction of the bed any longer, we wrestled the mattress inside and made the bed as well as two clueless blokes could.

Stowing the box of fly-tying gear in the fo'c'sle head, we then marched like guardsmen to the pub. Vernon sank two schooners in as many minutes, then attacked two meat pies as if he hadn't eaten for hours, which he hadn't. I was in a quandary about what to do with him; not that I was his keeper, but since Sharkie had told Vernon that Hugh would 'see him right', I felt obliged to keep an eye on him until Sharkie's mountain stretch has expired. Sharkie had really done his best to be in reasonable shape prior to being whisked away to altitude. He was happiest at sea level. He feared and hated heights. He had never slept upstairs and had recurring nightmares concerning ladders and of clinging to the edge of a cliff.

I began to notice that Vernon was shaking uncontrollably, a condition often displayed by those who suffer from Delirium Tremens, a severe alcohol withdrawal symptom. I had seen many men afflicted with the shakes but Vernon out-shook them all. He was becoming steadier slowly, but half the contents of the first schooner soaked his clean shirt. Thankfully, this incident went unnoticed, but his speech was fast becoming mangled and I feared Vernon was about to become a liability. There was no way I would inflict him on Sven's family as there would be children present and plenty of drink. The thought of what Schnapps and Aquavit would do on top of the toxic cocktail now coursing through him, I preferred not to dwell on. Soon after lowering his third glass by half, Vernon dipped into his taxi fare bag and slurred that he wanted something with a bit of an edge to it and carelessly shouted for a double whiskey. This did not go unnoticed and Neil serving at the end of the bar waved me down.

"Shall I get a cab for your mate, Hugh?" Neil asked diplomatically. I explained as quickly as I could that this would not be a good idea and filled him in on the details of Vernon's previous forty-eight hours. Once again, this good man helped me out. Had I been aware of Vernon's level of inebriation, I would never have suggested coming to the pub, but he was a toper of many years and well-practiced in concealing such a matter.

Without any protest, we got Vernon into Neil's car and between us we bundled him along the wharf to Sharkie's caboose. Gradually, things were becoming clearer to Neil. He had known Sharkie for quite a while and was aware that he had been barred for life by a previous licensee. The ban had long been lifted, but Sharkie never went near the pub. There is a possibility that he was unaware the ban had been lifted, or maybe he was just being Sharkie. The key to the shed was in its usual place, hanging on a nail outside, defying trespassers. Vernon was still conscious when we sat him on Sharkie's blow up bed and muttering as to the whereabouts of his shipmate having no recollection of the Yuletide arrangements.

Neil was silently taking in the scene as if he had just crossed the threshold of the Old Curiosity Shop and stunned by the latrine as I moved the Holy Mother reverently to one side for Vernon's convenience and placing the piece of tatting over her head. Filling the tub with a few bottles of beer and ice, I repaired to the boat and returned with the 'edge' that Vernon was desperate for, half a pint of Talisker. Neil shuddered on seeing Vernon despatch a third of the glass in a gulp that reminded him, he said, of a Baleen whale, about which he was well informed through an experience as a young man he has dearly regretted. My empathy with him was profound as was my concern for Vernon whose face had become heterochromatic. I knew that it had been unwise of me to give him the whiskey, but had I left him conscious, he could take it upon himself to search for the source where he may have tumbled overboard and drowned. As it was, he was fast becoming comatose so propping the door open for air, we left him. Positive he would not stir until I returned in the early hours, we went back to the pub where we resumed our positions on the opposite sides of the bar.

Looking forward to the evening with Sven's family, I took it easy and played darts badly with all comers. Everyone of course wanted to hear tidings of the girls who had made an everlasting impression, interrogatively questioning me with posers, such as "Did ya get ya leg over the pair. Hugh?" All unanswerable.

Towards sundown, I returned to the wharf to check on Vernon and clean myself up. I had left a hose coiled in the sun; the water was hot enough to shave, and with the remainder diluted with cold water, it was sufficient to perform my ablutions. I changed into clean new clothes, brewed tea then settled back to re-engage with the Financial Times, which I had stuffed hurriedly under a cushion prior to welcoming the sisters aboard. After three minutes, I gave up trying to expand my fortune. It would probably have made more sense had it been printed in Icelandic. I took the paper to the shed and laid it at Mary's feet. Sharkie would make good use of it. The sound of blacksmiths' bellows issued from Vernon's gaping mouth. I felt his pulse which was as regular as a metronome.

Leaving a frozen pie which would have thawed somewhat by the time I returned, unless the cats had snaffled it, I wandered off to Sven's in the approaching dusk. As I neared the illuminated boat, church bells pealed in the distance reminding me, for whatever reason, of Sharkie. Why had he subjected himself to this brief but torturous period of abstinence? He was a proud independent man who took and expected nothing from his sister. There was some special bond between them because as Jonah had pointed out Sharkie could not recall the names of the rest of the family who annually attended these forty-eight hours of aridity and prayer. I would have loved the experience.

Sven's boat, longer than Tex's and broader of beam, rocked in the disturbance caused by a maniac passing at speed. Unconscionable conduct. The boat bedecked with festive lights; a spotlight shone on the hatch cover upon which was spread a white sheet. Plates, trays and bowls filled with food that could not have been acquired in Hobart, it took me back to the delicatessen in

Fortnum and Mason's in London. The beautiful wee girls in national costume were singing a nativity song in their father's native tongue. Sven advanced to the gangway with a menacing bottle of clear liquid, vision of a riotous party in Stavangar three years before reminded me to take care. I took a baptismal dram as protocol required, promising myself to stick to beer of which there were fish boxes filled with ice cooling Heineken, Carlsberg, Tuborg as well as the local brew Cascade. I was introduced to wife Anna, heavily with child and very charming, and about thirty others whose names went in one ear and escaped out of the other as they are wont to do.

We then went aft where in a large container of seawater moped two of the biggest crayfish I had so far seen. I had forgotten about them. Sven point blank refused payment at which I stated that if he did not accept a couple of quid, I would leave immediately. Sensing I meant it, he snatched and stuffed the money in his pocket and poured out another shot of aviation spirit. As a responsible loving husband and father, he then wisely stowed the bottle in a craypot whence we re-joined the party which comprised mostly of fisher folk, talking shop as people tend to do who have nothing else occupying their minds. Piling high the largest plate available from the array of gastronomic delights, I eased into a comfortable space and enjoyed the nicest Christmas Eve since I had left the Cotswolds in that 'Sceptred Isle'. The girls singing, dancing and presenting gifts to the young ones and plucking a bottle of beer from the ice when requested.

Sven came over after he had made a brief welcoming speech as I knew he would. To converse with someone familiar with the things and happenings of your past became a hunger after a long period, and at the end of an hour of reminiscences of Norway, Scotland, the Kon Tiki Expedition, Ibsen, Grieg, Burns, Amundsen, William Wallace, Quisling, of Ivanhoe and the Middle Ages, the pros and cons and validity of Minke Whaling, we were well sated but equally refreshed.

At around 2030 Hours, most of the young ones were curled up asleep, not even Sven's rendition of *Click go the Shears* in Norwegian disturbed their repose. Parents soon began stirring their children, enticing them with the need to get ready as Santa was already over Launceston. I said goodbyes and thanks for the lovely evening and departed with the two crayfish in a hessian bag and enough choice leftovers for Vernon's Christmas dinner if he had the appetite. I quickened my step hoping he was still alive.

He did not appear to have moved a muscle during my absence. The untouched bottles of beer confirmed this and the scattered pastry flakes indicated feline larceny. I needed an early night and intended getting one as an early rise was called for in order to restore the shed and surrounds to a state that would be in keeping with the idyllic littoral vista. Vernon and the shed would need a tougher detoxing as his bladder had sprung a leak several times.

*You don't know how fortunate you are, Sharkie*, I thought. Hoping for the best, I tumbled into my bunk in the fo'c'sle.

Waking at first light after a dreamless night, happy that Tex's crayfish had been replaced in the freezer, I brewed tea, made a sandwich of gravlax from the leftovers and enjoyed breakfast in the stateroom. Fortified, I steeled myself for the labour of Hercules that needed to be faced. Vernon was awake and reposing in something similar to the lotus position but with spastic modifications, sucking from a bottle of beer which shook like a maraca. A pool of piss encircled, coupled with the smell of excrement that clung in the morning ozone that drifted in from the Derwent, suggested that Vernon suffered from a chronic olfactory malfunction.

Wishing me a Happy New Year, to which I re-joined that I trusted we both would in seven days' time, I managed to get him to his feet and led him to the Holy Mother's hole; quickly replacing the tatting over her head which had been disturbed by the high tide, creating a blowhole effect. Propping Vernon up somehow whilst he divested himself of his long-suffering raiment, the irredeemable underpants being consigned to the outgoing tide. With a gaff hook at arm's length, I dragged the fouled clothes outside and under the tap, turning it on full blast and wondering who else in the world would be doing this on the twenty-fifth of December.

Filling two buckets with water and washing detergent, we used a piece of towelling and started sluicing off the caked dung. Several buckets of rinsing water followed that left Vernon, shall we say, presentable. I found one of Sharkie's T-shirts and with the psychedelic shorts sat him in the sun, then swabbed out the shed with a gallon of disinfectant. Not surprisingly, Vernon had no appetite for solids so I left him with a bottle of beer while he kept an eye on his urine-marinated cigarettes drying in the sun. It would be some time before they did, and I had no wish to be in the vicinity when he set fire to one.

Returning to my boat, I shaved and scoured myself raw, dressed in clean clothes and admired myself in the full-length mirror in the stateroom. Sober, healthy, fit and smart as a guardsman, though not quite as tall. With an hour to go before Christmas lunch was due, I attached a note of gratitude to the hosts' wrapped gift. Attempting interlocution with a dejected Vernon, I noticed there were positive signs of improvement in his condition when he called me by name and demanded a bracer.

"Not a fucking chance in hell," I replied brutally. "I don't want a fucking corpse on my hands when I return," I said softening a little. "I'll leave you some beer on ice and sandwiches," I said even kindlier. I had a soft spot for the drunken old bastard, but he had fallen asleep and didn't hear.

Cloud was thickening, threatening a thunderstorm. I tried shifting him to no avail. A drum of diesel would have been more compliant. A storm water soak wouldn't harm him one bit I thought, as I ambled off to lunch with the gift in one hand and a magnum of Moet Chandon in the other. A big noter, in the Australian vernacular. I was enjoying it. I had never been rich before.

Christmas lunch was not the private family affair that I had expected. Joining the family were several acquaintances I had met around the wharves and slipways, mostly old fellows returned from the sea, and of no particular fixed address. No drunks or rowdies, just amiable old salts earnestly trying to outdo one another with decorated yarns of whales, wrecks, typhoons and torpedo and Kamikaze attacks. Pop would have loved it; he could spin a yarn, especially about the Bismarck and salvaging sinking and sunk ships in the Thames estuary.

The happy lunch party began to run out of steam at about 1600 Hours with a few of the older men beginning to doze off. Neil had arranged for a couple of semi sober fellows to ferry them back to their respective lairs, sheds and sail lofts where I eagerly lent a hand.

Neil and Janet did not embarrass me by over-effusiveness when I presented the gift. They were delighted. Soon after, Neil got a phone call from Jonah asking for me. He called to advise that Sharkie's bloody record was in Tex's fridge. He had stowed it when I had left the freezer shed unlocked and unattended for a few minutes. Sharkie would have fretted over its disappearance, which coupled with the enforced temperance, would not have made him the life of soul of the party. I know I would have enjoyed it in spite of the masochism it suggested; even so I was hard pressed to imagine what they were doing for laughs.

Boxing Day would be business as usual so my offer to help clear away all evidence of the party which had been held in the public bar was well received. An hour later, the pub was ready to pump beer once more. Anticipating the sailing on the next day, I had controlled my intake of beer as had the landlords of the establishment, who suggested that we deserved a celebratory bottle of champagne. How could I say no? Since my sudden wealth, I had acquired the reckless habit of turning up at invitations with a bottle of fizz or malt, mostly for the show, I might add, as the stuff itself did not fit comfortably with my plebeian tastes. I was twenty-six years of age at the time, beer and skittles with a drop of plonk occasionally; vintage rarely. We drank a toast to Christmas and whatever the New Year heralded, then topped up our glasses with the remains of the bottle, the three of us sipping silently. What were they thinking of?

I could not get John Kennedy out of my mind for long. Hardly anyone I had met had spoken of his death, maybe using the Christmas and New Year stampede to preclude dwelling on the possible and probable repercussions of the shattering event. Using Vernon as an excuse, I took my leave of the generous couple who thoughtfully had packed some lunch for Vernon. The three of us needed an early night.

A sudden surge of guilt overcame me as I strolled back to the wharf, which I could not explain. The thunderstorm had not eventuated but a light shower had woken Vernon in time for him to rescue his urine-soaked cigarettes which had dried partially. Cursing loudly in his attempt to ignite one, spent matches strewed the ground. I had bought him a packet of cigarettes as I suspected he would need the aid of napalm to get a puff from one of his. Thinking I may as well have a bit of fun at his expense, I retrieved a foot-long cigar from my belongings on the boat. I had bought it in Cuba two years earlier whilst loading a cargo of sugar in the port of Matanzas. It was expensive and encased in an airtight light metal cylinder. I had been waiting to meet a deserving tobacco addict. Vernon did not exactly fit the criteria, but as Mark Twain said carelessly, "A woman is a woman but a cigar is a smoke." Fetching matches from the wheelhouse, we between us performed the longed-for ceremonial incendiary act with three cheers to Fidel Castro. Prior to setting fire to the cigar, I had detected an all too familiar stench; so, leaving Vernon impersonating Stephenson's *Rocket*, I entered cautiously the inner sanctum of Sharkie's shed. As I suspected, Vernon had voided his bowel without the aid of a bomb aimer. A powerful solution of disinfectant and bleach accompanied by choking wafts of smouldering tobacco leaf successfully fumigated the premises to such an extent that I witnessed cockroaches scuttling out of the door.

For the first time in my life, I recall beseeching Odin and Poseidon to allow time to pass quickly and for the 27th to arrive as speedily as possible, in order for me to be relieved of my duty by a sober Sharkie. I gave Vernon the Christmas fare, cigarettes, two long necks of beer, implored him not to burn the place down and left him wreathed in smoke and smiles. In my bunk, I read a book until it fell from my hand. Awakening after a dreamless night, I used and scrubbed the 'Heads' in Tex's cabin then ducked my head under Sharkie's tap. It was Boxing Day; I was expecting to be picked up by a crew anytime for a day's sailing and for whatever else was heading my way. Vernon was awake and cheerfully brewing a concoction that vaguely smelt of coffee and other components that I failed to positively identify. Politely declining a cup, I ventured to the ecclesiastic latrine with an optimistic mind and apart from replacing the tatting over the Holy Mother's adoring eyes, found all was in order. Obviously, the rationing of the beer had assisted in restoring Vernon to something approaching normality.

When I spoke to him, his eyes lit up immediately with a spark of comprehension; he was talking intelligibly; something I had not heard nor seen since I had hailed his taxi. Taking advantage of the situation, I put a proposal to him that it was essential to see that the place was clean and shipshape for the following day, adding that the agreement with Sharkie when they were both in their cups was tenuous to say the least, and a renegotiation might possibly need to be convened. Clear headed now, and aware that he would never be employed as a cabbie again, he came to realise the situation he was in. With his spherical, ruined body, getting other employment would be nigh on impossible. Sharkie, in spite of his addiction, was a proud and responsible man. The shed was his castle. Vernon said he would ask God for guidance. I backed him up by consulting my two. We then broke our fast on refrigerated leftovers. Vernon drank two mugs of the villainous brew. I watched him; the three witches of MacBeth incantating in my head. I drank water and contemplated the day ahead while providing Vernon with half a dozen long necks on ice, a can of beef stew, some eggs, a frozen loaf of bread and *500 Miles*. I watched this enigma of a man as he stuffed the last two inches of the cigar into a briar pipe that he had purloined from Sharkie's sea chest. His packet of cigarettes intact, he was a picture of bliss and contentment. A vehicle trailing a sharpie honked from the street. I sped off with a wave. We drove out of town in a south easterly direction for some time, and soon were in convoy with several other sharpies, and sometime later after a pleasant drive, we came to a part of the coast the name of which I have long forgotten. The day flew past all too quickly and in the fair, often gusty breeze we succeeded in flattening our boat twice. In the afternoon, following lunch, we tuned in to the start of the Sydney- Hobart Ocean Race. We competed once more; this time remaining on an even keel and crossed the finishing line in third place. They were a fine bunch of men, boys and women and girls whose company I enjoyed for several days. Their friendship and the days are still with me. With a little guilt and a lot of self-searching, I had to acknowledge that I was more at home with the Boyds, Sharkies and Vernons, who decorated the planet like frescos on a rendered wall. I did not deliberately seek the companionship of oddballs; far from it. I had always enjoyed my own company, but it had increasingly become a luxury as if the lodestone of my make-up drew weirdos and misfits continually on a collision course. I remember as a small boy, I was forever bringing home tramps to tea. On one occasion, an Indian pedlar made chapattis in my sympathetic mother's kitchen. He had met with stiff resistance at other cottages he had tried to tempt with his culinary skills. Question, was I a weirdo or an oddball? No one had ever called me one to my face. Deciding not to allow it to bother me, I left it behind.

Vernon was in good humour when I was dropped off at the wharf. Apart from an increasing thirst which apparently no amount of water could assuage, I obtusely suggested tea, coffee and a tin of tomato juice; none of which were considered appropriate in combating and staving off the dehydration that threatened to put an end to his life. Unable to torture him for more than a few moments, I poured him a generous bracer from a locked depository, which vanished without being sniffed or savoured in one carp-like gulp. An icy bottle of beer followed, inverted and poured in an unceasing torrent down his parched gullet as if performing a Trumpet Voluntary. I watched in awe and sympathy.

Entering the shed, my nose on red alert, I discovered all was well, Hail Mary. On Vernon's insistence I lightened his taxi fare bag of two quid, confirming my belief that Vernon was not a freeloader. I had had no opportunity to assess his true character since his arrival on Christmas Eve. I was now getting glimpses of the real Vernon. Puffing away on cigarette after cigarette, whiskey and beer coursing through his blood stream, he opened up about Tobruk and the unforgettable horror of the Western Desert, a period of his young life he had shared with Sharkie. Remembrances that caused cataracts of tears to flow. Drink, seemingly the sole panacea that drew the blinds over the experience. I gave him another bottle of beer to accompany the dozen eggs I had whisked up in which I had added the rest of the gravlax. Vernon cleaned his plate with the vigour of a foxhound pup, burped, lit another smoke and sipped his beer contemplatively, knowing that his mate was returning the next day, completely dried out. He was maybe thinking it a nice gesture to begin the day on sober terms. There was a fair chance that Sharkie would appreciate it, and on the other hand, he could think Vernon a bloody idiot as well. Who knew? On his return, I knew it would be the first and last chance I would get to see him sober.

The effects of the day's sailing were beginning to make themselves felt so I took a second bottle of beer from Tex's fridge and without making eye contact with Vernon wished him goodnight to which he replied, "Your blood's worth bottling, Hugh." I had not heard the term previously and knew not what it meant. Visions of Bram Stoker and Transylvania flashed before me as I self-administered a night cap of Talisker in the fo'c'sle followed by the beer and a hazy attempt to read some Longfellow, a gem entitled *Evangeline*, I had picked up in a second-hand bookshop. Thinking of the many hours I had spent in those treasure houses, I fell asleep.

Vernon was up and mopping out the shed by the time I had climbed out of my bunk. Bent on taking his first drink of the day with his digger mate, he appeared not to have taken any drink since my departure the evening before. A remarkable effort. He was shaved, washed and clad in the bilious shorts once more, his trousers dripping in the sun on a nail. Not knowing when Sharkie would return, but sure it would be sooner rather than later, he had risen in the dark, set on beating the sun to the yardarm.

I drank tea upwind of Vernon; his foul coffee and the tobacco reeking clouds which tumbled away in the breeze. An old lady of unfathomable vintage came past wheeling a 'sit-up-and-beg' bicycle with a wicker work basket attached to the bows. She lived on a house boat which was festooned with pots of pansies and herbs. She was profoundly deaf, a disability that at the time must have been a blessing, with the rowdy gatherings that often carried on till the early hours and the fact that she enquired kindly after Sharkie indicating that *500 Miles* was unknown to her. The despised record was in position on the turntable, defiant, awaiting the maestro's baton. The old lady asked me if I wanted anything from the shops. I gave her a pound note and said, "Yes, please, a dozen eggs, a pound of bacon and fresh bread, and buy yourself something nice." She beamed, mounted her bicycle and glided off. Straight backed; Oxford blue stocking. We sat wondering what would happen first, the descent of the prisoner of the mountain or a dish of bacon and eggs. We spoke not a word. Sober Vernon with a tormented frown dragged nicotine into his lungs and bloodstream. His vermillion face in the morning sun, smudged here and there with chartreuse. He was suffering and trembling. I suffered also witnessing his plight. Should I break out the usquebaugh? Just the one! Deciding against it, I went for a 'turn around the poop' in order to think. I felt better not having to look at him. I could not think of cooking breakfast until Vernon had been partially restored. I ambled past the houseboat where Black Bhageera, the old lady's cat, yawned and sunned himself, then sauntered back to the shed in time to meet the old girl whizzing down the wharf, basket loaded with breakfast fare. Cornflakes and fruit for herself, milk and minced meat for her cat. A treat she said, as she normally fished for him. She was vegetarian and purchased the meat and bacon under duress. I empathised, recalling the surges of guilt as a boy shooting for the pot. "I spent the whole pound," she said, as if confessing a sinful extravagance.

About to ferret in the basket for our much looked forward to breakfast, she was the first to spot Sharkie and Jonah ambling towards us. Sharkie, parchment faced and sober as a Quaker, leaden visaged Jonah holding his arm, both squinting in the sun. The old lady greeted Sharkie with New Year wishes, and sensing that peace would not reign for much longer wheeled away to give her cat the surprise of his life. With supreme effort, Vernon rose to his feet, and they fell into each other's arms, blubbering their relief. I handed each an icy long neck, which they swilled down their arid throats. Beads of perspiration washed the tears away. With bacon sizzling, the tub of ice and beer, *500 Miles* suggesting a lament for the dead, the neighbourhood welcomed the king from exile.

Sharkie had a large, battered suitcase with him. On it a label stated that it would not be required on voyage. Inside were a dozen bottles of whiskey, two hundred cigarettes, some old clothes from his younger days, which would require extensive letting out, a loaf of white bread plus a weighty mound of sausages. To me, he presented with a smile and a pat on the arm, a neatly wrapped brown paper package. It contained a book by Oliver St John Gogarty, an Irish wit and author, who among his many achievements became one of the first senators of the Irish Free State. The book was titled, *Tumbling in the Hay*. Inside was the mesmerising inscription: 'To my brother's friend Hugh. Best wishes. Barbara Arrowsmith.' Why had she sent me this book with its suggestive connotation? Was she yearning for something long ago that had passed her by; an opportunity that her godliness had denied her, leaving her to fantasise about what might have been? I wondered whether after its publication, was Gogarty meant to cross over the road at the approach of a bishop? The book remained in my possession for some years until someone 'borrowed' it. I sent a note of thanks with Jonah and walked with him to the road where the Bentley purred, shook hands with both he and Ivan and waited while they motored silently out of sight and out of my life.

With Sharkie in residence once again, I could now relinquish my role as caretaker and free to re-engage with the sailing fraternity. Sharkie stated he intended getting back to normal, which I took to mean permanently half sozzled, which suited him rather than getting paralytic. I think this was for the benefit of Vernon, letting him into the privacy of his life without laying down the law. A certain order had to be maintained. The newspaper was scoured each morning for any interesting news that he may wish to discuss with passers-by, provided it was not political and concerned with what the incumbent government were likely to ordain or abolish in the near future or never. A loaf of white bread was delivered daily; every other day, a butcher's boy brought sausages. Beef one day, pork the next. "Variety is the spice of life," he sagely informed me. The supply of tomato sauce was stringently monitored. The largest and most important consignment of the week were the six half gallons of sweet sherry which came regularly at 1600 Hours on a Friday afternoon. The lack of space being the sole obstacle that precluded him from ordering the wine by the butt or pipe, which would have eliminated the weekly stress of uncertainty leading up to the appointed hour.

While Sharkie had been counting off his formula for the perfect life Vernon had dozed off. I took this opportunity to ask Sharkie to fill me in on some of the details of North Africa, as I did not intend broaching the subject when Vernon was up and about. Vernon had been invalided home a nervous wreck; Sharkie himself had been too close to a shell burst thus earning a steel plate in his head. He demonstrated its location by attaching a horseshoe magnet to his head. It was extremely difficult to keep a straight face, which I thought was appropriate considering the seriousness of his wound. So, when Sharkie smiled, I roared with relief.

The days leading to the New Year were spent sailing and fishing with Sharkie from his dinghy, after breakfast and before sherry. If after sherry, we fished from the old lady's boathouse under the supervision of Bagheera. The craypot was checked daily and rebaited with no success apart from a diminutive evil-looking octopus. The illegal gill net remained buried in the shed avoiding the risk of a hefty fine. One day, I invited everyone to lunch up town, but Sharkie declined as Vernon's legs had ceased to function properly by midday. The old lady was thrilled though, and we walked to town, she, wheeling her bicycle with the basket in case she spied something interesting to put in it. Lunch in a milk bar; salad, followed by a double order of rhubarb crumble made her day. I bought her all the rhubarb crumble remaining and the happy old thing whizzed off singing at the top of her voice, while I strolled to the pub to say hello to Neil and Janet. I had placed a huge order with Neil for Hogmanay and stocked Tex's fridge and freezer with enough food until Easter.

Plans awry, as they so often were in those carefree days, I did not see the climax to the Ocean Race which was won on handicap by the Halvorsen brothers of Sydney in 'Freya'. 'Astor' took line honours. This was due to an offer from a group of twitchers who were sailing to Southport and the South East Cape, with particular interest in fairy penguins.

I had not sighted nor heard from Tex since docking. Rumour had it that he was in Europe, an odd time of the year to venture north, unless a lady was involved. A tryst perhaps in Gstaad; with a ski instructress, abounding with energy by day on the piste and keen to tire a man out thoroughly by night. Pre-empting his return, and possibly casting off with my worldly goods, I had stowed my gear in his shed, along with a note partially explaining my circumstances.

Free to collect my thoughts and think clearly, not knowing or caring if we ran south until we came upon pack ice, I prayed for the well-being of the two damaged diggers, then put them out of mind in order to be a worthy crewman on the ornithological expedition.

A guilty memory flashed before my eyes as we harnessed a fresh north easter and sped down the coast in a beautiful gaff rigged top'sl schooner. A vision I swiftly extinguished. I had no need for redemption, I repeatedly consoled myself. I had not killed a penguin. We were going to tag penguins. I felt good about this as I would be able to hold one and everything would be all right forever after. I had not sailed in such a boat before; she was well seasoned and the timbers creaked as I lay in my bunk. A lovely sound, which very soon only a lucky few will fall asleep to.

Catching penguins at night, watching them waddle out of the surf with torches and cameras instead of clubs and hessian bags. They fell into our hands with a single squawk then calmed as we stroked, soothed, tagged and in my case, kissed them. Released, they padded to their burrows as if being tagged and kissed was an everyday occurrence. At anchor, we baited a craypot nightly with lambchops, and fished, catching large flathead, one was five inches between the eyes. Black snakes sluggishly slipped off sunny rocks at our approach. Some did not. One bold fellow grabbed one behind the head for all to examine, saying it was possible to tame one. I took him at his word as there was no likelihood of my putting his claim to the test.

We returned to Hobart mid-January, mahogany skinned, hair the colour of ripe wheat and dangerously fit. Drinking had been minimal as we had to be alert and sober going ashore prior to the penguins' homecoming. Back on board, we were rewarded with whiskey and discussed the day's proceedings with amusing thoroughness when I enjoyed the acceptance that those academics un-patronisingly bestowed on me. They listened to the tales of my boyhood in the Cotswolds, of the Blitz in London, of Scotland, my joining the Royal Navy at fifteen years of age and reaching the dizzying heights of Signalman. Taught to read at the age of four but still baffled with the hieroglyphical symbols of mathematics. One member of the party had served in the Indian Army and enthralled us of an evening with bloodcurdling reminiscences of serving with the Chindits in Burma. I suspect this admirable gentleman, who boasted a very expensive purple-veined nose, had a private supply of highland mist as his glass was never empty. Every so often, he would venture for'ard in order to ensure the anchor was not dragging. As the evening wore on, he began calling 'Chota Peg' to an imaginary turbaned houseboy. No one took any notice of this and nothing was mentioned at the breakfast table, which he presided over with charm and erudition. I had never mixed with folk like these and readily adopted their laissez-faire attitude towards life.

With difficulty I bade them farewell and made my way to my temporary home via the pub, where I found birthday and Christmas mail waiting. There was a card from the sisters, it contained love and kisses, and forty quid. I had told them that I did not lend money. They had chosen to disregard my emphatic directive. Rabelaisian they were, but very proud women. Neil was eager to learn of my trip of which he admitted to being extremely envious. It took four beers to fill him in between serving customers.

Eventually, I got away; keen to see how the Bacchanalian duo were faring. After three weeks' absence, I anticipated change, and I was not surprised to see the boat missing, but it was still like being kicked in the stomach. "Vanished one night," Sharkie announced resignedly. Tex had left early one morning while they were sleeping off a big night. Mysteriously, *500 Miles* had disappeared once more. I tried to catch Vernon's eye, but he refused contact. "How could you, Vernon?" I muttered to myself. I was moving on. What did I care if Sharkie played it until the turn of the century?

They were sipping sherry from half pint mugs and discussing a note from sister Barbara, which had been delivered by Ivan that morning. A terse enquiry, asking Sharkie where he would like to be buried. She must have thought the subject too macabre to bring to the table over Christmas. She was prepared to meet the cost of his interment but not those of his derelict associate. Vernon said he did not give a rat's arse and astutely observed. "Youse don't see too many left lying about on top." I did not think it my business to offer a solution to what would be an irreversible decision, so I turned to the empty berth where my home of the past few months had been secured. With a pang of desolation, I turned away from the spot, never to look at it again. Retrieving my gear from Tex's shed, I noticed the note had been read. I gave the key to Sharkie informing him that I was moving on and to avail himself of the booze and provender apart from the crayfish. We then solemnly and ceremoniously drank a bottle of whiskey between us. Shaking hands with the moist-eyed pair who were no longer capable of standing, I weaved my way to the pub and clean sheets in a comfortable bed and slept like Rip van Winkle.

I had never enjoyed farewells, usually resorting to poltroonery. This was the case the next morning upon realising I had not visited the old lady on the previous day. An impossibility now as it would entail running the gauntlet of the Chateau de Sharkie. I was not up to it. I was becoming too attached, a definite hindrance when one is young, wealthy and with new territory to cover. Farewelling Neil and Janet was easier. I would not sever contact; I would send them a forwarding address when I chose to tarry a while.

## Hobart to Strahan

Guilt forbade a taxi so I asked directions to a used car yard of ill repute that Vernon had mentioned, where awkward questions were not asked and any name would do for cash. I drew money from the bank and picked up a cheque book, something I had never had or needed before, then caught a bus in the general direction of the purveyor of suspect conveyances, trusting he was not behind bars.

Out of town and through suburbia, a mundane landscape which differs little in any city in the world, signs of industry appeared here and there. Alighting at the first halt, the conductor directed me to a side street where within moments I located my quarry. Armed with Vernon's vivid description, I was not surprised on coming upon a wreckers' yard, neither was I exultant with the discovery. A man had seen me coming; his eager anticipatory stride suggested he had seen many a gullible sucker coming. Reeking of diesel, he reached for and grasped my hand and shook it like an old friend. He was clad in overalls, heavily impregnated with grease, oil and paint. A fire hazard.

As I had arrived on foot and not coaxing a smoking, rattling Heath Robinson contraption to his yard, it was obvious he could smell money. I could definitely smell him as he shook my hand again, so ecstatic he was to see me, enquiring whether I was looking for a 'nice set of wheels'. It took a supreme effort not to reply that I was interested in purchasing a Cobb & Co stage coach and confirmed that I was indeed a little tired of walking. His extra sensory antenna ears immediately zeroed in on my Pommie accent and he began rattling off makes of British vehicles, Morris Minor, Vauxhall and Austin of various vintage and states of roadworthiness. A black Wolseley stood stoically and defiant in the front row of the phalanx of well-travelled wrecks that begged for attention as the unloved, lost or unwanted do in a dog pound. At some stage in its life, the Wolseley appeared to have covered some distance on its roof and had amateurishly disguised bullet holes in the bonnet, which added to its disfigurement or charm as the case maybe. Enjoying his Runyonesque spiel, which I had no wish to interrupt, I gave him plenty of rope. I had had invaluable experience in many ports from Tangier to Alexandria where I had majored in bizarre negotiations.

The most important lesson I had absorbed was that there never was a salesman who could bear watching money walk out of his yard or shop. Irrespective of the adage 'Buyer Beware', the buyer still has the advantage. The verbalistic flow was having little effect as I had already chosen a Morris Minor in the fourth row. This would require a fair amount of marshalling and would involve the resuscitation of at least half a dozen of the geriatric machines in order for me to test drive, purchase and set off on my exploration of the Apple Isle. The extrication of the Morris was achieved after thirty minutes of jump starting, ear-splitting detonations and the reinflation of many tyres. The air was becoming acrid and blue with smoke and even bluer with fluent Anglo-Saxon profanities. A prophecy of Vernon's eventuated on discovering a prayer book in the glove compartment proving beyond doubt that the vehicle had been religiously cared for by the church-going previous owner.

The battery of the Morris Minor, which had morphed into a block of blue vein cheese, refused to give any sign of life even with jump leads attached. Swapping batteries with an aged chariot, which had been shuddering with indignant rage on being disturbed, the Morris roared into life immediately, eliciting a joyous whoop from the sweating proprietor as if he had hit the jackpot, which in fact he had. He sensed a sale.

An enquiry as to the price was met with:

"It's a giveaway bargain at one hundred and forty pounds," he said magnanimously.

"I've only got eighty pounds," I practically whined.

"That'll do," he flashed back. He could feel my eighty quid already in his undernourished wallet. Eight red tenners (known as bricks); I knew exactly how he was feeling, he would do anything to seal the deal.

The gear stick was strange to me in the Morris, with the pedals seemingly too close together. It took some time to stop crow hopping around the yard, and when I finally had the car moving relatively smoothly, I headed for the gate. Pre-empting me by five seconds, the front entrance had been hurriedly shut. He was not letting me out of his sight. I was beginning to feel embarrassed. What kind of people dealt with him? I needed to get out and he wanted the eighty pounds.

"Fill her up with petrol and the money's yours," I offered. We both signed a filthy scrap of paper which indicated that the vehicle would require re-registering in four months. I knew nothing about cars or engines, they always were and remain an enigma. In my greenness and self-delusion, I convinced myself that the next four months would be plain sailing. Four months equalled one hundred and twenty trouble free days at fifty miles per day. I should cover a fair chunk of the countryside.

The money stuffed into his wallet, he gave a signal to a youth who carelessly splashed fuel into the tank. The young man then ambled over to the gate, which he opened with a supercilious gesture, as if releasing a bull at a Corrida. The Morris was revving in pole position, was it as Aston Martin or a Maserati? As I shot out of the yard, the spotty young cretin gave the V sign and mouthed a crude epithet which I lip read as Pommie Wanker. I took no offence. He was correct in both instances. However, I had the resolve to improve myself.

On the road, I slowed to get used to the gear stick and pedals; on speeding up, the car seemed to be running smoothly, albeit manifesting an air of impatience. Calling at a garage in a small village, all was explained by a mechanic with a smiling quizzical countenance, who emerged from a dark cavernous workshop wiping his hands on a piece of towelling.

"I 'erd ya coming 'arf a mile away; dya always drive in second gear?" he growled.

I said that I had purchased it that day and had driven it but a few miles.

"I know exactly 'ow many miles you 'ave drove it, mate, from that fuckin' burglar yard back in town, the last one. Am I roight?"

"Correct in every detail," I said.

"Well, ya dun orright getting 'ere. I usually 'ave to tow is fucken 'eaps of junk here."

"Do you mean to tell me the man's dishonest?" I sensed that the chap was feeling sorry for me.

"Dishonest, the cunt shoulda been in jail years ago," he growled.

He then enquired how much I had parted with and on being advised, muttered, "The fucken robbin' cunt."

It was clear that the two men were known to one another and were not on the best of terms, so in defence I threw in that I had had the petrol tank filled.

"Run 'er over to the bowser, mate, and we'll see if 'e's dun wun honest thing in his life."

It transpired that he had not, the tank was a quarter full. The petrol gauge was stuck halfway, and it remained so until the car's last gasp.

While filling the tank he asked where I was heading. Not having a clue, I replied that I was bound for Queenstown, which was the first place that came to mind and a considerable distance to the North West. Taking this in, I could see him weighing up my prospects as to whether I would get halfway or being taking in tow a couple of miles down the road.

Two small shops glared at each other a couple of hundred yards off, on opposite sides of the road. Both were newsagents and both claimed to stock the best ice cream and the iciest cold drinks in the Southern Hemisphere. Prominent placards announced, this was the spot to catch up with the news and quench one's thirst. Upon asking which one he would recommend, it appeared to be much of a muchness.

"But go to me daughter's one on the left or she'll abuse the shit out of me."

I thanked and parted company with this most forthright of men with his inspiring words ringing in my ears.

"Good luck, mate, don't speed. Keep 'er under a 'undred. Send us a postcard from Queenstown." I drove to the shop in second gear smiling at his droll farewell.

The daughter was holding the fly screen door open for me. Her father had given her a call, ensuring a welcome, lest I should patronise her competitor. I bought bread, fruit, dried and canned goods and a newspaper from the friendly woman who directed me to the pub, which stood off from the road and just around the bend. Thanking her, I confidently started the car and drove off with the owner of the other shop glaring at me. Leaving them to their private war of attrition, hoping that they would not take up arms, I decided that it was not worth searching for the top gear on the short trip to the inn.

Taking on a part cargo of liquid refreshments and discovering that like Bethlehem there was no room at the inn nor a stable, I resolved to press on to the next large town, as the thought of spending the night in a rattle trap of a car with the back seat piled up high with booze did not seem a good idea. I had no wish to incur the interest of the local constabulary as I could not be sure of the history of the Morris or if in fact, I legally owned it.

On sea voyages, as is well known, it is imperative to refer to charts, use a sextant and compass in order to pinpoint with any degree of accuracy one's precise location on the planet. Without these instruments to plot a course, should you wish to sail from Liverpool to Baltimore, in all probability you could make landfall in either Bermuda or Baffin Island. On land for the most part, navigational aids can be dispensed with, rules relaxed or completely ignored, unless by chance you should find yourself in the middle of the Gobi Desert or the Taiga. In the many ports I called at in my sea going years, I never once consulted maps or tour guides, finding that luck and haphazardness invariably resulted in unexpected adventure and delight. Such was the case as sans road map, the Morris, some hours later motored into Bridgewater.

A memory of Somerset and the West Country, a whiff of scrumpy and fermenting apple orchards. Who needs a map? Just follow your nose. You could not do this at sea, unless you were a Polynesian or an Arab dhow trader. I had followed the garage owner's kind advice and the speedometer needle had not recorded 100 miles per hour, in fact it had only exceeded 40 mph when occasionally I happened upon the elusive top gear and travelling downhill. The old car was enjoying herself and still in one piece, so was I. I could wish for no more.

I rely on memory of those faraway days having never kept a log book. Dates and place names vague and unreliable. Does history record the exact date Marco Polo pulled into Samarkand? I doubt it. The intrepid fellow had more on his mind than wondering what day it was. I had read several accounts of the battle of Agincourt. In all, three different dates are claimed, the 23rd, 24th, 25th. After the three-week march through the pissing rain of Northern France in October, this discrepancy maybe excused, don't you think?

Over a drink or two in a friendly pub, I gleaned information as to where camping gear could be acquired plus the necessities for surviving in the bush. I related my experiences with black snakes on Babel Island and my penguin study adventure to the South East Cape. One and all were emphatic that prevention was better than the cure and pointed to the Overproof Bundaberg rum bottles on the shelves. A very old, skeletal educated gentleman insisted that the apothecary's measure of eight drachms should be allowed to pulse through the blood stream constantly to ensure permanent immunity. They were a cheerful, helpful lot, full of valuable tips and advice, in addition to a fair amount of leg pulling and bullshit. At closing time, they wished me luck as I weaved my way up the stairs to my room, with the Morris parked safely at the rear of the pub.

I was unaware that the tariff included breakfast. In the morning, I was alerted to the fact by the landlady hollering from a window as I was about to seek elsewhere for my early morning provender. An urgent desire exacerbated by the saliva-activating aromas emanating from the kitchen. Three men were seated at the long deal table being served by a stout perspiring woman who cooked, waited on table and presumably washed up as well. Two of the men were encumbered in suits. Salesmen, I guessed. Neither spoke a word to anyone during the entire meal. Rivals, I supposed, hawking the same wares. One, without much enthusiasm, poked toasted vegemite soldiers into a solitary boiled egg. One egg! I was sure the smiling rosy-cheeked cook would have boiled him half a dozen, but then he did appear to be a little dyspeptic. The other cove was no trencherman either; dolefully spooning soggy cornflakes into a reluctant mouth. I could not envisage him getting very far before he collapsed. I moved a chair closer to the third man who sat like Henry VIII plundering the plates and dishes that the cook placed on the table. When his plate which had held a T-bone steak was removed, the T-Bone lay bleached, as if picked clean by hyena and vulture. Kaleidoscopic visions exploded in my head of the Kalahari Desert. The man was a thoroughbred. The cook-cum-waitress took my order as she placed a replica T-Bone in front of the giant. He grunted his thanks and enquired as to how I was going; vernacularised of course, in the customary Aussie idiom, leaving no doubt to its authenticity and sincerity. I replied, "Good thanks, how are ya going?"

Swallowing a mouthful of T-Bone, he replied, "Good mate, Pom are ya?"

"Correct, how'da guess?" I joked.

With his maw crammed to capacity, he laughed with his eyes then drank from a mug that a kitten could have drowned in. The bacon and eggs I had ordered were supplemented by a sausage, a mound of baked beans, fried tomatoes and a greasy pile of fungi. Not wishing to appear stunned in front of my breakfast companion, I plunged in with exaggerated gusto and looked up as if to seek his approval. Nodding his head as he gnawed at the T-Bone, he said, "If ya want ya steaks well done yer betta tell 'er ta stick 'em on now," he advised.

Not wanting to lose face, I worked my way laboriously through the meal that normally I would have carried away with me between slices of bread. Catching the eye of the cook, I conveyed by elaborate sign language that my appetite had been assuaged. My friend the voracious carnivore was now engaged in dolloping a stack of toast with alternate spoonful of honey and marmalade, sluicing it down with pints of scalding tea. Curious, I asked what his occupation was. He replied between gaseous eruptions that he was engaged in various pursuits, but that his main interest was in the stock exchange. My knowledge of business and finance was practically non-existent. Stocks and shares and the stock exchange conjured up scenes of shouting men in suits, sweating, collar and tie awry; and a platform of white shirt sleeved young men chalking Sanskrit on a blackboard and bafflingly erasing same a few seconds later. This amiable bear of a man bore no resemblance to my idea of a stockbroker. Maybe he was on holidays. I decided not to pursue the matter. Farewelling the cook, we took our leave. At the rear of the pub, it was like standing next to a Huon Pine as he said, "See ya later, mate – jeez, yer driving that. I was gonna give yer a lift."

He was picking up sheep in New Norfolk and transferring them to Richmond, then loading bullocks for somewhere else. Hauling his towering frame into the cabin of a juggernaut stock truck, he then sat rolling cigarettes while the engine warmed up, then extending a huge arm we shook hands and with a rumbling roar the truck snaked its way on to the road to continue its business of exchanging stock, leaving me wondering what he would enjoy for lunch.

The Morris chugged into life immediately, which was very encouraging and made me wish the truck driver had witnessed its eagerness after his disparaging remark suggested that someone had pushed it here and abandoned it. It began to shower; I would soon discover if the roof leaked. It did not. I activated the wiper blades, the sun-perished rubbery parts disintegrated after ten seconds, flinging pieces left and right.

I sat in the car reading yesterday's newspaper, watching runnels of water clean the windscreen. I had not noticed how begrimed it had been. The rain ceased after a few minutes, and I drove to the nearest garage, where in those days, garages could be relied upon for assistance as diverse as replacing a headlight or mending a broken axle, not merely a fuel outlet-cum-grocery store-cum-newsagent.

Topped up with petrol and sporting new wipers, we were prepared to weather the monsoon. We! I had subconsciously let the little Morris into my life to such an extent that it was now us and we. She was the only companion I had. Snails no doubt felt the same way. Small wonder she took her time getting anywhere.

Following the directions given by the previous evenings' merry makers, I located an army disposal store, a fascinating barn of intrigue. Baffling equipment and gadgets filled the shelves and hung from rafters. Clothing from the Korean conflict and the Second World War; topees and pith helmets from the Boer War; fur hats for Polar regions. An ancient sledge waiting for snow and may have slid with Mawson. Iron cooking pots that I was informed were capable of producing an Irish stew or a birthday cake; the heavy lid doubled as a frying pan. I bought one, snared by its diversity and apparent indestructibility. For fifteen shillings, a moth-holed tee-pee-shaped Army tent was added to the pile of essentials. It weighed half a hundred weight dry; immovable after rain, I suspected. A swag, I had been informed was a must, and it was what the Americans call a bedroll. In fine weather, no need for the tent. Just lay it out, zip it up to the chin, gaze at the Southern Cross and put the thought of snakes, spiders and maybe a Tasmanian Devil, eager to keep you company, right out of your mind. Sober, I did not think that I was up to this. Sleeping in the swag sounded fine, but in the tee-pee tent. I was keen to erect it. There was history in its musty smell.

Panoramic scenes of Spion Kop and Magersfontaine glided past. I searched for bearded Boers bullet holes.

Sundry items including a four-gallon fuel can, kept the store assistant on his toes and the store owner happily ringing up the damage on the till. Fitting it all in the Morris was a challenge. What with booze and supplies on the back seat. Finally, the swag and fuel can, wedged in the boot, the tent crammed in the front passenger seat, I was waved off into the hinterland by two bemused individuals, who I could see in the cracked rear vision mirror shaking hands and probably making wagers with one another or congratulating themselves on the day's turnover.

With my pocket compass, I laid a course to the north west, abandoning plans to visit the convict barracks at Port Arthur. Wrestling with my conscience, I asked myself repeatedly why would I wish to explore a settlement of infamy and misery, where men were treated sub-humanly? I acknowledged that for the most part the prisoners were guilty of heinous crimes and largely intractable. The lash, used for the slightest misdemeanour, appeared to be an act of revenge. They had been punished enough. I readily confess to a morbid infatuation in historic battle grounds. I had gazed on the field of Agincourt visualising swarms of arrows and the fluttering banner of St George. As a Royalist boy at Edgehill, close by my birth place, on Midsummer evening, sounds and cries of combat could be heard if you were a believer, and I was devout. In both these conflicts, the opposing armies were willing participants.

Satisfied that I had made the right decision, we motored at a pace that a post-chaise or a Hansom cab would have had little difficulty in exceeding for an hour in a part cloudy and showery day with occasional shafts of sunshine lasering through. We passed and disappointed several hitchhikers, guiltily indicating the tent. Once I pulled up for two young women to advise them that I had no room in the car for them. They suggested that I should get an apparatus that could be attached to the roof. A roof-rack, unknown to me. A village of great charm welcomed us, where we topped up with a pint of petrol and filled the fuel can. A roof rack not being obtainable, I was advised that the risk of additional weight to the stoic Morris may well be the proverbial straw that brought the camel to its knees. A scruffy wayfarer loitered near as I was about to leave, who insulted the Morris for the second time.

"Sorry, no room," I said, stating the bloody obvious.

"That's okay, mate, I'm in a hurry anyway," he sneered.

We ignored the slur and drove off determined not to bother with top gear as she seemed perfectly content the way things were. She felt safe with me, confident that she would never be borrowed by would-be bank robbers but to enjoy a Romany life for a while. At around noon, following the Derwent River in another small town or rather a sizeable village, a pub adjacent to a bakery invited me to partake of Australia's favourite snack. The esteemed meat-pie. Ravenous, I devoured one in two minutes, stoutly abstaining the offer of the tomato sauce. Next door, cold beer the mandatory soul mate of this culinary delight, rather than take the edge off my hunger pangs brought on a surge of hoggishness that only another pie would satisfy.

Enticing aromas wafted from the patisserie, customers barged in to choose their lunch. Every kind of pie, including apple, came forth from the kitchen on steaming trays along with pasties and sausage rolls. Pies the dimension of manhole covers ticketed family pies. I pictured my breakfast acquaintance unfazed by its size with no family in sight. I bought two more normal-sized pies, in case of an emergency, I told myself. Letting the fly screen door crash shut for the twentieth time in two minutes, allowing very nippy flies only to invade, I drank two middies and toyed with the idea of parking outside for a week. Lethargy and sloth, while not firmly established character defects, had often lured me towards a wayward path.

Idle thoughts dismissed. There was a campsite to be found. The erection of the tent. I imagined veldt dust besmirching the verdancy of the meadow by a babbling stream where brown trout rose for flies.

### Making Friends with a Farming Family

This vision soon became a reality. A laughable fiasco was enjoyed by a brawny sheep farmer, his wife and a gaggle of kids whose amusement kicked off with the sight of the Morris lurching up their rutted track. Feigning alarm, the kids hid from view behind rainwater butts and chook sheds, aiming make-believe firearms at our noisy approach.

Exiting the car cautiously, hands in the air surrounded by hysterical collies and kelpies, I was assured by a small girl that my life was not under threat and I could put my hands down, whereby the rest of the bushranger gang emerged from their places of concealment with the exception of one persistent brigand keeping up murderous machine gun fire, until hauled from cover by his mother and advised to desist in no uncertain terms. With the cease fire, question time commenced in earnest.

"How far 'ave yer come in this bomb?"

"Where yas headin?"

"Wherever it is, ya can't be in a hurry."

We took the banter in good heart; the kids' noses pressed to the windows and being swatted about the ears for doing so. A wonderful welcome, I thought. The ice being truly broken, I was swept, pulled and pushed into the house for afternoon tea. Hot scones, butter, jam and a wonderful crab apple jelly together with a capacious teapot were placed on the table that would have accommodated a rugby team. Only then did the introductions begin.

Ted and Diane were royalists through and through and had named their seven children accordingly, which is the sole reason I recall their names. Three girls were the eldest of the brood. Anne, Victoria and Elizabeth, followed by Johnny, George, Eddie and Harry. The three girls, the eldest being fourteen years of age, were very pretty and polite and would have sat well on the throne of England. The boys were strikingly handsome and had Sicilian bandit written all over them. Fortunately, they were well under the control of their big sisters and a very handsome mother.

Apart from the sounds of mastication, silence reigned for a few minutes. With crammed mouths, interlocution would have proved difficult and an utter waste of eating time. I had noticed a huge piece of meat, presumably a part of a sheep carcass, in a baking dish on the wood stove. Potatoes, pumpkin and carrots encircled it as do pilot fish squire a shark, obviously this tea party was merely a prelude to more serious gourmandising. Tea over and not a crumb remaining, boys licking jam from fingers, girls conscientiously dabbing lips with hankies, boys laughing at them, mother rising with plate hiding a smile. Dad stifling a burp and then deciding against it causing more laughter which brought on a salvo of volcanic flatulence, driving all female members from the house in giggling protest.

The working day being far from over, we trooped outside. There were sheep in several pens patiently waiting for something to happen. The youngest girls were collecting eggs from the hens' hiding places and the eldest one was driving a tractor out to a paddock on an urgent mission, judging by the pace of it. As we walked to a wooden fence where an old horse was chewing the top rail, followed by sniffing dogs and the four bandits, Ted prompted me by asking if I was wanting somewhere to camp. I said I was, and with his arms outstretched pointed to three thousand acres in which to pitch my tent. We had been joined by the two younger girls by then, who in unison with their brothers loudly acclaimed that the tent should be erected on the front lawn. I was in a bit of quandary especially when Ted offered the use of the shearers' quarters. Embarrassed now with the choices, I protested that I did not wish to be an inconvenience.

"You won't be, mate, I need a hand at the moment if ya wouldn't mind, the kids are too young and Mum forbids me to put 'em at risk."

I could have shouted with joy.

"I am a born and bred country boy," I said, "but I know bugger all about sheep husbandry."

"No matter," he said. "As soon as I saw ya get out of the car, I sez to meself, 'ere's a stroke of luck, fit as a Mallee bull, with Mum's cookin' 'e might hang about for a month. Watcha think?" he said pleadingly.

"It would be an honour," I said, and meant it.

We shook hands and with a wallpaper brush he daubed sump oil on the top rail of the fence. The old horse shied away.

"Poor old bugger's mopin'; his mate died a month ago, gotta a donkey cumin' in a couple of days; he'll be alroight then."

The boys were keen to conduct me to the horse's grave site, adding that it was not very deep and we could dig some of it up. At that, Ted told them to bugger off, and they did for a few yards to keep out of the way of his boot.

The shearing quarters were ideal, with shower, lavatory and a radio. Five-star lodgings in my book. At the insistence of the kids, the tent still had to be erected, something I was keen on too. I drove the Morris to the front of the house. Excitement mounting, fastenings untied with difficulty, finally the tent lay rolled out to reveal 'bullet holes' and hornet's nests.

"Bullet 'oles ya reckon, Hugh, more like bloody cannon balls, mate," said Ted, laughing.

The boys were oblivious to the state of the tent; joining up the centre pole sections and laying pegs in a large circle. All hands were engaged in raising the tent and loud cheers rang out as the pole and the battle-scarred remnants of what once had been living quarters came to the perpendicular. Pegs hammered in, kids yoo-hooing each other through the gaping holes, she had been pitched for the last time and appeared to be resigned to the fact. I blamed no one but myself for its dilapidated condition. I had not inspected it. The store had not labelled it 'in pristine condition'. Diana flatly refused to allow the boys to spend the night under what remained of the canvas; literally sleeping under the stars. The weather was warm; snakes were on the move even at night. The tent was bundled into the Ute, ready to be taken to the tip. The pegs would come in useful one day, and the boys had their own ideas for the pole sections.

There were a few more days of the school holidays remaining, which could not pass quick enough for Ted as the renovation and repairs of the shearing shed could not commence with the boys on the loose. Their mother alone had complete control over them, but that was in the house. Outside, they were a constant concern to Ted and short of sewing them up in chaff bags and suspending them from tree branches where he could keep an eye on them, he was at a loss as to know what to do. Remembering my boyhood, village kids at large, a troop of baboons; intent on fun. I understood his worried frown perfectly. Parking the Morris alongside the shearing shed, Ted helped me unload the car. I was slightly embarrassed by the large amount of booze.

The lock to the shearing shed door was loose and due to come adrift at any time.

"Better put a padlock on this lot," he said. We filled a veteran fridge, which I had not noticed before, with beer. It was a kerosene apparatus; new to me. The kids were down at the river where they cooled off and swung from ropes prior to dinner. The eldest girl supervised them. They all swam like dolphins. We took the opportunity in their absence to sample a couple of bottles already residing in the antique cooler. Ted did not keep drinks in the house for reasons that did not need explaining. I thought about broaching a bottle of whiskey as Ted was perusing the display on hand. Shaking his head slowly, indicating it would not be a good idea, I thought better of it. Until a new lock could be obtained, a padlock and chain were utilised as a temporary measure, with Ted declaring,

"That should keep the nosey little buggers out."

The peace and serenity ended with the arrival of the aquatic seven whose stomachs had heard the dinner gong heralding the evening repast. Dry clothes replaced sodden bathers, the eldest girl assisting her mother; the boys' hands hovering in readiness over their utensils. Obedient in front of their mother but not subdued. At the word go, they would metamorphose into a quartet of wolverine cubs. On entering the kitchen-cum-dining room, I had immediately detected a culinary aroma of the Hellenes. Mutton or lamb cooked slowly for three or four hours, the tang of lemons and herbs, the meat failing from the bone, potatoes and vegetables added towards the end. Heaven.

Before I could pose the question, Diana owned to having been shown by a Greek friend some of the finer points of Aegean cuisine, which was welcomed by all. Much preferred to the customary mutton stew, or roast mutton which remained so tough resulting in the meal being drawn out by an extra half an hour. Lamb was rarely eaten, unless it had suffered a broken leg or been maimed by a wild dog.

We talked on the front veranda after dinner, watching the sunset. The boys, weary now, engaged in a game of Ludo with noise and exuberance. The girls were helping Mum clear away and attend the various domestic duties. Unfair, really. I have three brothers; we helped Mother wash up. Lack of sisters was an unfair blow. Boys who were blessed with sisters often wondered why we took so long over dinner. In summer, there were three hours of daylight left to create mayhem. We maintained a vow of silence. Exile in Paraguay being preferable to washing up after dinner becoming public knowledge.

Ted mentioned that a rabbit warren needed attention with the tractor and back hoe about a mile away. He rallied enormously when I said why waste diesel. I'll take the boys, dogs, picks, spades and a crowbar in the ute and spend a joyful day digging out the colony of vermin, and I will ensure it takes all day.

"Jeez, you're a bloody genius, Hugh, why didn't I think of that?" he exploded.

"Get in the tub ya dirty mongrels, you're going rabbiting termorra with Hugh."

The speed with which they obeyed was astonishing.

A little later, I said good night to everyone including the boys who were wallowing like otter pups in a large tin bath on the back veranda, soap suds and gallons of water from a hose attached to a tap inside, flowing onto flowerbeds. Showered and dry in the shearers' quarters, my thoughts dwelt on the happy healthy family. I would ensure Ted had the day to himself tomorrow.

In my new accommodation, I began a letter to Neil and Janet, explaining of my luck in finding this piece of rural bliss and asking them to forward any correspondence in a fortnight and hold anymore until hearing from me, adding whether they had heard anything of Sharkie and Vernon but not to put themselves out. I don't know why I had added those last few words because I knew he would make a point of calling at the wharf.

The radio was announcing unpleasant details of the Vietnam War with President Johnston's blustering. I listened to the news about peasants being carpet bombed and the defoliation of their forests. Australian young men were compulsorily drafted and US draftees, too young to vote and legally drink alcohol, being slaughtered for reasons unknown to them and countless millions.

Such pointless deaths in the line of duty brought home the horror of the sinking of HMAS Voyager at Jervis Bay a few weeks earlier. The destroyer was taking part in a naval exercise when a tactical blunder by the Voyager's Captain put the ship in the direct path of HMAS Melbourne, an aircraft carrier. Eighty crewmen perished.

For what? Theirs not to reason why. Theirs but to do and die.

And here was I living the hedonistic life, looking forward to one day at a time, three thousand pounds in the bank and life's smooth running hindered only by the occasional stab of conscience that the immortal Bard wrote of – it doth make cowards of us all.

In my shearer's bunk, I tried to concentrate on Huxley's *Antic Way*. I had always preferred books written before my time. I loved history; I could discover something about the past. I had a pretty good grasp of what life was about in the now. The future held no interest for me in the slightest, apart from what lay over the hill. I put the book aside; one needed an unclouded mind to read Huxley.

It was Thursday; school began again on the following Monday. We had two days in which to rid the warren of 'underground mutton'. Sunday being the day of rest, in theory only, was reserved for the multitudinous preparation of the much anticipated, by Mum and Dad anyway, new school term.

I fell asleep and dreamed the night away of my school days, or ferreting, of the powerful palpable scent of ferrets, yapping terriers, badgers, fox cubs and sweaty hobnailed farm boys, and boisterous girls who would often join in wearing frocks and dresses as they did in those days. In their enthusiasm, they would treat us to glimpses of their knickers and bottoms, and excited beyond measure by the ones that wore nothing underneath. Boys would put rabbiting aside, watched behind bushes and view the scene while masturbating.

With quite an interesting night behind me, I was awakened at first light by my crew of rabbit hunters, with a rowdy chorus of 'come and get it'. Three of the boys were preparing for the day by gobbling large bowlfuls of oats smothered in sugar and cream, the fourth epicurean had opted for 'Cockies Joy', a brilliant pseudonym down under for golden syrup. In the bush and in the out-back stock camps, Cockies Joy is considered an essential and is consumed after every meal with damper and flies. Scalding black tea is then administered to ease its passage through the oesophagus and kill the flies. Burping loudly is not only permissible but mandatory.

The girls were digging in too but considerably less voraciously than their uncouth brothers. Mother on duty at the stove frying slabs of bacon cut from a piece of muslin covered ham that hung in a meat safe on the veranda where Dad sat, mug of tea in hand contemplating his day. He called out, "Morning, Hugh, sleep well?" And without waiting for a reply barged into the kitchen; I use the term barged because he seemed ill at ease and awkward inside and lumbered from room to room as if assisting in the relocation of a grand piano. Outdoors, he was as nimble as a gymnast.

The boys were now hoeing into the bacon steaks, rashers they were not, fried eggs were slipped by Diana onto plates as deftly as croupier's chips. I accepted a bowl of oats from Diana and stunned the household into silence when I politely refused the popular garnishing. Jaws slowly began to masticate after the initial shock of witnessing their weird guest sprinkle salt on his oats. I made a great show of how much I was enjoying them and explained that caber tossers put salt on their oats. I could see they were having difficulty believing me, but I am here to say that for the duration of my stay they applied a tentative pinch of salt to their oats along with sugar, cream and Cockies Joy.

The rabbit diggers put the finishing touches to their plates, mopping up with chunks of bread as I ate the last of the doorstep bacon sandwich. Ted was chomping at the bit like a shire horse straining between the shafts at harvest time. Diana and the eldest girl had filled a cardboard box, with specific instructions, not to be touched before midday, more than four hours away.

"What about mornin' tea?" the boys whinged.

"Ya not stopping for no mornin' tea yers had enuf tucker to last yer a bloody week," Ted growled. Tools, boys and an old dog that Ted hoisted in the back and tucker box in the passenger seat, as a necessary precaution. Diesel fumes belching from the exhaust, we were off. "*Vaya con Dios*," saluted Ted. "That means go with God," he said reassuringly. Rattling and bouncing across the paddock, kelpies and collies streaming astern, thinking God was outnumbered by Tassie Devils today, he'd have to be on his toes.

Running adjacent to the Derwent, our destination became visible at eight hundred yards; a monolith among giant trees on the bank of the river. Not wishing to drop a wheel in a burrow, I pulled up fifty yards short of the rabbit citadel. The eager exterminators had bailed out and charged the mound, shrieking a la Tuareg, bent on the destruction of the infidel legionnaire fort. Dogs insane with joy; sand and earth flying everywhere from their frenzied excavations. What did the rabbits live on? There was not a blade of grass to be seen.

It was common during the summer months for a fire ban to be declared, and Ted had warned against attempting to smoke them out, not that there was anything to burn, but if the neighbours got a whiff of smoke, alarm could set in. Horrific bush fires were annual occurrences, loss of property and life were practically part of folklore.

Oh, for a couple of ferrets, that would keep the dogs busy. I nosed the ute closer and digging commenced in earnest. Once the crust of the hillock had been broken, it was surprisingly soft going, even four-year-old Eddy with sand castle bucket and plastic spade was determined to make his presence felt.

I knew from the start and I was sure that Ted was aware also that we were embarking on a mission of futility. The whole escapade was designed to give Ted the time and freedom to prepare the ground work for the repairs to the shearing shed, which a couple of weeks before had come off second best in a disagreement with the tractor. Eldest girl at the helm; foot slipped off clutch. An accident. No recriminations. We were merely keeping the boys from under his feet. He loved his sons, especially when they were asleep or at school. He lay awake at night thinking how useful they would be in a few years. He would love them more then.

We mined unceasingly for an hour without disturbing one rabbit. There may have been a hundred, possibly more in the underground labyrinth. The dogs, tongues lolling, had not let up for a second. The boys, smothered in sweat and sand, suddenly demanded dinner, two hours before the promulgated time. I put it to them that maybe a swim would be beneficial with a drink of cordial to follow. They looked at each other to seek agreement and accepted the compromise. It was not that long ago that I was their age. Bullying and shouting never worked. The adoption of guile cannot be over-emphasised. Little Eddy took part in the aquatic interlude, assisted by two rubber life belts in the shape of a duck, which he called Mother Goose. The belt was attached to a length of rope of which I had a firm grip. A few of the dogs, noticeably the collies, took a break from digging and were cooling off in the river. The geriatric Welsh collie, who would have been a nonagenarian were he human, lay panting with exertion from witnessing the energy being expended and no doubt recalling his puppyhood.

Keeping my part of the bargain, I doled out mugs of cordial from a churn which had inadvertently been left simmering in the sun, With an hour and half until noon, I suggested that we continued digging or sit in the shade for half an hour, but not to enter the water with half a gallon of steaming cordial onboard. They had obviously been drilled well and agreed that it was dangerous to do so, insisting they have another dip prior to dinner. As there was no possibility of a swim for hours after they had disposed of the cubic foot-sized box of comestibles, I gave the thumbs up to that. Then like all good boys, they sat patiently under the river gums for about forty seconds then recommenced excavation. The dogs had more sense and equanimity, sleeping with one eye open. Eddy slept also, enveloped in Mother Goose, the other end of the rope secured to my ankle, lest I too should drop off.

Feverish gouging of the warren continued for some time when on the main trench-tunnel an antechamber was disturbed from which two rabbits bolted and fled across the paddock and over the horizon with the hysterical dogs in pursuit. We stood and watched in silence as the dogs too disappeared from view. The old collie had tottered a dozen paces, gave a feeble bronchial bark then lay down once more. His brief but gallant show of enthusiasm earning cuddles and terms of endearment from the boys. My heart warmed to them. I expected them to enquire about dinner at any moment, but they bent to the task at hand. Their appetite for blood had been whetted and they dug like wombats, unearthing a little later, a piece of stone that they convinced themselves was an axe head. Rather than convene a serious anthropological discussion, the discovery resulted in a ruckus as to who found it first. Ten minutes of arbitration followed, during which it was agreed turns would be taken to take care of it for twenty-four hours, which included sleeping with it, that way they would each have it twice a week. Eddy, who was still asleep despite the row, was not included. Despite some protests, George, the older and biggest, assumed the role of the curator of the supposed artefact. He brought up the subject of dinner and the preceding swim, a necessary procedure in order to remove the stuccoed alluvial detritus which clung to them.

All the dogs bar one had returned to the fold and set about drinking the Derwent dry. Having no time piece, it was unanimously decreed that it was near enough to noon and into the water they plunged for a few minutes until their synchronised stomach chronometers rang the dinner gong. I managed to get the dripping wet three musketeers to sit down and behave somehow, as the distribution of the longed-for dinner would be akin to feeding riotous earthquake survivors from the rear of an Oxfam truck. One-inch sandwiches, colloquially referred to as sangers, were eagerly and politely handed around. Leftover jam-filled scones followed by a marvellous fruit cake with the density of Aberdonian granite. The churn of cordial had cooled somewhat in the river and their thoughtful mother had included two thermos flasks, one of tea, the other of coffee.

Eddy, still attached to my ankle, woke suddenly and announced that he had done pooh in his bathers and that he was hungry. George dexterously relieved him of the soiled article with one hand, the other refusing to part with a large wedge of cake and set him adrift with Mother Goose on a string. The boys were quite blasé about Eddy's lapse of etiquette at the 'dinner table'. He was four years old and as advanced and normal as you would expect any four-year-old to be. Sensing my puzzlement, George explained that Eddy had been house trained in his first year, as indeed they had all been, but the aberration in Eddy's behaviour began with his mesmeric fascination with the method of body waste disposal employed by their horses. "Outdoors they shit and piss where they like," George said, surprising me with his crude explanation. "'E only does it around the yards, not when we go to town," George added, with obvious relief. Fishing Eddy out of the river, he laid his bathers on the bonnet of the ute and sat him in the shade, warning, "Stay there or yer arse'll get sunburnt." George was ten years old. A responsible lad; he would be of great assistance to his father in a few years. He endured the role of watchdog with great patience, aware that in his way he was helping his dad.

Bursting at the seams, no one felt like rabbiting so we sat in a circle examining the axe head. Blood thirsty comments ensued. "'Ow many 'eads had it chopped off?" "Is that blood there?" Abounding conjecture flowed, becoming more gruesome and inventive by the second. To steer the subject to an alternative course, I asked how old did they think it was. It was pleasing to see that this question brought about a seriousness to the debate.

They knew about 'Truganini', widely believed to be the last of the full blood Aboriginal in Tasmania. The Aboriginals had lived here for thousands of years, until driven off their land, shot, poisoned and forcibly removed to nearby islands, such as Cape Barren where in the nineteenth century they had mixed with whaling crews from America and Northern Europe. The boys' knowledge and feelings about what happened to Australia's original inhabitants was matter of fact, and how could it be otherwise? They were children.

They showed their interest in the natural history with an account full of feeling for the Tasmanian Tigers. Thylacine shot, trapped and poisoned to extinction in the 1930s. A neighbour had a skull of one that an ancestor had trapped. They swore me to secrecy as they had been sworn to secrecy themselves. The neighbour feared the relic would be confiscated by a museum. Why anyone would want to keep a constant reminder of a relative who had assisted in the total elimination of a beautiful marsupial was beyond my comprehension.

I felt a little overwhelmed by the trust that their parents held for me, knowing that without George I would have baulked at the escapade and not even suggested it. I had taken my training ship days in the Royal Navy seriously and carried out my duties to the best of my ability, often being 'verbally' commended for exemplary behaviour, but I had never felt in myself that I was a responsible person. Judge for yourself by the previous pages. Carefree, devil may care, a tincture of arrogance. It was all about me. As long as my way of life did not impinge on another's, I was happy. Arrogance, not a trait to be proud of but my awareness of its existence could help me exorcise it from my character. A fervent desire.

Restlessness hung in the air, food and drink all gone, forbidden to swim and tired of poking about for rabbits, we packed up the gear. Taking a circuitous route, I got an interesting guided tour of the farm which provided Ted with an extra hour of preparations. As we neared the homestead, I suspected that our early return was not only expected but also welcome. Diana had seen us coming and was engaged in reversing the tractor into the machinery shed. A mother's peace of mind restored. Ted was beaming, the girls had been dropped off by a neighbour from shopping in town, then they were all set for afternoon tea except Eddy, who was immediately immersed in a tub of suds and a liberal dash of disinfectant. Afternoon tea was taken on the veranda keeping Eddy under surveillance lest he slip under the suds with fatigue and drown. The boys replenished the brown Windsor soup that Eddy was sitting in with the hose; pieces of unidentified flotsam floating over the side and drifted down to the thriving flowerbed. After all defecatory signs had been banished, Diana then put Eddy in the house bath.

Then it was chore time which included the afternoon quest for the chooks' elusive nests and the feeding of pigs. Everyone was occupied in some capacity. Ted and I adjourned to the shearers' quarters to check on the temperature of the beer. I could feel that Ted was desperately trying to express his gratitude for my willing assistance without actually mentioning that he still had Saturday to contend with. His concern was plainly written on his amiable face. I already had a solution in mind.

Ted had been sawing planks of timber from a seasoned log while we were rabbiting. The circular saw was driven by a belt attached to the tractor. Diana had been helping him; constantly on alert should we return unexpectedly. Normally, the saw was never operated other than on school days or when it was guaranteed that the boys were at least fifty miles away. I volunteered to take the boys in the family station wagon and fill them up with ice cream in a milk bar in town.

"'Aven't yer 'ad enuff of the little buggers yet, mate?" he asked.

"I'm sure George and I can handle them," I boasted, petting the kelpie that had gone AWOL. It was limping and in a sorry state, a deep gash on one of its pads. The girls were bathing it in neat antiseptic. It must have been in agony but did not flinch, panting fiercely, looking at the girls with trusting loving eyes. Ted told them to chain the dog up.

"She'll be right in a few days. Can't afford the vet. They either get better or they die," he said philosophically. This seemed to bring him around to the question of money and payment, as the work on the shearing shed plus the renovations would take about a fortnight. I told him that if he thought I would accept payment for helping him, he was wrong. I added that if he brought the odious subject up again, I would with reluctance pack up and leave. Before he could protest, I filled him in on the past few months, omitting the Melbourne Cup saga, the social maelstrom I had been caught up in. Barely a minute to myself. Late nights. An excess of booze. I was a reader, a thinker, I needed time to write. What I had learned from the few hours I had been with his beautiful loving family was invaluable and payment enough.

It was agreed that I take the three eldest boys to town, my treat I insisted. I thought he was about to hug me, but men did not do that in those days. That settled, we celebrated with another beer, after which I shaved, showered and wrote letters until the evening repast was announced. The letter I wrote my mother I adhered as many stamps as there was space for and tucked two ten-pound notes in the folds of the missive. I had done the same with each letter since the previous November. She had expressed surprise as well as thanks for this as she had only known me as a spendthrift, generous on the first days' home from sea but mostly penurious in the latter part of my leave. I made up stories lest she thought I had taken up bush-ranging.

The fifty yards that separated the house from the shearing shed were insufficient to avert the tantalising aroma of fish frying which wafted from the kitchen. Home cooking held so many memories. On the veranda, the elder members of the brood were putting the finishing touches to the various school assignments they had been burdened with; my grouchy sentiments entirely as they seemed to be enjoying themselves. I never had homework and I was glad of it. Holidays were for holidaying in my book. I learned little during school hours. Was that the fault of the education department or my disinterest and boredom with the curriculum, I have never decided. Bit of both most likely.

"Tea's ready," called Diana, and we all bustled inside. On the table rested two large serving dishes, one piled high with steaming battered fish, the other with glistening golden chips at an equal angle of repose. Tomato sauce, a bottle at both ends of the table stood in sentinel attendance along with vinegar, salt and two jugs of cordial. What more could this happy band wish for? "We're not Cathlicks but we always 'ave fish and chips on Fridays. A mate drops it off on his way one from 'obart for the weekend," Ted explained.

On the veranda, we watched the sunset. Children giggling at Ted's tall stories and becoming sleepy. The boys were ignorant of tomorrow's plans. The dogs were snoozing at the end of their chains, bar the geriatric collie lying at Diana' feet. He would not be straying too far. Ted and Diana would be sawing timber the next day as more was needed for the partially completed second bathroom that he had been busy with. The plumbing was in place but could not yet be used by the modest and bashful. Bathroom or shearing shed? It was a question of priorities. School term morning ablutions were chaotic. The boys use the shearing shed amenities. "I always get up a foive for a shit and wot 'ave ye cos once the girls get up yer got no hope and the boys fighting and shoving in the shed I've driven down the paddock in the dark for a crap, no bloody joke on a frosty morning." His poeticism entranced me.

During weekends and school holidays, the morning stampede was replaced by a more leisured approach to one's personal toilet. For the boys leisured to the extent of not bothering to wash at all. A waste of water. "The dirt'll cum off 'em

212

at bath time, a fair bit of it anyway," Ted opined. With a chorus of 'goodnights' we bid farewell to a happy day. On my way to the shearers' quarters, the lonely horse was waiting at the gate. I stroked his muzzle and gave him an apple core. He snickered thanks. The sump oil Ted had dosed the fence with had rendered it unappetising.

I awoke at sunrise to the sound of pigs squealing and snuffling over their swill after dreaming of giant rabbits chasing dogs for what seemed like most of the night. At breakfast, it was apparent the boys hadn't a clue as to what had been planned, in case overnight I had changed my mind, I supposed. Ted let me break the news. "I am going to town this morning. Ice cream, lollies, pies for dinner, anyone interested?" I offered.

"Me, me, me," rang out, arms shot in the air. I should have thought of Eddy but had not.

"You're not comin', Eddy," George informed him tactlessly. Eddy began howling. I took my notebook out and sitting next to the youngest of the happy band of brothers, asked him what we could bring back for him. His grizzling instantly ceased and he began an extensive list of requirements. A bucket of ice cream (strawberry), 20 Mars bars, big bag of lollies, 20 donuts (the jam ones), 20 bags of crisps, 20 bars of chocolate and heaps of Jaffas. What had begun with giggles and sniggers around the breakfast table had now increased to guffaws and shrieks of laughter which rather than discompose Eddy's train of thought, acted as a cattle prod to his hopes and inventive imagination. Running out of edible ideas, I now added cap gun and thousands of caps to the lengthy list along with a pedal fire engine, bow and arrows, cricket bat, ball and stumps plus an Aussie Rule football.

The girls of course were not included in this foray into town. They had been the day before and hadn't the slightest wish to be in the company of the odoriferous brothers in whom there resided mutual sentiments. The girls would adhere to the rules and stay well clear of the circular saw keeping Eddy under strict surveillance.

George pumped the Holden tank full from a forty-four gallon drum, and we were away, waved down the driveway with not a tear from the wavers. The station wagon was not twelve months old. The power of it startled me; it was as if I had been transported in time from a model T Ford of 1909 to an E Type Jaguar of 1960. A spasm of unfaithfulness swept over me when I thought of my little Morris which had carried me thus far. The homestead fast disappearing in the rear vision mirror and in a clear stretch of road, the needle swiftly reached one hundred miles per hour. The reckless milestone reached, I dawdled for the remainder of the trip much to the annoyance of my three urgers whom I had forged a pact with before putting my foot down. Don't tell Mum and Dad until I've left the island.

It was sixteen miles back to town, a fact that had failed to register with me as the dashboard in the Morris, apart from the miniscule light indicating that the engine was running, kept all vital information a close secret; no speedometer, no mileometer, the fuel gauge stuck on half full or half empty according to one's state of positivity or negativity. As the town came into sight, the two back seat drivers commenced a rundown on the best ice cream vendors. It appeared the citizens were well provided for in that department. George in the passenger seat told them to shut up and directed me to a colossal Greek milk bar that bristled with attractions of every kind. I had given George all the change I had, to be going on with and the boys pushed their way through the madding crowd of kids, punching and shoving their schoolmates who wanted to know what the fuck they were doing in town. I returned to the car to peel a tenner from my roll of five hundred pounds. It made no sense to advertise my wealth to these rampant squander bugs. It hadn't taken George long to carve a gangway to the counter where he tipped out the shrapnel and demanded the equivalent in ice cream of a dark-eyed smiling heartbreaker his own age and a fellow classmate. The girl's eyelashes fluttered like butterfly's kisses, and with another beautiful smile, she told George to sit and she would bring the order to the table. From where I stood, the tables all seemed to be occupied and such was the case until George emptied one with a few shoves and threats, and the three then hoed into a gallon of multi-coloured ice cream, heads down and arses up. Surely, Ted and Diana were unaware of this side of George.

The dark-eyed girl had George by the balls figuratively speaking. She knew his louche behaviour was primarily to impress her. To some extent, it probably did, but it was unlikely to get him anywhere in the long term. He would have to discover this on his own. While the three were satiating at the trough like foxhound pups, I changed the tenner at the counter, purchasing a large bag of toffees from the dark-eyed girl's mother, who I found later was Diana's friend who had taught her how to render a ten-year-old sheep into a special Greek dish. I then slipped next door to split another tenner on something I didn't need.

I found my charges waiting at the car, the designated meeting place. Save the milk bars, most shops and businesses closed at noon on Saturdays so it was agreed to partially fulfil Eddy's wish list. George reckoned that the cap gun, lollies and the ice cream should be enough for the greedy little bugger. They were being so compliant that I gave them a ten-shilling note each, slipping George, my First Lieutenant, another five shillings while the other two were examining their sudden windfall. They had probably never seen a ten-shilling note close up before, let alone own one.

A local Derby cricket match was scheduled to begin at eleven o'clock. George was very keen to be a spectator and had a score book ready. We intended to spend the afternoon under the 'spreading chestnut' tree; to be followed with tea, cucumber sandwiches and sponge cake at some stage of the proceedings. First things first, however.

The cap gun and about fifty yards of caps swiftly secured from somewhere; together with several bags of confectionery from a grocery store, all safely stowed into the station wagon. The ice cream, we would pick up on the way home from the milk bar which was open all day and half the bloody night according to George, who made it his business to be conversant with these useful fragments of knowledge. The milk bar was where the dark-eyed Aphrodite lived and in whom he pretended not the slightest interest. Come off it, George. Wouldn't you like to be sitting with her under the shade of the tree at the cricket match? Of course, you would, George. "To thine self be true."

We drove to the cricket ground and parked in the shade; the boys licking ice cream cones and carrying their respective booty possessively, broke and happy. I had bought two pies each for lunch plus an obscene amount of chips, dolloped with tomato sauce of course. Ice cream finished, they began stuffing themselves in earnest as they do geese in Strasbourg. I noted Henry with a pie in one hand, a large bite taken from it, in the other a Mars bar at the ready, a bottle of Orangeade with a straw between his knees. My eyes swivelled to George and Johnny who were similarly engaged. George's prospective mother-in-law smiled when I asked her for a tomato, feta cheese and Greek bread. I mentioned I had been to Greece and knew Cyprus quite well. She smiled again, refusing payment. The match had begun a few minutes before. George had not taken his eyes from the proceedings, food bombarding his mouth like guided missiles. I strolled away to eat my goat herds lunch sans Retsina; maybe a nap to follow, to dream of years before, of Cape Andreas and Fontana Amarosa.

I dozed behind a tree after lunch lest an errant ball bounce off my skull. This happened years before to a fellow villager in Duns-Tew. He was padded up and next man in when the unfortunate event occurred. He was never the same again; folk said it may have done him some good. I met him some years later while home on leave. He appeared bright, humorous and happily married to a buxom farm girl. Far removed from the dull, monosyllabic boy I sat next to at school, who couldn't remember the year of the Battle of Hastings. Four digits indelibly tattooed on most school boys' brains. He copied word for word everything in my exercise books apart from my maths, which he wisely chose to disregard. We received identical marks until our education ceased at the age of fifteen and we enrolled in the University of Life; I to enter the Royal Navy, he to follow the plough.

Waking to the clamour of cheering and clapping, I was alarmed by the sight of a flannelled fellow groping between my spreadeagled legs. Fearing sexual molestation, I sprang to my feet with such vigour and agility that it unbalanced the suspected deviant and set him on his arse clutching a cricket ball which had been skied in to the upper branches for six runs, descending to earth bagatelle like, to nestle in close proximity to my scrotum. George had followed the ball's trajectory from bat to tree top and in anticipation of a spectacular, though null and void catch, had outsprinted the fielder and witnessed the missiles potentially emasculating landing, which I might add the little bastard found highly amusing.

From what I recall, apart from the lusty six which almost deprived me of the powers of generation, the batting team were dismissed for less than a hundred runs. At this point, it was decided by whoever decided these matters to call a halt for refreshments, as the promising day the Bureau of Meteorology had pre-ordained, had the look of menace about it; clouds banking up, turbulence afoot. Mother Nature countermanding the weather prophets which as usual she excelled in. Why allow rain to interrupt cricket? A rugby fixture would take place on a ploughed field. Imagine a fast bowler hurling a Zeus-like thunderbolt a yard in front of the crease. Too funny for words. I thought of a poet whose name eluded me, who wrote:

"The flannelled fools at the wicket and the muddied oafs in the goals."

Can't you just picture the scene? Betjeman, maybe?

The covers crew were frantically sought and found in the beer tent, where they had been sheltering from the sun's rays since the umpires had placed bails on stumps. Anticipating an afternoon of redundancy, they had staved off

216

dehydration by sampling the contents of a nine-gallon keg. By the time they had tumbled onto the ground, thought processes way out of sync along with their lower limbs, rice plants could have been successfully sown on the wicket.

The boys and I sought the sanctuary of the car while a crowd of about two hundred packed into the beer and tea tents, with a frenzy one would normally associate with a Stuka attack. Twenty minutes later, the Niagara rain ceased, leaving a painstakingly curated oval a lagoon upon which a skein of duck had alighted. Nature had dealt a decisive blow to the afternoon's sport; the ankle-deep water being insufficient for water polo. Folk emerged from the tea tent, trousers rolled up, those in the beer tent conscientiously monitoring the keg lest it be cast adrift. Kids and dogs splashed, yapping and shrieking with delight in the hot steamy afternoon. No catastrophe for them.

The storm had abated just in time, the car was a sauna. We leaped from the vehicle; Harry clutching a brown paper bag of vomit, George and Johnny looking pale and delicate, hurried to a copse of eucalyptus, with an urgent need to regurgitate in private. I strode to where the waters were irrigating the hallowed turf and bathed my head, cooling; I watched a bail bob past my nose. I looked for more sporting flotsam. Should I keep it as a souvenir? I thought better of it. Nothing tangible would ever be needed to bring back a memory of this monsoonal pastoral day.

Having divested themselves of their saturated white coats of officialdom, the umpires were indistinguishable from the rest of the soggy crowd. After several enquiries, however, I was advised to investigate the beer tent which by this time appeared to be hosting several rampaging elephants. Fearing its imminent collapse, I repaired to the temperate tea tent where several harassed ladies were busily engaged in cleaning up a riotous bun fight. The lone male in the vicinity was a blazer and straw boater-clad military gentleman with a well-maintained white moustache and as sober as William Booth. A badge on his blazer indicated membership of a cricket club. He was the man to entrust with the rescued ball. We enjoyed a bit of small talk, and yes, he would indeed see that the all-important piece of cricketing accoutrement was returned to the umpires who were most probably in the beer tent, he said sniffily. I wondered if he could smell the stale beer on my breath. Surely, the goat's cheese would have nullified it.

I mentioned that I had not come for the cricket but was enjoying the day immensely. Cricket just was not my game. I preferred rugby, which rain doesn't interrupt. He attempted a feeble protest, which tapered off on hearing of my few hours with a lovely girl at the 'Bat and Ball' Inn in Hampshire, the birthplace of cricket and of a school excursion to 'Edgbaston' where I had secured the autograph of Donald Bradman. At this point, obviously feeling that he had encountered a pathological liar or that I had spent too much time in the sun, he excused himself and marched off shaking his straw boater-ed head. How selfish. I wished to hear his stories. Advancing on Rommel in the turret of a panzer tank, face burnt black in the Western Desert sun. Maybe storming Montecassino in company with Uncle Wal and his medical bag, who would stop when coming across the fallen, to check for a pulse. Many an aficionado of the game that I idly teased over the years regarding my cricket experiences, though a little envious never doubted the veracity of them. Maybe the old curmudgeon was jealous; a destructive trait.

My good deed accomplished, I paddled across the waterlogged area to where the scene of Caligula excess had taken place. I recalled my occasional gluttonous intake as a boy at Christmas and birthday festivities, followed by the inevitable bilious attacks thence to the hollowness that had to be swiftly addressed. Thus it did not surprise me to find the boys having voided the entire contents of their cast iron stomachs, looking famished and feverishly counting the remaining change they had pooled. They were keen to commence further assault on their bodies. Pre-empting any plans that would be hatching in their anarchic heads, I ordered my First Lieutenant to break camp. Cars were beginning to vacate the aquatic sports ground, wheels spinning, mud caking the shins of willing pushers. Vehicles underway but not answering the helm slithering sideways and executing 360-degree pirouettes. I thought of the Dodgems at Banbury Fair. It took about ten minutes before it appeared safe to weigh anchor. George understood the folly of engaging with the exiting chaos and the risk of being sideswiped. I would have required shackles and a knout to control his brothers without his assistance. All clear at last, I made a charge for the gate, fish tailing, wheels spraying mud and gravel to port and starboard. The escape dash took a mere twenty seconds to where I ran aground on bitumen.

A garage beckoned down the road, I asked George to walk the boys there and hose themselves down. I followed slowly, leaving the quagmire in the hands of the curator. Everyone seemed keen on going home so after washing the mud off the wheels we returned to the Greeks, where a speedy replenishment of empty stomachs took place. I bought two dozen pies plus the biggest box of chocolates on the premises for Diana and the girls. Driving home at a fast but safe rate of knots, lest the tub of strawberry ice cream liquefy, I mentioned to George as we left town that I had seen Aphrodite in company of a boy. Not only that but they were holding hands. George said he didn't give a shit, adding that he'd punch the boy's head on Monday. I didn't doubt him. He really did give a shit.

Sound of gluttonous mastication alongside and behind me kept the moans of displeasure at our funereal pace to a minimum. We were travelling at sixty miles per hour; the speed limit. They would not be satisfied unless telegraph poles whizzed past like a paling fence. I mouthed a silent prayer of thanks to all pie manufacturers. Cadbury's got a mention also.

At the farm gate, Eddy on a dog leash was being restrained by a sister. They hopped in the back seat; Eddy grabbing a Mars bar and demanding his promised ice cream. George told him to shut up or he'd give the ice cream to the dogs. Eddy shut up.

The wood sawing had ceased, judging by the joyous pack of dogs that had been slipped of their chains. As we drew up to the house, Ted and Diana approached, dusting themselves off like millers after a day making grist. Elizabeth had a king-sized pot of tea on the veranda with hot scones she had turned out on a large platter. With as much decorum as we could muster, we adults and the girls gave the repast our immediate attention; the boys munching away at whatever. I couldn't bear to watch the revolting wee gannets. Eddy's strawberry pink face beamed over the bowl of ice cream. At least I think it was a beam, it was difficult to ascertain. I detected future artistic talent when he added several 'Liquorice Allsorts' and sat back in his chair in order to better appraise his masterpiece. The little chap was quite loveable, really.

Ted and Diana had not stopped once and were guzzling mugs of tea with the thirst of shipwrecked mariners. The gustative interlude was interrupted by Henry maintaining that the ceremonial handing over of the axe head was long overdue. George, anticipating the demand, snapped that he had lost it. This disclosure caused unrest and annoyance in the ranks and disbelief in Ted and Diana, who knew George very well. George stalked off, and I followed him. We strolled down to the hay barn where we miraculously discovered the axe head hiding under a bale. I reminded George that he was the leader, not a dictator and explained the difference. Ted and Diana had not seen the supposed axe head before but as sensible, peace-loving parents, silently gave the ancient tool and weapon their nod of authenticity. The artefact in the hands of its caretaker, Ted rose from his chair accompanied by the usual burps and explosive farts of appreciation, resulting in giggles and sniggers from the boys and the rapid disappearance of the females.

I quoted 'Burns':

"Where ever ye maybe,

Let your wind blow free."

Not very amusing or original, but he didn't stop laughing for ten minutes.

"Come and look at wot we've dun, Hugh," invited the contented patriarch.

I was not prepared for the stunning scene. The huge old seasoned trunk had been converted to planks, ready to be cut to size, drilled, nailed and screwed. Work would begin tomorrow on the new bathroom, enabling ablutions to be taken in private. Did I mind working on the Sabbath? I thought he was joking, but he wasn't. I said that all days were the same to me. The sun rose in the east and set in the west, during which between meals we occupied ourselves in various ways. It mattered not a bit to me. Noticing the seriousness on his amiable face, I immediately regretted my self-centred careless rambling.

"You're a good man, Hugh," he said, which did nothing to ease my guilt.

"The moving finger writes, and having writ moves on," according to Omar Khayyam.

Seven kids and countless sheep; the enormity of his responsibilities weighed heavily upon him. The thought made me shiver.

In my quarters preceding a long neck of 'Cascade', we each took a generous pull at the malt bottle. I related my carpentry prowess at school; how a spade scraper was the sole article of woodwork I was permitted to take home. Other boys in my class were turning candle sticks and rolling pins on lathes, as well as walnut veneering cigarette and jewel boxes. Don't expect any master joinery from me. Humping timber and holding the other end of the tape measure was my forte. Far from disappointing him, Ted took the news of my ineptitude with relief, as it would rule out any possible outlandish design suggestions I may harbour.

The plan of action decided for the next day. The dogs, chooks, ducks, the whole menagerie fed by whoever's task it was. All scrubbed, Eddy in his pyjamas. Dinner was served. Not surprisingly the boys' usual trencherman appetite was well below par; a point that their parents did not question. They knew their boys. Ted demolished two pies in half a dozen bites. "Horses Doofers." He burped. Diana had made a pastry at breakfast time. It had been in the fridge all day. Rolling it out, in a few minutes it was in the oven. Egg and bacon pie, she said and it will ever be known by that name. She had friends who had travelled abroad who on their return from Europe and the mother country now referred to the dish as Quiche Lorraine. Diana agreed that they could be transgressing the 'appellation d'origine' laws. Ted of course didn't know what the hell we were talking about and cared even less. He was deep in thought, weighing up the probability of having the second bathroom ready for the modest, in time for the Monday morning stampede. Eddy apart, the boys sought exemption from the evening meal with no protest from anyone. The rest of us fell upon the egg and bacon pie in earnest. With their brothers in absentia, the girls deemed it an opportune moment to review the box of chocolates from where they had secreted it. I watched with pleasure their picking and choosing with decorum their particular fancy. I pictured the four boys cramming their mouths and regurgitating like a flock of fulmar. I would have done the same at their age.

All was quiet. We drank tea on the veranda with the sand flies and talked of the day ahead. With the sinking of the sun, the flies were becoming scarce, the swallows called a halt to their incessant hunting and twittered for a while under the eaves. Then good nights all around. With the last of the sunlight streaming through the window, I finished off the two remaining chapters of Norman Douglas' *South Wind*, which I had begun one quiet afternoon on Babel Island. A captivating writer.

I awoke to the squealing of pigs at the trough, the cacophony of geese and ducks and the geriatric horse snorting the chaff from his feed bag, the rattle of buckets. The 'Enigma Variations' of my boyhood. The three 'gannets' had had a disturbed night. Diana had administered a tried-and-true purgative before turning in. The physic also doubled as an emetic, and here they sat at breakfast replenishing their heroic bowels. The day as aforementioned had been allocated for the preparation of the new school term. Uniforms clean and ironed, shoes polished. Home work had included an essay on how they had enjoyed the holidays.

The girls would have plenty to write about with their enquiring minds, whereas their brothers just ate. Ted was straining at the shafts like a grain fed shire horse. "Tuck in, Hugh, don't be shy, we'll get stuck into the bathroom first up," he enthused.

A ute load of timber was driven up to the wall-less bathroom and we got 'stuck in'. For the initial ten minutes, I slaved away holding the end of the tape, while Ted jotted down measurements. Simple enough. I was then entrusted with the plane, which I had enjoyed at school for half an hour one day. I had no idea then why or what I was planing the unsuspecting billet of deal for. I just kept planing until I was ankle deep in shavings; the piece of wood the width of a tram ticket. So engrossed was I that I failed to keep an eye on Billy the wood work teacher and received a wallop on the arse as he crept up behind me like Dr Wackford Squeers of Dothebys Hall. All in good fun though. He was a kindly man who had great patience with me. It must have been very trying for him. Years later, I bought him a pint in a village inn. "Aah, the wood butcher," he mused.

As I planed away, I had entertained Ted with the pencil sharpening escapade at school. He was experiencing difficulty in concentrating on the job at hand and begged me to desist in slightly more robust language but welcomed further anecdotes at a suitable time.

We hammered, sawed, nailed and screwed all day with a break for lunch – dinner and a cup of tea at three o'clock in the afternoon. I planed more timber under the watchful eye of the forewarned foreman but was denied at first the thrill of operating the destructive-looking weapon called a router, which outpointed the pencil sharpener by a long chalk. With a bit of imagination, it could achieve feats of mayhem that its inventor never thought possible. Sensing my disappointment, Ted relented soon after, and I was permitted to have my way with an off cut, with artistic effect.

Everything in order for school, the kids were let slip for their various farmyard activities. Ted and I instinctively headed to the tavern where we eased our parched throats. The bathroom needed another day's work but could now be used by all but the very coy, and we had eliminated the need of Ted to void his hyperactive bowels al fresco when the South Pole threatened with frozen breath once more.

The dinner-tea table was bedecked with 'leftovers' Diana announced, almost apologetically. I said it looked ambrosial and smelt the same. Ted said it was ambrosial also, adding, whatever that means. Cold Greek-style mutton, roast potatoes, a garden-fresh salad plus a steaming plateful of the surviving meat pies and of course, the tomato sauce. Dinner over, we adjourned to the veranda as usual, the wind of change palpable. The girls talkative and happy; pleased to be seeing their friends once more the next day. The boys were swatting flies morosely. George muttering now and then about which kind of retributory action he would take against the poltroon who sneakily sullied Aphrodite's fair hand, ignoring all advice that his intended assault would not impress the girl one bit and to seriously reconsider.

I thanked Diana for dinner. Ted agreed again that it was ambrosial and roared with laughter. Later, when I asked him if I could use the brace and bit in the morning, he laughed even more. As I yawned my way to bed, his voice followed me until I closed the door on it. Too tired to read, I thought of Diana as I constantly had since the day I had arrived. Diana, educated, mother of seven; Venus to me. I, shamelessly dining at the family table watching her at the stove bending over the fire box with billets of wood, her mesmerising thighs and derriere, the outline of her shapely body, myself in semi-permanent state of arousal, waiting for a moment's wilt in order to make my escape. I would concentrate on the work I had promised to assist with, then leave this happy family. It was time to move on. Waking early with Diana on my mind, I needed a cold shower. I would hail Diana good morning, then eat breakfast, eyes averted, my mind on other matters. As a custom on the first day of school term, we all went to the gate to wave the children off to school. The school bus was due at the gate at 08.05; at 08.00, the boys reluctantly traipsed, the girls' excitement mounting.

Downwind of Diana, the scent of roses hung in the air. She was in her best shoes, stockings, Sunday dress, long hair glistening in the morning sun shimmied to the gate and posed almost provocatively, defiant, childlike and beautiful. She had erred some years before when she saw George off on his first day of school wearing gumboots covered in pig shit, with chaff in her wind tousled hair. George copped plenty from the boys on the bus but fought back well. He came home with a fat lip but with a glint of pride in his eyes.

It was necessary to resort to my wilt tactic; jumping out of an aeroplane with an umbrella or resuscitating a warthog. Walking back ahead of Diana and Eddy, and leading by five yards, I partially resolved my embarrassment, until Diana called, "In a hurry to get to work, Hugh?" This jolted me out of my trance. I broke into a trot, lest she saw my rampant member, a questing bowsprit.

"I need to use the lavatory," I shouted over my shoulder.

Restored once more to a state of equanimity, I joined Ted who was patiently waiting for me to hold the other end of the tape measure. I had noticed with some puzzlement certain aspects of the plumbing seemed to be missing, spaces where an appliance could be installed later. I mentioned the matter to Ted, and I was fortunate that Diana was not around when I did. He replied and I quote: "The girls found out from their schoolmates of an apparatus called a 'Biday' that French sheilas used instead of toilet paper. Bloody dear, but think of the money we would save on toilet paper over the years. They even use paper after they've peed. Whereas we just have to shake the old fellow." And that was how I learned what bidets were for.

By dinner-lunch time, the bathroom was functional for the bashful as well as the brazen. Ted was well pleased. After the break, we spent half an hour cleaning up then advanced on to the damaged shearing shed to prepare a plan of action for the repairs needed the next morning. It was a particularly hot and humid day, sweat poured from us in runnels. Ted had commented on the heat several times in various epithetic terms. Eventually it sunk in that he was extremely thirsty. We downed tools, stuck our head under the horse trough tap and enjoyed an hour in the cool of the 'Shearers Inn'.

It was obviously puzzling Ted why I had refused payment. Originally, he thought I was an itinerant fruit picker looking from somewhere to camp for the night. In this assumption, he was partly correct, but this was my fifth day with them. I was just touring, I explained, after a busy cray-fishing season. I intended to get to the mainland somehow by sea and then try fishing in Port Augusta or somewhere in NSW or in Queensland. I loved the sea and preferred to spend a month sailing to somewhere than fly. Imagine sailing with Conrad or Masefield in a tall ship or in company with that cranky old bastard Somerset Maugham on a steamer out of Yokohama bound for San Francisco, I romanticised.

He shook his head in utter incomprehension. "I've never bin to sea. I've never been far at all; I tried before I met Diana to enlist in the Army and maybe get to Korea, but they knocked me back when they discovered a heart murmur." I was stunned. Here was this brave man running three thousand sheep with the vagaries of the weather together with innumerable problems associated with farming and he had been deemed unfit for Army service. I felt ashamed thinking of his family and the lascivious fantasies I held for his lovely wife. I pushed the bottle of malt under the bench. Small wonder that apart from our first welcoming tot he had refused all subsequent offers.

I said, "Everyone had accepted me as family. I felt at home."

"Stay as long as you loik, forever if yous want," he affirmed. Then with a sudden change of subject, he exclaimed, "The donkey's coming tonight, it's in foal, if that's wot ya call baby donkeys."

He had me stumped there, but I replied, "It would do for now."

The barking of dogs indicated the arrival of the school bus. Three hot, panting boys came galloping down the drive, socks encircling ankles, shirt tail flapping in their wake, ties awry, grazed knees, the lot. At a distance astern promenaded the girls as if they'd been to chapel. Diana had orangeade in readiness on the veranda; the boys were guzzling it in pints, the dogs in ecstasy. I wondered whether George had carried out the retributive threat on his hapless rival. I did not seek verification, instead I asked him which King George he'd been named after, hoping to catch him out. Immediately, he answered, "The last one, the sixth. King George the fifth was shitty with his son 'cos he stuttered. The rest were fucken nuts and only spoke German." Quite a historian, our George.

We finished off the orangeade while the brood ticked off their jobs. Dinner-tea followed, then the usual hour on the veranda, the fun part of the day. I thought of Sharkie and Vernon, the Maori girls, Boyd and Tex, the little old lady and Bagheera. I would write Neil and Janet before turning in advising them to hold my mail until further news. Where I would be in a month's time, let it be a surprise.

I don't recall how long we worked on the shearing shed. I do know it was well into February when one afternoon we stood back admiring 'our' handiwork, which included new guttering and down pipes. A thousand-gallon rainwater tank stood expectantly waiting for rain. The old water tank that had served the farm for eighty years was about to embark on a new career, cut in half for animal shelters.

I had a bottle of Moet Chandon that had been simmering in the Morris since I bought it. Hoping it was still drinkable, I put it in the freezer for the celebration once the children arrived home from school. I thought it meant to get into the party mood a little earlier by downing some beer and trusting that the cooling champagne would have no effect on a heart murmur.

While the building and renovations were in progress, I had picked up a few useful pointers. Handy hints. Nothing too complicated. With mallet and wood chisel, I had succeeded in cutting a large dove tail joint for one of the roof beams exposed for all for years to come. I admit it did look as if a beaver had been at it before Ted smartened it up. I was proud of it and kept a photograph of it for some years.

Barking dogs signified the approach of the school bus. Diana had resurrected an emperor-size punch bowl and had installed it near the horse trough but out of

225

reach of Dobbin. I had jokingly suggested using the champagne with the cordial. Taking a glass and deeming it below par, she was delighted to take my advice, adding soda water, extra cordial and a large block of ice. The unique concoction went down well with no ill effects. Ted and I stuck to Cascade and basked in the accolades leaving Diana and her daughters chattering animatedly.

After the grand opening, I helped with the animals taking the opportunity to farewell the old horse and his donkey companion, who had stumbled from the float. It was not exactly love at first sight and only the biscuit of hay I tossed over the fence brought them to a bit of horse-donkey play. Nothing violent; neither had much kick in them.

After showering, I prescribed a generous ball of malt and another bottle of beer. Any other time, I would be feeling a little jolly but not so on this occasion. I needed Dutch courage to break the news of my imminent departure. For the better part of my life, so far I had always suspected that folk were pleased to see the back of me after a few days' stay. I was reckless, impulsive and compulsive, traits that tended to nullify eventually everything I had going for me; my integrity, generosity and fair-mindedness. I felt I had blended in well with this wonderful family, the one stigma being my lustful desire of Diana. My integrity had been severely tested.

Dinner was a fairly sombre affair after I had announced my leaving. Ted did his best to lighten the mood with jokes about how Hugh had been away from his girlfriend for too long. The girls giggled at this and said in unison, "Lucky girl." I didn't know where to put my face and lied about meeting up with a mate at Eden. I had never had any qualms about slipping my moorings before. This was the hardest by far, but it had to be.

Pigs breaking their fast woke me from a deep undisturbed sleep. I had a shower, not sure when I would get another and joined the breakfast table for the last time. George told me he had topped up the Morris from the fuel drum, shook Ted's vice-like calloused hand followed by seven smaller ones, then Diana's, which sent a tingling sensation to the extremities of my body.

The Morris' battery being flat, willing hands push started it down the paddock then at a funereal pace, drove to the gate. I waited until the kids had boarded the bus and it had moved off; the girls and boys waved from the back window. George gave me the thumbs up. He was way too big to wave. When they were out of sight, Ted with a serious breach of protocol at the time, grabbed me in a bearlike hug, leaving me free to return the gesture. I picked up Eddy, who was crying, then turned to hug Diana. Upon releasing her, the Morris obliged by supporting my failing legs. Jumping once more out of my aeroplane with a parasol, I avoided disgrace. Unable to speak, I left like Georgi Zhukov and did not look back.

## Destination Strahan

With my average speed of 25 miles per hour and hugging the edge of the road, I was unlikely to incur a ticket for reckless driving or obstructing traffic and could confidently predict that my stoic little Morris would not attract the attention of would-be bank robbers. I was steering in a north westerly direction with the main objective being the fishing port of Strahan, a fair way further on.

As expected with a new horizon before me slowly changing, the pangs of separation and loss soon began to dissipate. It was ever thus. Paying off a ship in the Royal Navy or the Merchant Marine, parting from mates one had spent eighteen months or longer with. Messmates, drinking mates, mates who thought your thoughts, mates who would never understand you but could laugh with you all the same. Never to be seen again. Vows and promises to meet up some day, to canoe the McKenzie River in beaver pelt caps when our time is up, maybe marry the daughter of a publican. Where were they all now? Dead? Or worse still, paying off a mortgage. Happily married or happily divorced? Or footloose and free like me? No, freedom is having a goal, to pursue a dream. I hadn't one as yet.

Nursing the old girl along, we pulled up in a long-forgotten town around noon. Ducking my head into a couple of pubs to see if any of the clientele appeared to be men of the soil, I found one where several drinkers were Akubra hatted. Following the usual procedure, I approached the bar adjacent to the farming forum, clearly and decisively beseeching the innkeeper for a much-needed beer in my Pommy accent.

"Where ya from?"

"Hobart?"

"Dya come in that?"

"Where ya headin'?"

I explained I intended getting the car over to Melbourne and then to Darwin. Bullshit like this normally attracted immediate interest. I pointed out that I was touring the island on a working holiday and I was not in a hurry, at which there came a chorus of:

"I'm fucken glad to hear that."

Someone enquired where I was staying the night. Seeing that there was some concern as to where I intended laying my head during the coming night, I said that you gentlemen appear between you to own a fair portion of Van Diemen's Land and I would be very grateful to be allowed to park my faithful vehicle on a couple of square yards of it for a few hours. Upon my request, it was generally agreed that I looked harmless enough for one of them to run the risk of allowing a Pommy bastard on their property. My offer of a beer was politely refused as they were in a 'Shout'. There were five of them and had they accepted, custom demanded that I imbibe a further half a dozen beers, or I would not only be a Pommy bastard but a Piss Poor Pommy Bastard. They convened weekly, same time, same place to discuss the weather, fat stock prices and horse racing. Their respective wives did the shopping, then sat with other wives in the ladies' lounge.

It was resolved that I would camp fourteen miles out of town in the direction I was heading and not to drink anymore as the Police Sergeant lay in wait for the unwary and pissed, especially on market day. He was a 'proper' bastard, one of the worst categories apparently, and also a cunt, someone added.

Equipped with a roughly drawn map on the back of a beer mat, I thanked them and left them to await their wives to ferry them home. A morose drinker at the end of the bar got up from his stool, came to attention and stiffly saluted as I passed. I acknowledged him Douglas MacArthur style and went out of the door; the farmers' laughter following me.

In the bottle shop, I bought a case of cold beer and from a grocery shop, a loaf of crusty bread and a chunk of cheese that would have delighted Ben Gunn, then drove out of town in search of my haven for the night. Keeping a vigilant eye out for the over-zealous copper, I spied the officious bastard lying off the road around a sharp bend snoozing in the sun. He could hardly have booked me for speeding, but even a cursory inspection would have rendered the Morris unroadworthy. The fact that the old girl bowled uncomplainingly along at 25 mph would have meant nothing to this martinet, so I had been made to understand. Apart from the aquatic cricket match, he was the first upholder of the law that I had come across since Hobart. Fearing his afternoon nap in the sun may have been interrupted by the rattling of my passing, I risked more pressure on the accelerator, nothing supersonic but enough to increase the mysterious rattle which had developed soon after leaving the pub. Keeping my eyes on the cracked rear vision mirror, I returned to safe cruising speed preparing to seek refuge in the first farm gate that was open if a flashing light should appear astern.

A little further on the yellow letter box that I had been told I could not miss came in view on the right-hand side. Glancing in the rear vision mirror for any sign of the gendarme or a semi-trailer attempting to shatter the world land speed record, I resorted to the pre-war method of one's intention to alter course by sticking my right arm out of the window horizontally, as the Morris had no other mechanism in working order to perform the task.

The gate had been left open, leaving the cattle grid to prevent the straying of stock. Crossing the grid, I parked to one side of the track and returned to inspect the innovative mail box of which I had seen many of various designs but of comparable cubic capacity. Ted had explained the logic of using cavernous diesel drums or clapped-out refrigerators as depositories for deliveries other than letters, of which there were many, including the collection of a variety of goods going both ways, i.e. twenty dozen eggs or half a sheep. Rural improvisation at its best.

De-capping a beer, I took a lengthy pull reducing the contents by a third, which elicited an acute desire for solid sustenance. Ripping a chunk from the fresh baked loaf and a savage bite from the cheddar, I despatched lunch like a navvy sitting by the side of the track, near a fence of lamb netting, which afforded scant relief from the sun. Thinking it advisable in order to avoid heat stroke and possible dehydration, I de-capped another beer. As I guzzled the long neck with the ease and manner that I had absorbed from Sharkie and Vernon, out of the corner of my eye, I caught sight of the police car racing by, blue light flashing on the roof, presumably in fierce pursuit of bank robbers.

Feeling pretty happy after knocking the beer off, I was about to relieve myself on a rear wheel of the Morris, upholding a lawful practice of centuries that alleviated the appalling scarcity of public conveniences, my imagination running riot as to how the ladies coped. A car drove through the gate with a woman at the helm. I frantically adjusted my dress with one hand while clutching the empty beer bottle with the other. Speechless, the bug-eyed lady attempted to arouse her soused spouse who evidently had not enlightened her of his friendly offer. So alarmed did she appear that I was loathe to approach her lest her agitation increased. I called to her in my usual charming manner hoping to put her at ease just as her husband surfaced from his stupor ensuring his good lady that I was a mate.

"Yer might have told me, yer bloody piss pot!" she shouted with obvious relief. Reassured at last that I did not pose a threat, she smiled wanly and accepted my proffered hand. I apologised for the embarrassing state of dishabille she had discovered me in, to which she shot back, "Oh, don't worry about that 'e pisses all over the place," dismissing my concern.

"Only outdoors," the husband replied defensively.

"Come up to the house, no need to camp out, yer can sleep on the veranda," he said. "D'ya reckon yer Rolls-Royce will make it?" He grinned. I vouched for the Morris' reliability by declaring I would be prepared to wager a testicle on it. He replied that that was a punt he would never take. I had to agree that it was a little rash.

The homestead was out of sight but a mere three-minute drive up an incline, around a bend brought us to 'Dingley Dell', the astonishing scene bringing instant tears to my eyes. The stone-built house was encompassed by a deep veranda, armchairs and sofas studded with cushions welcomed along the walls. Majestic old trees stood here and there shading fine-looking stock horses with a glistening chestnut blood stallion standing imperiously close by. Stone farm buildings sat stubbornly proud of their immovability and allegiance to the big house. The woman swung the car around and reversed through the yawning doors of a barn with the expertise of a semi-trailer driver.

The car was pre-war American, a Dodge I think; she said she had been driving it since she was ten years old when her feet reached the pedals. Her father had imported it before Hitler invaded Poland. Apart from dust, it was practically in showroom condition and only ninety thousand miles on the clock. It did not get a run very often as the officious copper for reasons known only to himself had endeavoured to have it put off the road from the day he had been posted to the area. Today, it had succeeded in being registered for another twelve months. The Morris would have fitted in the boot.

The lady's father was a cowboy from Nebraska who was sent as a soldier to Europe in 1918. Fortunately, the Armistice was signed before he could be sent to the front. Playing up in London to celebrate his luck, he had met a Tasmanian girl who had been trapped over there at the outbreak of the hostilities. Delighted on hearing that she lived on a 'ranch', he wooed and won her and apparently they lived very happy lives.

I assisted in the unloading of the groceries and a dozen cases of beer. He obviously had no intention of going thirsty before his next trip to town. I wondered what she drank and soon found out. The building that served as a garage had once had loose boxes installed each side with a tack room the width of the one-time stable at the rear. The tack room was stacked, deck to deckhead, with enough grog to put a battalion of the Highland Light Infantry to sleep for a month. Case upon case of whiskey, gin, vodka, brandy and rum.

We carted the shopping over to the house, where the lady stowed everything away, bar half a dozen bags of crisps. There were a number of refrigerators in the vast kitchen. The farmer opened one which was crammed to capacity with 'Cascade' and grabbed two long necks with one dexterous hand and taking two glasses from a shelf with the other, we adjourned to the shady part of the veranda and took an armchair each. Since the farcical introduction at the front gate, the woman had not stopped talking for more than five seconds and that was merely to refill her lungs with air.

At the first cessation of her nonstop chatter where I had learned her family history, I took the opportunity of reintroducing myself. Still drowsy from the pub, he surprised me by remembering my name. I of course had not a clue of his but recalled it when he leaned over to shake hands once more. "Gerry," he said. "Never forger a name pissed or sober," he affirmed. Something to really brag about that, normally I could not recall a person met casually two seconds later unless they had been blessed with one green eye and one brown, or had impressed me by achieving something notable and stupid like paddling across Bass Strait in a bathtub. A minute passed and I was finally introduced to Phoebe when she brought out a huge bowl of crisps. Unable to speak, as her mouth was busy masticating making it impossible to utter her name without an awful mess occurring, Gerry did the talking by ordering two more bottles of beer. Phoebe complied, disappeared and returned drinking from a capacious brandy balloon, filled to the brim with her own special cocktail, which caused her face to screw up at first contact with her oesophagus.

The next five minutes were wordless but not soundless as we did justice with the crisps. Phoebe drained her glass, rose to get dinner going, leaving Gerry dozing, and I to request permission to look around. Given the go ahead but to watch out for 'Joe Blakes' down at the creek, I strolled around the convict hewn stone buildings built during the days of transportation when prisoners were assigned to landowners and various other free settlers, thereby setting them on the path to a ticket of leave and eventual emancipation. There was hope for some who arrived in irons.

The rear of the house did not surprise, I expected and came upon a formal English rose garden. Trellises for climbing varieties, a sundial and stone paved paths led to the creek. I stamped my way to the water's edge; any snake would be long gone. Children never got bitten, I heard Diana saying, they make too much noise. City folks creeping about or attempting to kill them are at greater risk. Along one wall stood several headstones. Much loved pets, dogs, cats, possibly a budgie or goldfish. Not human resting places unless they had been christened Hondo, Ringer and Belter, names etched with care, pride and love.

A well-tended vegetable garden separated from the rose garden by a stone wall. Tomatoes were thriving ripe against the wall, runner beans clustered on a trellis, lettuce in semi shade among currant bushes, cucumber grew fat on mounds of horse manure and old lichen-encrusted fruit trees promising a bountiful autumn. An ancient sheep dog padded up behind me, visiting old friends maybe, although he did make a feeble attempt to cock his leg on Hondo's headstone. Phoebe followed him, announcing dinner.

Gerry had had a shower after his nap; its restorative effect amazed me. Plate-sized T-Bones were sizzling on the wood stove. "I always cook my steaks charred, no blood dripping out of 'em. Phoebe likes 'em not quite dead. She does her own." This suited me fine I told him, which was true. I recalled Tex on the occasion he had shot a bullock at an isolated location near Cape Barren Island. One and a half inch slabs of beef, seared for no more than fifteen seconds on either side, on a hot plate. Blood in rivulets down each side of his mouth where at the confluence of the chin coursed down his hairy sweating chest. I had never been that hungry for meat, so Tex's savagery partially explained why cannibalism occurred even where seafood was plentiful.

"We should bring up some wine for our guest," ventured Gerry.

"The light bulb's gone, take a torch and mind the steps yer not sober yet," Phoebe cautioned. *Christ, there's a cellar here*, I thought. Of course, there would be.

"I'll come and help, Gerry." I followed him out of the kitchen. "If we're not back in an hour don't come lookin'." Phoebe's reply was up with anything I had encountered in the Royal Navy.

The cellar door was identical to several others in a long passageway. There was no indication as to what lay behind them. The door to the cellar opened onto an alarming black abyss, a sugary mustiness wafted up my nostrils. Gerry seemed oblivious and aimed the torch beam onto three wide wooden steps, the fourth and remaining ones being chiselled from natural rock. The light fitting was within easy reach, but they had no replacement bulb. I removed the expired bulb and handed it to Gerry, thick with dust. He could not remember ever changing it since the wiring was installed in the twenties. I asked how old the house was. "Eighteen sixty-six," he said. What liquid treasure lay down here? This cellar was being built two years prior to the Franco Prussian War.

"Hope yer like red, mate, cause that's all there is." Recent vintages by the dozen lay in racks authentically dusty and cobwebbed. A daughter had brought them as an investment, I fail to recall the vintage year. "How many d'ya think you'll want?" I replied that I thought one would be sufficient considering what I had sunk already, but two in case one is found to be corked, I said for effect only. And only if you think your daughter would not object. "She doesn't drink," he said in an annoyed manner. I did not think that that was the point, but I let it rest. "Yer right, mate, wouldn't want to drink it if it was corked." He pointed to a vast rack, apparently full but hidden by a dense cocoon of cobweb resembling the material used to cover weaponry on mothballed warships. "That's likely to be corked, had some mates come once, knocked a few off. None of us could dry fart for three fucken days. Fucken nightmare at the ram sale." I wondered if they were all corked and if not, how old they were and what value a connoisseur would place on them.

I realised that come the dawn I must leave. I could feel the tentacles of attachment coupled with nostalgia insidiously taking hold. In the poor light, I selected two bottles with the most attractive labels and tentatively ascended the steps praying for a safe passage to the dining table. Gerry staggered up the steps behind me with another bottle. "In case yer dropped one," he said in a concerned tone. I asked again if his daughter would object to our pillaging and as before, he growled that she was teetotal and a nun. This got me thinking of nuns of a different stamp in Roscommon, Ireland, sitting one rainy day in the snug of a pub, drinking tea surreptitiously impregnated with John Jamieson and Son's finest. I see their serene angelic faces now.

Phoebe had picked a healthy salad; the table was set, and she had replenished her glass which would have comfortably accommodated several goldfish. The glass commanded attention like Big Ben and the coat hanger in Sydney Harbour. Her steak had been momentarily introduced to some heat for not much longer than Tex's, and Gerry declared our steaks sufficiently rested. What that meant I had not the foggiest and was too embarrassed and arrogant to ask. I had never eaten steak until I visited ports of sophistication in the Royal Navy. I grew up on the cheaper cuts supplemented by relentless poaching.

Often when debating the merits and origin of the 'Sonsie Haggis' with the 'Sassenach', Americans or the generally ignorant, I found it necessary to point out when the Laird had an animal slaughtered he had no intention of sharing the choicest parts with the peasantry. Evisceration followed the hapless beasts' demise; the result being spilt on the ground for his clan folk to fall upon like starving Comanche on bringing an arrow-bristled buffalo to its knees.

We sat, steam rising from a bowl of new potatoes, a large lump of butter slowly subsided among them. I waited for one of them to fire the starting pistol to raise a toast or offer thanks to the Almighty, but it appeared that such ceremony had long been dispensed with. I raised my glass of burgundy and thanked them for their hospitality. Gerry took up his beer glass and Phoebe hers, with both hands. Good luck, good health and I added 'Tirpitz', explaining its significance. Gerry liked that.

"Not corked is it, mate?" said Gerry.

"No," I confidently replied.

"How's its aroma and aftertaste?" he said teasingly. The wine was up there with the Commodores in Hobart.

"The finest wine in the seven seas," I declared. I showed my appreciation by sniffing and rolling it around my tongue, as I had seen folk do. I had sampled wines in many unhygienic locations in the world, some with an acridity and astringency all of their own, redolent of burnt shag feathers. These bottles were not sealed with corks, often they were stuffed with bits of rag. And then there were the fly-rimmed carafes in jungle bars far up the River Plate. I knew what bad wine was; however, three or four weeks at sea tended to nullify any epicurean senses one thought one had.

I mentioned the plonk with the aroma of burnt shag feathers, he laughed and spilt beer on his steak. Phoebe told him to leave me alone, but the banter continued, and we had a lot of laughs. We repaired to the lounge after and shared life stories.

Phoebe had cooked for the shearers over the decades and held formal dinner parties, the premier attending on one occasion. They were on their own now, all farm work and shearing were contracted out. Another daughter was married with three children and living in Nebraska, where she had gone years before in search of her grandfather's roots. I shared their unremitting sadness of their only son's death in Korea. Phoebe was active with the Country Women's Association with Gerry on the board of the local Race Club and keeping abreast of the fat stock market. Both of them getting on with their lives but ever with the lingering look of loss and what might have been. We talked for hours. Phoebe brewing coffee to keep us awake. They had not stayed up so late for years.

Awakening from one of his intermittent naps, Gerry declared it was about time we hit the sack. I prepared to unroll my swag on the veranda. Phoebe insisted that I use their son Denis' room, with no protest from me. Apart from the occasional dusting and vacuuming, the room had been undisturbed for a dozen years. Sober, I would have refused, and sober, Phoebe may not have offered, but with the lateness of the hour combined with the excellent wine, I would have happily reclined on a bed of nails. I recall little until I awoke in the shrine-like room well after sunrise about six hours later, aware of the palpable presence of Denis. An Australian Rules football sitting upright in a vase, a signed guernsey hanging on one wall along with boots, photos of mates and girls, himself in uniform, diggers hat tipped back. Fly fishing rods, cricket gear, tennis racquets. A Winchester rifle and a twelve-gauge double-barrelled shotgun lay in a rack. I had not undressed, still shod in fact. I tumbled from the room with a lump in my throat. Unsurprisingly, my hosts had not risen. I quietly used the bathroom then let myself out of the back door and made my way to the tool and tack room to locate the pliers and fencing wire. Gerry had suggested that I should fix the Morris' tail pipe which was dragging on the ground after the bumpy drive to the homestead.

Running repairs completed in fifteen minutes with an audience of stock horses and the geriatric sheepdog looking on. The stallion was as usual aloof and a little way off. He had raced but never been placed. Intractableness and over keen interest in lady horses, Gerry had said. Gelding him would have altered his behaviour somewhat, he well knew, but how could he do that to a mate? Upon frequent requests, the stallion was loaded on the float and taken on excursions of pleasure.

I returned the pliers to the tack room intending to make a run for it, poltroon that I was. Reason prevailed however, how could a silent, swift getaway be accomplished by my gallant little chariot? Phoebe solved the dilemma by announcing breakfast in the strident eardrum shattering decibels of a drill sergeant. Saved from another cowardly decampment, I headed for the kitchen. Forty yards from the screen door, I detected sizzling rashers and bread toasting.

Far from suffering from the late night, they were raring to begin the new day. Phoebe laid a piled high plate in front of me that would have challenged the stock truck driver, as I pondered how to break the news of my urgent departure. She averted the need, however, by placing a parcel of sandwiches by the side of the plate, saying, "That should keep yer going for a few miles, sonny boy. We know yer wanna get going. Itchy feet. Like all you young folk. Yer know yer always welcome back here."

I could feel her yearning for her lost boy. Full of regret that I had slept in their son's bed and not the veranda, we said our farewells as bravely as possible. The horses who had manifested an absorbed interest in the Morris skittered off as I picked my way through their droppings. Dilapidated but stoic my brave conveyance sensing my need from a speedy departure sprang to life on command. We rattled to the farm gate, not once looking in the rear vision mirror.

Turning to starboard, we set off at a risky 25 mph, heading northwest where somewhere the fishing port of Strahan lay. A sheltered harbour where the roaring forties pounded continuously on the west coast. Boyd's deckhands had mentioned that they had had no trouble getting work there, but the weather was 'shithouse' and they had returned east. We passed several hitchhikers during the bright warm morning, apologetically signalling no room. Many of them thought I was slowing down for them, not realising that the old girl was on her last legs, a fact that even I was reluctantly acknowledging. Giving the Morris a well-earned break, I pulled off the road when my stomach suggested lunch. Broaching the sandwiches that Phoebe had thoughtfully prepared, drank some warm beer which was becoming increasingly more objectionable by the mouthful and vowed to never partake of it again once civilisation had been reached. Late afternoon, I approached another farmhouse and successfully negotiated a deal to swap six of my simmering bottles of beer for cold ones, offering a bottle of whiskey to seal the deal. It was accepted with smiles.

Sometime later, in a hamlet I refuelled the Morris and myself and bought sandwiches of mysterious content. I allocated my parched throat one bottle only, wishing to get to the coast as soon as possible, hopefully in two days. Buying ice, I laid out my Drizabone, arranged half a dozen bottles like a Naval kit muster, covered them in ice with the sandwiches atop, stuffed the weighty bundle into the Morris feeling well pleased with myself. I would sleep soundly tonight in my swag whatever was slithering about me.

Motoring on for some time, I noticed what appeared to be a neglected and unused farm gate. There was not a farmhouse in sight and after a bit of tussle managed to gain access. Leaving the car by the roadside may have suggested abandonment, not that I feared she would be stolen, but she was beginning to look as if she was resigned and possibly looking forward to her retirement as a hen roost. Wrestling the Drizabone from the front seat, together with my swag, I made camp. The beer was tooth numbing, just the temperature that I was becoming accustomed to. I fell upon the sandwiches, then read Huxley until dusk.

Soaked with dew, I woke at sunrise, ate the remaining sandwich and two apples, washed down with tepid water. I was able to show restraint when the occasion required. Sensing and smelling what lay ahead, it seemed the Morris could too, throbbing into life on command.

Wrestling with the gate. I took a couple of minutes to check that no detritus or signs of inebriety remained. We took off at our normal pace. It was apparent that the Morris was experiencing difficulty in climbing; often second gear was unable to meet the challenge, resulting in first gear being called upon, heating the engine to such an extent I was prepared to abandon ship should a sudden conflagration occur. The thought of buying a new car I deemed tantamount to treachery whilst old faithful continued to serve, no matter the slow rate of knots. No. She had become a friend. Soon to be left in a wreck yard. No tears as when having a pet euthanised, just walk away without looking back.

The Morris was beginning to use more petrol now also exhaust fume were becoming more visible. I now decided to motor for half an hour at a time, stopping around noon for fuel top up and ice, then resting and reading until sundown. Haste was no longer a priority. Eventually, I would be afloat.

Drinking cold beer in the evening, seriously wondering what I was going to do with my life. Small fortune in the bank. Maybe I'll get married, but who to? These beer-fuelled reveries were not providing answers. Should I meditate? How do you meditate? No, forget it. Was it Huxley or Norman Douglas who said that meditation was the doze's first cousin? Dozing came easily.

I was on the road at first light. I caught a whiff of the sea when I stopped for a pee and a short time later caught a glimpse of the southern shore of Macquarie Harbour, breathing a huge sigh of relief. Strahan lay on the northern edge of the harbour; how far I could not say. Down a rough farm-track, we bumped our way to the water's edge with the tail pipe just maintaining its fragile grip by the sound of it.

I made camp on what I thought was a deserted beach as I had not seen a soul in miles. A man and a woman suddenly appeared out of nowhere, dressed in hiking apparel and wished me good day. With the billy boiling furiously, I asked them if they would like tea, realising at the same time that I had one tin mug. They said they would, but after a dip to cool down. The unlacing of sturdy boots was followed by the shedding of everything else and stark naked or 'in the bollocky' to use Naval terminology. Hand in hand, they sprinted for gentle waves. Catatonic with shock, I stared after them until they disappeared into the briny. I did not wish to be seen ogling when they emerged from their swim so I busied myself around the camp with jobs that did not need doing. I swiftly helped myself to a bracer from the medicine chest when I heard the thump of footsteps in the sand and heavy breathing. The woman who looked in her mid-thirties asked if I had had a swim. Not thinking very clearly due to the unusual turn of events, I uttered the inane comment that I had not any bathers. Her glistening wet naked body had aroused me. There was no eye contact; my gaze riveted on the region below her navel.

"Well, I am sure we can overlook that small oversight, you're not shy, are you?"

"No," I said defensively explaining that I had served in the Royal Navy and was well used to communal showers with the Rabelaisian ditties that accompanied them.

"Well, that was with men only," she challenged. They seemed a pleasant couple; academics I guessed, and unnerved by their brazenness, I decided to retaliate by confessing that I had no control over my manhood and became immediately aroused at the sight of an attractive naked woman. With that, I let my shorts drop to my ankles, hoping to shock. It had the opposite effect. "Would you like to come for a little walk?" she said, offering me her hand. Knees knocking, I looked at her husband. He was reading Amis' *Lucky Jim*. I recall thinking, not the first time surely. It had been published ten years before. "Come," she said. "He's a very liberal man and not a voyeur." She walked, and I staggered through low shrubs for about twenty yards to an area pockmarked with mutton bird burrows. The woman laid a beach towel down, prostrated herself, bringing back a vivid image of the officer's wife in Malta. About to fling myself upon her, she suddenly leapt to her feet, and terror stricken, ran screaming

238

back to the camp. I turned to see a black snake emerging lethargically from a hole, about seven feet in length and as thick as my forearm. It offered no menace and gradually disappeared.

I remembered the towel, there was an indentation where her derriere had reposed so wantonly and wiped the dripping sweat from my face with it. So near, yet so far. Understandably, the husband had sprung into action on hearing his distressed wife's cries and in doing so had tossed *Lucky Jim* aside, too close to the campfire where embers were scorching it. Comforted in her husband's arms, all was well. Quickly retrieving my shorts as my member becoming revitalised at the sight of the woman's nakedness, I mentioned tea once more for want of something to say and then suggested a bracer might restore her composure. Her brazenness had vanished in her terror, which surprised and rather disappointed me. Refusing my offer rather churlishly, I thought, they scooped up their belongings up and hurried off, their bare arses winking at me until disappearing out of sight. I cursed the bloody snake. Why couldn't he or she have stayed down the hole? A splash of whiskey in the tea help things along a bit. There really was only one thing to do. Get married. Here I was, nearly a quarter of a century old and still playing with myself. Retrieving *Lucky Jim*, I re-read the final chapter which had remained legible, then consigned it to the embers. Ensuring that I was still alone, I walked to sea's edge to wash the stink of days from me.

The remainder of the day was spent reading and writing letters. At sunset, I turned into my swag, not giving the spoilsport reptile a thought. During the night, it began raining hard. I leapt up and swiftly crammed the swag and myself into the Morris, grabbing the towel I had fortunately stowed inside and dried my streaming head. The cloud burst continued for about three minutes then eased off and finally abated. Winding down a window, I saw the glimmer of dawn towards the east. Waiting until there was sufficient daylight to gather my scattered belongings, I scavenged around in the Morris for whatever provender was available to break my fast with, coming up with a stale but edible cheese sandwich, a Mars bar and two apples. By the time I had polished off the apples, cores included – another peculiarity of mine – the sun had snared the Sultan's turret in a noose of light, apologies, Omar, and I quickly skirmished about for any detritus.

Possibly sensing this was its last hurrah, the Morris burst into life with an uncanny enthusiasm and we were chugging along the road to where I confidently expected to come across Strahan. The first couple of miles were accomplished in top gear, but soon the familiar steam and sounds of protest began reducing our rate of knots to 15 mph and climbing even more gentle inclines in first gear. Finally, a decision had to be made as the heat reminded me of the foot plate of the 'Flying Scotsman' I had stood on as a small boy. Before I could cast the deciding vote however, the heroic Morris pre-empted me and stopped. A few strangulated gurgles and she never made another sound. Unloading my worldly goods, making it easier to push her on to the grass, I sat cogitating my next move. This was easy, having no alternative. A motorbike and a small bus were the only traffic I had seen as it was still early. Someone would come along before I starved to death.

I was reading *Shane*, a fine Western I had found abandoned on a park bench when the small bus returned and drew to a halt at my request. With my swag, Drizabone bulging with bottles, kit bag crammed with clobber and books heaped alongside my dilapidated vehicle, a swift explanation was required with a dash of guile. Pulling a handkerchief from my shirt pocket together with a brick (ten-pound note), I kept on hand for such emergencies; I mopped the sweat from my brow. If the driver held any negative thoughts about the scene confronting him, they quickly dissipated on spotting the tenner. With great effort and practice, he freed the biggest beer belly I had encountered while sailing the seven seas. Such was his feverish haste in extricating himself that I could only conclude that he was converting the tenner into a quantity of schooners. It was evident that I was going to get a lift, and having used the big note as bait, I was quite prepared to part with it. Despite his tremendous bulk, within thirty seconds he had stowed my chattels aboard, showing brief puzzlement with the Drizabone which overnight had sprung a series of leaks. The bus zoomed off, at an unaccustomed pace for me, and in the rear vision mirror, I watched the forlorn Morris recede from view. I had removed the number plates on the driver's advice, the suggestion being that it would not be traceable. I replied that it was not my intention to sully the beautiful countryside, and if he would convey me to a wrecker's yard for a tow truck, I would make it worth his while. My strategic cajoling had an immediate effect on the speedometer and the Falstaffian driver who burst into uninterrupted song for the remainder of the journey. I decided to give him twenty quid, not from generosity but curiosity. If ten pounds caused him to sing, what would twenty do?

I don't remember the driver's name. He was part Aboriginal and came from the east coast. His ancestors from years past had been Norwegian sealers. The driver's incessant singing, crooning and humming would have sent most normal folk raving mad after a while but had a lullaby's soothing resonance because I do not recall a thing until waking up to find a tow truck operator exchanging g'days with my driver. Sensing that money would soon need to be produced, I asked if I could use a toilet. I needed to relieve myself urgently but also wanted to avoid exposing my wad of a couple of hundred pounds in their presence, lest the cost of living would suddenly inflate. Bladder lightened considerably, I found the driver waiting expectantly and slipped him 40 pounds. Goggle-eyed and bereft of speech, he began recounting the four big notes in apparent disbelief. The tow operator emerged from his office with a thick book of bumf in his hand. "Stow the money out of sight," I pleaded to the driver. He quickly shoved the notes in his shirt pocket. Negotiations followed. The charge ten pounds. Robbery of course. How could I trust him to pick the car up? Agreeing to the extortion as I felt it useless to protest in this land of long dead bushrangers, I offered him an extra fiver on sighting the Morris once more. Triumph spread over his face. He had been correct in his analysis of me. One green, wet behind the ears, Pommy bastard. We shook hands, and he roared away. The bus driver did not seem to be in a hurry anymore, offering to conduct me to the boarding house where he resided. I said I would settle for a ride to the boat harbour where I was confident of securing a berth. Understandably, he was reluctant to part company with me and doubted my chances of success.

Instinct bade me to stop where a fishing boat was berthed with its mast un-stepped. Panting like a stag at bay, the driver eagerly helped to unload my gear, not uttering a word about the leaking Drizabone. The leakage had turned a darker shade and smelt of hops. Mopping up the pool in the bus with a towel from my kit bag, still with a smile on his face and singing a happy tune. Giving the towel a final squeeze, he wished me good luck and crushed my hand. It took him a couple of minutes to get underway leaving with a wink, another smile and a salute.

I turned to the job at hand. It was obvious that the fishing boat was not operating at the moment. Paint pots and various tools lay around. I called out several times and got no answer. I was about to enquire of a group of men fifty yards off when one of them broke off and headed my way. Once again, fortune favoured me. The man informed me that the boat was up for sale. An interested buyer from the mainland was due to arrive in a few days to inspect. Benson invited me to bung my gear aboard as his deck hand had buggered off on hearing the boat was changing hands and did not want to waste his time fucken painting. "What the fuck have yer done to ya Drizabone?" he said. I explained that it had been very useful on my journey in the heat to ensure my beer remained cold. He understood he said. "It could be pissing with fucken rain but cold beer is the main priority. I understand completely," he agreed. He nodded, interested and satisfied. "Yer any good at painting?" he quizzed. I said I liked nothing better than working on masts particularly on un-stepped ones. We then stowed the paint pots and tools away.

"Let's go for a beer, I feel happy, very happy," he said as we shook hands. "Benson's my name, pleased to make your acquaintance," he said as we marched purposefully to the pub where he was well known. I had not noticed how hungry I was until halfway down my first beer. We bought pies. Benson watched with amusement as I wolfed them down. "Jesus, I'd rather keep fucken St Bernard's than foot your tucker bill." He laughed. He drank quickly. Guzzling his third before I had finished my first. I meant to catch up when I had bolted the fourth pie. Slowly, the beer and pie intake eased to a succession of loud burbs, and we began exchanging histories. I told him I had joined the Royal Navy at fifteen years of age and about the Mediterranean and Cyprus and threw in a bit of bullshit regarding the Suez Crisis for effect, and he trumped me by having served on the Destroyer Arunta during World War II. Then it was all beer and skittles until we lurched back onboard in the dark, with me wondering about the tow truck driver.

I was pissing over the side of the boat as the sun made an appearance and almost fell overboard when a cat rubbed itself around my bare ankles. A smell of bacon frying caused the gastric juices to gush forth. The cat followed me aft where Benson had a pile of rashers crisping nicely in a serious frying pan. A loaf of bread cut into doorstep chunks lay in wait of adornment. "Wrap your chops around this, Hughie boy," he said handing me a three-inch sandwich, bacon poking out an inch all around. Pint tin mugs of tea were slurped with satisfaction, then breakfast was cleared away. Keen to impress, I began scraping and sanding the mast. I felt good. The man trusted me. I was determined not to disappoint him.

Benson had gone off somewhere, turning up at the same time as the bus driver and the tow truck operator with the Morris on tow a couple of hours later. I gave the fiver to the extortionist who began babbling about accrued costs. I had seen the Morris, my old friend. Satisfied, I turned away without answering, joining Benson on deck. The bus driver hung about for a bit making small talk about the weather, then deciding that the bank had closed, said, "See you later," and was gone.

Benson left me to it. He was gone for the following two days, unnecessarily reminding me to not leave anything lying around and to secure the wheelhouse door. He left me the keys saying, "You're the boss, Hughie," adding as an afterthought, "Till I get back." The pub beckoned in the late afternoon. The publican remembered my name from the previous night and asked as to how I had scrubbed up this morning.

"That Benson likes the taste of the suds, don't 'e?" He laughed. I had to agree. I then lost four games at pool. I had never played before. It broke the ice however, which was my objective. The bar steadily filled up with fishermen and women, labourers, all sorts, even men in suits. The folk were friendly. I wandered around the bar making myself known. Some had seen me with Benson the evening before and asked me how my head was this morning. There were nice-looking girls too, but they were all with husbands or boyfriends, except one who was drinking alone. A solid healthy girl, the type that appealed to me, well used to the sun and wind in her hair. I took a bar stool at a polite distance from her. I needed to know why everyone seemed to be avoiding her. I said hello, she smiled and asked me how I was going. Preliminaries over, we chatted for about an hour until I felt the beer creeping up on me. Taking my leave with the excuse that I had things to attend to on the boat, I left, picking up two long necks as my surviving bottles would be at an undrinkable temperature. A bottle of cold beer washed down some leftover breakfast and that was the end of me for the day.

The next morning, I heated up a couple of congealed fried eggs then carried on with the sanding. The Drizabone no longer a beer cooler, was drying nicely in the sun. I had dumped it overboard attached to a heaving line to rid it of any shards of the shattered bottle. Hosed down with fresh water, it appeared new once more. At midday, I shopped for provisions. I had no idea when Benson would return, not that I was reliant on others to meet the expectations of my wolverine appetite. Scrubbed and shaved with my Tarzan-length hair tidied up, I approached the pub at six o'clock with anticipation in my step. The pub was quite crowded. I nodded and g'dayed a couple of drinkers and the pool sharks who appeared keen to strengthen our brief acquaintanceship. Later, I promised, moving away through the throng in time to witness a leering inebriated lout attempt to whisper something in the solitary girl's ear. A big mistake. A lightening left jab had him sitting on his arse holding his head, the girl calmly sipping her beer, which had not spilt a drop. The thump and crash interrupted the hubbub, the general clamour returning within seconds. No one took much notice. The publican did not say a word, sweeping and mopping as if it were a regular event, which it probably was. The girl had not seen me as I made my way around the pool table. I was coming up behind her, not a wise move I decided, so I veered a little to my left to ensure recognition, which she did with a smile. I felt fortunate that I had seen her deck the fellow or things may have turned out differently. She was a loose cannon with a pretty wild upbringing judging by her conversation for the next couple of hours. That I could be a friend I was in no doubt, but I did not seek a life that required a shillelagh permanently down my trouser leg.

Two days later, Benson arrived with the prospective buyer. The mast gleamed with three coats of paint and ready for stepping. All gear stowed away. Paint work washed down inside and out of the wheelhouse. I was introduced to the buyer then kept out of earshot while the negotiations took place. The boat had been hauled up the slipway a month previously and a certificate of seaworthiness issued. An hour's run around the harbour apparently sealed the deal as Benson was all smiles when he arrived at the pub. "We're taking her to Warrnambool day after tomorrow," he enthused. "Can yer drag yerself away from herself?" he whispered, grinning. How gossip spreads around small communities. He had not seen me with her. Apparently, I was a cross between a hero and an idiot.

The owner had flown back to the mainland as he had not had any experience on the open sea. I thought that he was missing out on an ideal opportunity to put that to rights, so did Benson, who had hired another deckhand to take the boat over.

At the usual hour the following day, I took my swag and Drizabone to the pub to see if I could get a couple of quid for them, but changed my mind when I saw the girl looking with interest at them. I put them down beside her. "Could you use these? I have no need of them any longer." She seemed delighted. Several folks were observing us in excited anticipation. Waiting for her to lash out and flatten me. I had told her about my fiancée in Sydney, she had shrugged and made no comment. We drank several more beers between games of pool. We played doubles, the jittery opposition keeping well clear of her cue. We lost the first three games, then managed to fluke two consecutive games, which the girl enjoyed immensely. The opposition emboldened by her friendly demeanour and the beer, began engaging her in conversation but at a safe distance. Other fellows wanted to play against her and did. It was costing me money. But who cared? It was my farewell party. Leaving the pub with Benson, I offered her my hand. She took it, pulled me towards her and planted a plump juicy beery kiss full on the lips to a stunned silence, which in seconds turned to thundering applause.

We left McQuarrie Harbour at first light for Warrnambool on the south coast of Victoria. Benson taking the boat out to sea while I perused a chart which was never once referred to in the crossing. The deckhand had his priorities in order, namely his stomach. A strange fellow, but I quickly warmed to him as he fried steak, eggs, bacon, sausages and God knows what else. "She cuts up rough, we can't cook," he emphasised, as he piled hefty sandwiches into a meat safe. I felt his concern. We were as one.

Euphoric at being at sea once more, I have no memory of the duration of the voyage. Benson and the deckie were happy to allow me hours at the wheel, even a trick at night with Benson in the wheelhouse bunk with his eyes open, I was sure. A busy shipping lane, the Bass Strait. It could be very rough. I recalled the day running under the South of Crete. However, the weather remained fair until about three hours from land fall a bit of chop developed. At the wheel, I had been engaged with my constant soul searching and self-analysis. I had been aware from an early age that I was flawed in many ways. I needed to read *Steppenwolf* again and possibly again. My chief aim was to have character, not be one.

The new owner was at the wharf when we docked at about midday. He eagerly scrambled onboard with two teenage sons. His wife bravely followed after removing her unsuitable footwear. Two magnums of champagne were uncorked which we quaffed from tin mugs. A merry hour ensued. On Benson's recommendation, the owner kindly offered me a job. I declined, declaring that I was going to rinse the salt water out of my socks. "Why?" they enquired in unison. It is something I feel I have to do, the champagne said. Bewilderment and pathos flashed across their faces.

A look normally reserved for the deranged.

I recalled some lines of Constantine Cavafy:

*"Keep Ithaca always in your mind. Arriving there is what you are destined for. The traveller should set out with hope and at the end you may find Ithaca has no more riches to give you. But Ithaca gave you the marvellous journey."*